D0979479

UNDERSTANDING
THE FAITH OF THE CHURCH

THE CHURCH'S TEACHING SERIES

Prepared at the request of the Executive Council of the General Convention of the Episcopal Church

UNDERSTANDING THE FAITH OF THE CHURCH

Written by Richard A. Norris
with the assistance of a group of
editorial advisors under the direction of the
Church's Teaching Series Committee

THE SEABURY PRESS / NEW YORK

1979
The Seabury Press
815 Second Avenue
New York, N. Y. 10017

Printed in the United States of America

Library of Congress Cataloging in Publication Data

Norris, Richard Alfred.
Understanding the faith of the Church.

(The Church's teaching series; v. 4)
Bibliography.
Includes index.
1. Theology, Doctrinal—Popular works. I. Title.
II. Series.
BT77.N68   230'.3   79-4039
ISBN 0-8164-0421-6   ISBN 0-8164-2217-6 pbk.

Foreword

The series of books published for the most part in the 1950s and known as the Church's Teaching Series has had a profound effect on the life and work of the Episcopal Church during the past twenty years. It is a monumental credit to that original series and to the authors and editors of those volumes that the Church has seen fit to produce a new set of books to be known by the same name. Though the volumes will be different in style and content, the concern for quality education that prompts the issuing of the new series is the same, for the need of Church members for knowledge in areas of scripture, theology, liturgy, history, and ethics is a need that continues from age to age.

I commend this new Church's Teaching Series to all who seek to know the Lord Jesus and to know the great tradition that he has commended to us.

John M. Allin
PRESIDING BISHOP

THE CHURCH'S TEACHING SERIES

Introduction

This is one of a series of volumes in the new Church's Teaching series. The project has been both challenging and exciting. Not only is there a wide variety of opinions regarding the substance of the teaching of the Church, there are also varying and conflicting views with regard to the methods of communicating this teaching to others. That is why we have tried to pay close attention to the various movements within the Church, and to address them. The development of this new series, therefore, has involved hundreds of men and women throughout the Episcopal Church and is offered as one resource among many for the purposes of Christian education.

While it is neither possible nor perhaps even desirable today to produce a definitive series of books setting forth the specific teachings of a particular denomination, we have tried to emphasize the element of continuity between this new series and the old. Continuity, however, implies movement, and we believe that the new series breaks fresh ground in a creative and positive way.

The new series makes modest claims. It speaks not so much *for* the Episcopal Church as *to* it, and not to this Church only but to Christians of other traditions, and to those who wait expectantly at the edge of the Church.

Two words have been in constant use to describe this project from its inception: affirmation and exploration. The writers have affirmed the great insights of the Christian tradition and have also explored new possibilities for the future in the confidence that the future is God's.

Alan Jones
CHARIMAN OF THE
CHURCH'S TEACHING SERIES
COMMITTEE

UNDERSTANDING
THE FAITH OF THE CHURCH

Contents

Preface

This is a book about the church's creed. It is not, however, a commentary on the language of any particular text, such as the Apostles' or the Nicene creed. It operates on the assumption that the historic creeds are more than forms of words for intellectual assent—that they are in fact declarations in which people identify themselves as standing in a certain relationship to God. It asks, accordingly, about the structure of that relationship as the creeds portray it. Who or what is the God with whom believers are involved as they make these confessions of faith their own? What events or experiences are the basis of the faith and hope which the creeds express? What is the shape and posture of a human life lived out within this relationship?

There are no absolutely final answers to these questions. Christian theology is not a body of teachings which never change. It is the church's continuing effort to articulate, explain, and communicate the character and meaning of the relationship which it has to God in Christ. What is settled and given, therefore, is not what Christians have to say about this relationship, but the structure of the relationship itself, the mystery into which theology peers.

Consequently it is not the aim of this book to legislate about the church's faith or to make it clear what every Christian is bound to agree with. Its function is, in the proper sense, introductory. It seeks to lead people into the issues about God, and about human persons and their relation to God in Christ, with which Christian doctrine is called, generation after generation, to deal. The disagreements it evokes, and the questions it inevitably raises, are thus part and parcel of its business, if they serve to deepen people's understanding of Christian faith and life.

In writing this book, the author was greatly helped by the advice and criticism of others. In particular, a grateful tribute is owed to the Rev. Professor Charles Winters, of the University of the South, for help which he gave both in the designing of the book as a whole and in the reshaping of several of its chapters; to the Right Rev. Donald J. Parsons, bishop of Quincy, for a variety of acute observations and suggestions; to the Right Reverend Arthur Vogel, bishop of West Missouri, for many enligntening observations and criticisms; and to the Rev. Professor David Lotz, of The Union Theological Seminary, whose criticisms of one chapter helped mightily to clear the author's mind. None but the author is responsible for the result; but without this help—and that of many others—the result would have been a much poorer thing.

Thanks are owed to the warden, the director of studies, and the staff of the College of Preachers in Washington, D.C., where most of the book was written during a semester's sabbatical leave. Only superlatives can describe the quality of the hospitality which the College dispenses.

This book is dedicated with gratitude and affection to the graduates of The General Theological Seminary, 1970–1978.

Richard A. Norris, Jr.

Introduction

There is such a thing as Christian faith. The world contains innumerable evidences and signs of its reality. Almost anywhere you look there are assemblies of people met to hear Scripture read and preached, to strengthen their common life in Christ through eucharistic worship, to confer about Christian courses of action in the world, and to learn from one another how better to understand their shared life and calling. There are buildings, books, musical performances, all of which are understandable only if one sees that they are expressions of Christian faith. There are social institutions, some useful and others perhaps past their usefulness, which are historical products of Christian believing and acting. Above all there are individual men and women whose lives testify to the present reality of this faith.

That is where this book starts: with the fact, the reality, of Christian faith. Its aim is to suggest a way of understanding that faith—to say what sort of thing it is, what is involved in sharing it, and what it tells us about human life and destiny in the world.

In order to do that, however, some preliminary reflection is necessary. We have to take that phrase *Christian faith* and ask ourselves two important questions about it. First we must ask exactly what sort of thing it refers to. If people want to examine or inspect Christian faith, what kind of phenomenon can they expect to be looking at? Then second, in the light of the answer to that question we must ask what people have to consult in order to understand Christian faith. What sorts of data, what sorts of evidence, have to be considered and weighed in the process of getting to understand the faith?

These, of course, are in the strictest sense preliminary—introductory—questions. To discuss them is not to get down to the job, but to ask what the job is and how it ought to be done. Many readers, therefore, may prefer to skim over, or even to skip, this introductory material. Nevertheless it is probably best to put the preliminaries first. In that way, people who want to understand the assumptions on which this book is operating, and why it proceeds in the way it does, can be satisfied.

What Does Christian Faith Refer To?

Our first preliminary question, then, concerns the reference of that phrase Christian faith. What kind of thing does it denote? Most Christians, if pressed, would probably find it hard to give a perfectly clear and satisfying answer to that question; and there is good reason why this is so. The term faith as we customarily use it has a confusingly wide range of meanings.

Most frequently, perhaps, people take faith to refer to a system of teachings and beliefs. On this understanding, the words Christian faith would signify something like "all the things which Christians agree are true," or "the set of opinions which Christians for the most part hold." In other words, the Christian faith is something thought—a set of beliefs.

No sooner is this said, however, than a second meaning of the phrase Christian faith comes to mind. This time faith is not something thought or believed: rather it is the very act of my believing. It is the trustful assent which a human being, or a group of human beings, give to God and to what God does for them and says to them. Here, one might say, faith is a subjective act—an attitude or disposition of a human being.

There is, however, still another, a third, meaning of Christian faith, and one which embraces and includes the other two. On this understanding, Christian faith does not just mean an interior attitude, any more than it merely means a set of opinions. It involves both of these, but is bigger than either of them. Christian faith means *the relationship which people have to God and to one another on the basis of what God has done for them in Christ.* What is more, it means this relationship with all of its components—and they are numerous and various. My believing (and yours) is obviously involved in it. So are the statements made in the creeds. But then Jesus is involved in it also. Bread and wine, and the water of Baptism, and the books of the Bible are involved in it. Prayer and worship and Christian action are involved in it. The Christian faith, in short, is a complex actuality in which human beings get connected in a particular way with ultimate reality, with God.

And this is what we set out to deal with when we try to understand the Christian faith. Obviously it is not an easy thing to make sense of. People can give, and certainly have given, inadequate or false accounts of it. The fact that they have done so, however, does not mean that the faith itself therefore disappears or is totally destroyed. For, as we have said, Christian faith is not simply a set of ideas or teachings; and least of all is it identical with any account or explanation which we give of it. It is a lived reality—a *given*—which it is our business to understand, and which does not cease to be real when we partially misunderstand it. Human beings are in fact related to God through Christ by the work of the Holy Spirit; and the faith *is* this shared relationship.

Theology— Religion's Search for Understanding

If, however, the faith has, for Christians, the status not of an ideal or a hope or a theory, but of something given and real, it is bound to create problems and raise questions. Mere ideas can always be thoroughly grasped and mastered; but the relationship which people have to God in Christ is not so easily understood. It has the simplicity, but also the opacity, the depth, and the mystery, of something which comes from beyond us. Consequently it gives rise to doubts and troubles and questions, as people try to explain it, comprehend it, and defend it.

Out of such doubts and questions the discipline called theology is born. *Theology* (which literally means something like "talking rationally about God") refers to the sort of reflective inquiry which arises out of people's search for, or their engagement with, the ultimate, the "beyond." Put it another way and say: theology is what happens when religion begins to ask questions. It can take many forms and serve many particular purposes. Whatever its immediate purpose, however, theology is distinguished by the fact that it is not so much *a way of looking at religion* as it is *a way of inquiring religiously*. Theologians, we might say, want answers to religious questions, not answers to questions about religion. It is this fact which distinguishes what they do from what, for example, historians or psychologists of religion do.

On the other hand, what distinguishes theology from other forms of religious activity is precisely the fact that it is a form of inquiry. It is rational activity, and its goal is knowledge and understanding.

To say this, of course, is to evoke all sorts of questions. What, after all, has reason to do with faith? Is not faith an intuitive "hanging on" to something, and thus alien to the questioning and calculating attitude of reason? Recent experience, after all, has taught us to associate reason with natural science and philosophy. These, however, are secular activities which have little need for faith and little concern for the question of God. Furthermore, is it not dangerous and misleading to suppose that reason can "know" God? We rightly contrast "the God of the philosophers" with "the God of Abraham, Isaac, and Jacob"—the God who is merely an idea, an abstraction, with the living God who escapes our efforts to comprehend and control him. What place, then, has reason in religious understanding?

A great deal depends, where this question is concerned, on the way in which reason is understood. Most fundamentally, reason is the capacity to think and talk about things—a fairly basic endowment of human beings, and one which seems to have a role in all kinds of human behavior, not excluding religion. Apart from reason, people cannot make sense of things, or share with one another the meanings which they discover in their experience.

Furthermore, reason is not to be identified simply with highly abstract and specialized activities like calculation or the construction of logical proofs of various sorts. These are, needless to say, essential ways of finding and expressing the sense of things; but the range of their relevance and applicability is limited. Reason is no less at work in musing and imagining, in reflective appreciation, and in purposive action. It is reason, after all, which sees and formulates the difference between "the God of the philosophers" and the living God—and which knows that faith does not work in exactly the same way as scientific inquiry. Reason, in fact, is functioning wherever people find or search for meaning in their experience. Therefore it is at work in faith itself. Faith grasps and knows something; and it identifies and speaks of what it knows. To just the extent that this is true, however, faith involves reason and reasoning. Faith alienated from reason would not be faith at all; for it would be blind and could not make sense.

To say, then, that theology is an activity which is both religious and rational is not to utter a contradiction. It is to assert (1) that faith has something to say, (2) that it wants to say this something truly, and (3) that it wants to say it clearly. Indeed, this threefold statement can very well be taken to define the business of theology and the sense in which theology is rational inquiry. (1) That faith has something to say is evidence of the fact that knowing and understanding are intrinsic parts of it, and that faith naturally tries to articulate what it grasps. (2) That faith wants to say this something truly means that it cannot be satisfied to speak carelessly or superficially or uncritically. It must be sure to say only what is justified by the reality of what it grasps. Consequently, theology systematically questions, reflects, reconsiders, and argues—all in the interest of making sure that the truth is told. (3) Finally, the fact that faith wants to say something clearly means that the truth it grasps is not a private truth, but a truth which in principle holds for everyone and which therefore belongs out in the open—in the public realm. The rational task of theology is not merely to identify and articulate the truth which faith grasps, but to do so in such a way that its truth can be shared and communicated.

Where Theology Starts: Tradition

Theology, then, to speak in the most general terms, is inquiry into the meaning of the faith. Further, it is inquiry which aims to establish and clarify the sense of the faith critically, both for believers and for others. Once this is said, however, a further question rears its head. How does theology go about this task? What tools does it use, and what sorts of evidence does it appeal to? In any sort of inquiry, the people engaged in it have to know not merely what sort of thing they want to find out, but also what means they have to use to get at it. A biographer has to know what sources to consult in order to appreciate the events and ideas which shaped the life and thought of his subject. A physicist has to know what observations and experiments might be relevant for testing a particular hypothesis. Similarly, the theologian must have a fairly clear idea of what he has to look at and consider in order to get at the truth of Christian faith.

Now, at first glance, the answer to this question must seem perfectly obvious. The theologian wants to understand the faith—that relationship of people with God which happens through Christ. Presumably, then, all he or she has to do is to look at that relation, to inspect it. But then, where is it available for inspection? What does one look at when one looks at the faith?

Well, clearly enough, the first—or at any rate the most natural—place to look is at people's experience of that relationship. The theologian might, for example, consider his or her own experience of it; or accept the living testimony of others who speak as Christians. Such a procedure, however, has its limitations. For one thing, the experience of any particular individual may be, and to some degree almost certainly is, incomplete and distorted. An individual's experience of something is always shaped to a significant extent by subjective factors; and it is shaped to an even greater extent by the kind of perception and understanding which is allowed or imposed by a cultural background. Consequently— just to take an example—what I make of other people in my experience of them will depend in large measure on deeply rooted psychological factors in my own make-up, and also on the way I have learned to interpret and react to a certain kind of looks or behavior or language. Hence it is quite possible for me to have an experience of someone, and still to get that person wrong, whether through positive misunderstanding or through failure to understand as completely as I might. Individual experience and the kind of understanding it produces always needs to be tested and confirmed—and, if necessary, corrected—when it becomes an issue in the public forum. And what is true of ordinary human relations is bound to be true also of people's experience of that relationship with God in Christ which we call Christian faith. It is not enough to consult either my own experience or even the experience of my immediate circle.

In any case, as already suggested, the faith is not, except secondarily, *mine* at all. It is something shared. It does not belong simply to me or to any individual. As a human phenomenon, it is a community's faith—the church's. At this very moment, my relationship with God in Christ is shared by myriads of people who do not look, talk, think, or behave like me. In fact, participation in this relationship is not even confined to my contemporaries. The church has a fairly long history; and that history recalls to me the fact that this faith which I call mine has been shared, experienced, and interpreted by long generations of believers whom I can never meet in the flesh. Indeed, if it had not been for things they said and wrote, institutions they founded, languages they formed and handed on, I could not even have this experience of mine. My faith is all tied up with theirs.

Theology, accordingly, must cast its net very wide when it consults experience. In order to see the true sense of Christian faith, it must allow its understanding to be fed in the first instance by *tradition*—by ideas, forms of expression, and convictions which arguably represent the experience of the whole church. Tradition refers here to persistent, public expressions of the faith through which that faith is not merely preserved but actively transmitted. There are many such forms: standard shapes of prayer, established confessions of faith (creeds), and definitions of doctrine which have proved themselves as guides or pointers to the truth. The value of such forms does not lie merely or principally in the fact that they represent the experience of the past, or even that they are widely agreed upon by Christians. More important is the fact that their use and understanding generates and maintains Christian experience and commitment. To use them seriously is to enter into the faith.

Among such forms of expression, the established creeds of the universal church are, for our purposes, central. The reason for this is that they—both the Apostles' and the Nicene Creeds—have for centuries had a triple use. They have been employed universally as a basis for the instruction of converts and believers alike. Further, they have been used as forms in and through which people actively relate themselves to God in faith by an act of trustful commitment: "I believe in God . . ." Thus they are not merely statements of doctrine. Rather, they are vehicles through which the individual identifies himself as one of God's people; and the words which they use to perform this function indicate what is involved in being one of God's people. Finally, the creeds have been used as forms of praise as well as of self-commitment. This use is, of course, secondary from an historical point of view; but it is not for that reason unimportant. The way in which people praise God is a very good pointer to what God is and means for them. There is good reason, therefore, to think that anyone who wants to explore the logic of the Christian's relation to God in Christ would do well to take the creeds as a starting point; for they function as ways in which that relation is realized and enacted.

Of course this does not mean that such texts as those of the Apostles' or Nicene Creed are infallible, or that they settle all questions, or that their language is beyond criticism. Far from it. In fact the creeds are criticized every time they are interpreted or explained. On the other hand, it does mean, as we have suggested, that they are reliable. Their authority does not lie in the fact that anyone who just repeats their words is *ipso facto* right. It lies in the fact that when responsibly understood and used, they really do provide access to that relationship with God which is Christian faith. This is the reason why they have a special status. And for theology they are necessary "givens"—focal articulations and expressions of what it sets out to understand. The creeds, therefore, are not only guides and norms for individuals in their growth into faith. They are also guides and norms for the theologian who tries to give a public account of the sense of Christian existence.

Theology's Primary Source: Scripture

Common Christian experience as contained in tradition and focally expressed in the creeds—that is our starting point, and quite rightly. Here, as we have said, there is an immediate and reliable expression of the church's practical understanding of the faith. Nevertheless, theology only begins with the formulas thrown up by tradition. To understand, test, and develop what such formulas say, it refers elsewhere to the one source of teaching which the church has always placed in a class by itself: namely, the Bible, the Holy Scriptures of the Old and New Testaments.

Why is this? Why is the Bible placed in a class by itself and treated as the final authority for faith? Certainly everyone knows today that the Bible, like the creeds, is a human product—a product of the church's historical life and experience. Its several books, and the collection as a whole, reflect the mind of the Old Israel and the New. They are not independent of the people, the times and places, or the circumstances which produced them. What then is so special about them? We might say that they are special because, human as they are, they are inspired. In fact, however, the reason why Christians say the books of the Bible are inspired is precisely because of their special character, because of what they are and what they do for the church; so that account of the matter does little more than carry us around in a circle.

The fact seems to be that the Scriptures have special status because for the believing community they are, in a distinctive way, originative. Christian existence in relation to God is not something which the church itself invented or created or got started. People's life with God in Christ has its source in what God does—in God's love and grace. The fact that human beings can respond to God and be with God depends, therefore, on the prior fact that God *speaks* to them. He utters a Word which makes this relationship possible. Hence we can and must say that what is originative for Christian faith is God's Word.

Now if, in the pursuit of this theme, we ask where this Word is found, where it is that God communicates himself to people, the answer is clear. His Word is found in the call to Abraham, in the liberation of the Hebrew people from slavery, in the ministry of the prophets, and—finally and definitively—in Jesus the Christ, whom Saint John simply calls "the Word of God." In other words, what is original in Christian faith is an eventful history in and through which God has called and created a people, and whose center point is the ministry, death, and Resurrection of Jesus. These "events which speak" are the basis, the point of origin, and the presuppositions of Christian existence; and for just that reason they provide the one point of reference from which it can be finally understood, or from which understandings of it can be tested.

On this basis, it can be seen why the church treats the Bible as something special—why it always reads the Bible in its public meetings, teaches and preaches from it, and constantly meditates on it, studies it, and interprets it. The fact is that the Scriptures are, for the church, the place where God's originating Word gets spoken. The writers of the biblical books recount, interpret, react to, and try to explain those "events which speak"; and in their doing so, God's Word is repeated for us. That Word is not simply identical with the human words of the Bible; for God's Word cannot be made and kept automatically available. God's Word is always a happening—an event which creates faith and sets people free for hope. But the human words of the Bible are the occasion and the possibility of God's speaking to us: they get us involved in the events and with the person in which God speaks. We must therefore say that while the creed has the authority of a formula which is reliably expressive of the faith, the Scripture as the human mirror of God's speaking is constitutive of that faith, and hence constitutive of the Christian community itself.

Obviously this does not mean that the Bible is a handbook or a textbook which automatically answers all religious and theological questions. Nor does it mean that the Scriptures are word-for-word accurate in their historical reporting or their accounts of natural phenomena. The people who wrote the books of the Bible were speaking of their relationship with God—the things God had done in relation to them, and what they had heard of God's "Word" in these events. When they spoke of these things, they did so within their own time and culture. They pictured the universe after the fashion of their own times, not according to our current understandings of things. They remembered their history for its importance to them—for the "mighty works which God did for our fathers." They were not dispassionate chroniclers of ancient facts, but proclaimers of a message. Yet they tell us accurately of the "Word" they heard in the events of their lives.

In short, the books of the Bible are themselves, and not what we should have tried to make them if we had been writing them in twentieth-century America. To understand them, therefore, we have to enter their world, and not pretend that they belong to ours. When we do enter it, we discover a rich panorama of literature: legal texts and poems; legend and history; myth and theological argument; letters, and epics, and sermons. We find changes of outlook, theological debate and disagreement, and constant reinterpretation of older beliefs and ideas. In short, we find the intellectual and spiritual product of the history of an entire religious tradition—but one which has, for all its variety, a clear thread of unity. This literature has one central theme: God in his relation to a people whom he has called, to whom he has spoken. And since the relation of the present-day church to God belongs to the same story, God's calling and speaking as it is encountered through the Bible is the source of the Christian community's self-understanding today. There is no need to pay the Scriptures superfluous compliments. It is enough that in them, in and through all their human variety, we learn to recognize and respond to the God and Father of Jesus Christ. When that happens, they are seen to carry God's Word.

Theology's Context: Culture

But theology does not depend for the understanding it seeks solely on tradition or solely on Scripture. It also depends, though in a quite different way, on its own social, moral, and intellectual setting; for this both evokes and conditions its inquiry. The faith which is expressed in tradition and grounded in God's word must be understood and lived out in a particular cultural world which has characteristic ways of seeing, explaining, and valuing things. The way people habitually think; the way they organize their common life; the things they naturally want or admire—all these factors inevitably have an effect on the way they see Christian faith and on what it means for them, whether negatively or positively. Every cultural world in which the church exists (and such worlds are, and have been, many) has its own way of appropriating, and its own way of being troubled and challenged by, the faith.

Thus the culture within and to which the faith is interpreted is part of the *matter* of theology: and this in two quite different but equally important ways. In the first place, it is part of the matter of theology because the ideas and values which dominate a given society will also dominate the minds of Christians in that society. Quite naturally, therefore, and, to one degree or another, unconsciously, Christians will make sense of their faith in the same way in which they make sense of everything else in their world. They understand the faith in terms of their particular culture's normal way of seeing things; and this means that "what everyone knows" in that cultural world has a tendency to become part and parcel of what the faith is understood to say.

But, in the second place, culture is part of the matter of

theology because at least some of the values and ideas which dominate a given society become issues for theology. The reason for this is that there are always, in the tradition of Christian faith, established beliefs and ideals which do not easily fit into the world picture of a given culture. Sometimes, these differences are suppressed and forgotten. Just as often, however, they raise doubts and questions. The faith is perceived as inconsistent with obvious and widely acknowledged truth; or it is seen to challenge central cultural values. In either case, a dialogue or debate ensues in which the faith's understanding of itself and the culture's understanding of its world are both liable to significant alteration.

Culture thus becomes, in one way or another, a matrix and source of theological understanding. To say this is not to utter an exhortation to theologians or Christians generally to "get with it." Cultural values and ideas affect theological understanding automatically and as a matter of course: exhortation is scarcely needed to bring that about. Nor is this fact a matter either for regret or for rejoicing. The way in which a culture induces people to "see" Christian faith may indeed, and frequently does, result in distortion of it; but it may also bring out dimensions of it which had previously been ignored, or bring it to terms with hitherto unrecognized truth. The task of the church—and of theology in particular—is neither to glorify nor to repudiate a given cultural world, but to permit its ways of understanding and the problems it occasions to clarify and advance, both positively and negatively, people's grasp of the faith in idea and action.

Conclusion

Theology tries to spell out the meaning of that relationship to God which people have in Christ and which, as a shared relationship, constitutes the Christian community. The goal of this undertaking, at least from one point of view, is to help each of us make sense out of his or her own experience. If this goal is reached, each of us will find his or her belief at once strengthened, enlightened, and corrected.

This aim cannot be achieved, however, simply by reference

to our own experience or to the normal assumptions of our own belief. Theology accomplishes this goal by bringing us to see our own faith in the light of the common experience of the historical Christian community as that is exemplified in the traditional creeds. Furthermore, it understands and tests this common experience by reference to its foundation: the Word of God conveyed in the Scriptures. This scriptural testimony is thus, for theology, the definitive word. As it interprets Scripture, however, and thus enters into the "sense" of the common faith, theology carries with it the problems, issues, and insights contributed by its own cultural world. Since this cultural world is different both from those in which the Scriptures took shape and from those which formed the tradition, theological inquiry takes the form of a continuing dialogue. The tradition is appropriated and reinterpreted critically both in the light of its foundation and in the light of the questions raised by its cultural setting. For this reason, theological inquiry never comes to a final answer. The faith is always questioned and questioning, always relearning and reappropriating its foundation and seeing it in new lights.

In what follows, we shall try to be true to this description of theology. Our thinking will follow the structure of the creeds. It will take notice first of all of the fact that the creeds enact a relation between God—Father, Son, and Spirit—and the human beings who profess it. It will therefore begin by asking, in the light of Scripture, what picture of God and of humanity is involved in this relationship. It will then continue by looking at what the creeds say about the basis of this relationship—about Jesus and the meaning of his ministry, death, and Resurrection. Finally, in the third part, it will ask what this relationship with God in Christ means for the people who share it as their lives are caught up in the re-creative work of the Holy Spirit. In all of this, our thinking will rightly and inevitably illustrate both the dependence of theology on the Bible, and its involvement with the ideas and values which dominate contemporary culture.

Part One

· 1 ·

Human Identity
and the Question of God

The church's creeds are the starting point for our enterprise of understanding the faith. But what are these texts, and what do they do? If we imagine a group of Christians reciting one of them, what do we conceive to be happening? When a person "says" the Apostles' Creed or the Nicene Creed, what is that person doing?

At the most obvious level, people who recite one of the creeds are *saying* something. They are making statements which claim to be true in some sense, and they are asserting beliefs. At a deeper level, though, they are also *doing* something. An action is taking place, and one which involves far more than just the making of statements, however interesting or important those statements might be. What is more, this action, which the words of the creeds both express and carry out, comes close to the very heart of Christian faith. People who say "I believe in God . . ." are in fact entering into a certain relationship with God in Christ. What is more, this relationship is one which gives them a particular identity; and in reciting the creed sincerely, they are taking on that identity voluntarily.

Maybe this sounds strange—as though we were trying to find a very complicated way to describe a simple, and even

17

ordinary, sort of act. Yet it is important to remember that the creeds open with the words *I* or *we;* and these are words which not only signify the people who are speaking, but involve them with what they are talking about. In fact, the man or woman who says "I believe in God" is in some respects exactly like the man or woman who answers "I will" at the significant moment in a wedding ceremony. By saying "I will," the bride or groom does not just express a view, but enters into a relationship—and a fairly deep and serious relationship at that. By the same token, the person who says—honestly, and not mockingly or insincerely—"I believe in God" is thereby involved with God; and that too is a deep and serious matter, which determines who I am and how I understand myself.

Notice that in neither of these relationships does the speaker acquire identity—that of wife or husband, or that of God's child—just by his or her own say-so or by a unilateral decision. Real identity never comes by unilateral decision. It comes through a relation to other people, whose demands or calls evoke the response in which my identity is decided. Christian identity, in other words, is not something I make up for myself, or a role I determine to "try on." It is something appropriated. One discovers this identity—this truth which is oneself—through Baptism. There God claims me as he calls me by the name of the Christ; and I appropriate that identity, make it my own, by answering God with an "I believe." It is this action which is repeated every time the creeds are said.

So Christian faith is, as we have tried already to say, something like a connection which comes about between God and human beings through Christ. It is a relationship, established as God's call evokes human response. This relationship is the datum, the "given," which Christian theology tries to understand. It is also the datum which Christian behavior tries to live out and which Christian worship enacts symbolically. That is one reason why the creeds are important. They are concerned with this core reality of Christian existence. They portray the relation of God and human beings in Christ—but they do so only because, at a more fundamental level, they are forms in which that same relation is acted out. "I believe in God . . ." both says this connection and makes it.

The Question of God

If we are to understand the creeds, however, and this relationship which they portray, we must begin by recognizing that they make a significant, strange, and arguable assumption. They speak of God, and they claim to put people in a certain relation to God. At one time—indeed in just about any time save the present—this might not have seemed strange at all. In other ages, it is true, people might have found the sort of God Christians speak of an unfamiliar one; but they would never have thought it strange or problematic that human beings should set the symbol *God* at the center of their way of understanding things. At present, however, for many people, this is a very puzzling policy indeed.

For it is true, just as a matter of fact, that in the cultural world which the church now inhabits, there are many people who are genuinely unsure whether it is possible to speak meaningfully about God at all. This does not mean merely, or even primarily, that there are people who doubt or deny the existence of God. No doubt there are. More important, however, is the fact that there are people who do not know how to speak of God because they do not grasp the point of talking about God. The word *God* does not have a significant function in their vocabulary.

To be sure, not everyone feels this way. Public opinion polls continue to show that a great majority of Americans believe in God in some sense; and presumably this means that they see some point in such belief. Nevertheless, the cultural and mental world in which they live continues to be structured in such a way as to make belief in God seem irrelevant for most purposes. People in other times and places have been convinced that God—or gods—impinged on their lives at every possible point. Events in the natural order were divinely ordained or "sent." Political and military success and failure were conceived to depend directly on the divine will. Through dreams, visions, and prayer, every individual's personal life felt the influence of the divine; and indeed, the destiny of every individual, both for the present and for the future, was thought to depend on the way in which he or she conducted relations with the divine powers. For such people, the question of God was an immediate and a practical issue. It could not be ignored.

Our picture of the world, however, is different from this. Even religious people see things in a different way. Except for those who belong to some subculture in which an alternative picture is self-consciously preserved, the assumption nowadays is that things in the natural, social, and personal orders work according to their own inherent logic, without the interference of gods. Consequently, it is not strictly necessary, either for understanding things or for taking effective action in the world, to reckon with the divine. To be sure, what is not strictly necessary may seem wise or desirable to many individuals. A devout person in government or business, for example, may regularly pray for guidance and support; and such prayers may be heartfelt and genuine. Nevertheless, if his or her associates think that a particular decision is based only on prayer, the likelihood is that they will regard the person in question as professionally incompetent, as not understanding how things really work. Referring things to God is acceptable, but essentially superfluous, behavior; what is necessary, though, is human awareness and control of facts and circumstances.

Why is this the case? Why is it that, at most, the notion of God is allowed a place only in the private, interior life of the individual and has no role in the significant public business of our cultural world? Quite bluntly, it is because the picture of the world which dominates our culture is one in which there is no room for God.

By "picture of the world" here is meant an habitual way of seeing things which is rooted in the common symbols by means of which people learn to understand and evaluate what goes on around them. As human beings grow up and get educated, they acquire a language, a way of talking and thinking about things. This language structures their experience and provides them with a certain way of being related to the world. Implicit in this language, therefore, is what we have called a picture of the world; and it is this picture which, for the most part, decides what sorts of questions people think it important to ask, and hence what sorts of beliefs or convictions normally make sense to them.

Imagine, for example, a culture which sees the world as a vast, mysterious arena in which mankind is very weak and alone; and in which rocks, trees, rivers, mountains, seas, and meteorological phenomena represent or embody personal "powers" of some sort. In such a culture, with such a picture of the world, it makes sense to *talk* with the rocks or the rain. It makes sense to *plead* with the rain, or the power behind it, to come down upon the parched ground and give it life. It makes sense to give presents (bribes, if you wish) to the powers of nature on whose good will one is wholly dependent. To moderns, of course, such behavior appears primitive and superstitious; and so it is—from the point of view of their picture of the world. From the point of view of the culture we have been imagining, however, it makes good sense. To act or think otherwise, in fact, would be nonsensical.

The modern western picture of the world is, by contrast, a thoroughly secular one. That is to say, the powers of nature and the processes of the cosmos are thought of as objective, predictable, and (in principle) comprehensible. They are not, and do not represent, personal powers of any sort. They are things which can be understood and analyzed and thus predicted or controlled for human purposes.

The point of contrasting these two pictures of the world is not to suggest that one is good and the other bad, or that one is old-fashioned and the other up-to-date, or that one is Christian and the other not. The point is simply to call attention to the fact that our contemporary picture of the world is one in which the symbol *God* has very little functional importance. That symbol belongs to Christian language, and to the way of experiencing things and asking about them which Christian language involves. It does not, however, figure very prominently in the official mental world of contemporary western culture.

To speak of God in today's world, then, is no easy task. The language of the creeds does not fit in with our ordinary ways of talking and thinking, with our everyday assumptions. If "God" were merely the name of a particular item, or a particular kind of item, which is "there" in the world but which modern people tend to ignore or not to notice, the task might be easier. In that case, all one would have to do would be to call people's attention to the existence of this particular reality as a part of the world. God, however, is not an item, a particular reality, within the world, at least not according to a Christian understanding of God. To put it another way, the word *God* is not the name of a particular thing or a particular kind of thing in the world. It has a much wider and more encompassing sort of meaning than that. It is a symbol which pulls together and articulates a vast range of experiences and ideas. What is more, it sets these experiences and ideas at the very center of people's thinking and living. When the word *God* is seriously used, therefore, it carries with it, at least in an implicit way, a complete world picture.

It will not do, then, to explain this word as though it could simply be added to the active vocabulary of contemporary culture without further effect—like (say) the name of a new model of automobile or a new form of plant life. No doubt the contemporary world picture, and the way of talking which belongs to it, can provide people with occasion for asking and speaking about God. It is also true, however, that any significant speaking of God must in the end result in a radical transformation of that world picture itself.

This means that Christians must do some hard thinking. They, after all, are as much products and carriers of modern culture as anyone else. They too share its way of seeing and valuing things. If they mean to speak seriously of God, then, they will find themselves in a dialogue in which they stand on both sides of the discussion. They will have to ask what their own world—the world as their ordinary language teaches them to see it—would look like if it were understood theologically; that is, if it were looked at from the standpoint of the experiences and ideas of which the creeds speak. Conversely, they must try to discover what their understanding of God would be like if God were known as the mystery of *this* world and not some other.

Consequently, they must be rigorously honest. They cannot pretend that *God* is just a name for some value or concept current in today's culture; and they cannot pretend that this culture really believes in the God and Father of Jesus Christ. They must be satisfied initially to identify points where the question of God can be meaningfully raised. Agreement, either about God's existence or about the importance of the question of God, cannot be expected; a starting point for a dialogue must suffice. *To establish the meaningfulness of the question of God* is the immediate goal: when that is reached, at least the point of the creeds' language can be seen.

Looking for a Starting Point

This sort of difficulty is not one which is peculiar to the present age. When the earliest Christian missionaries—Jews, all of them—began to preach the Gospel to the gentile world, they faced a not dissimilar problem. Some Gentiles had already been attracted to Judaism and could understand themselves and their world in terms of the world picture carried by the language of Jewish religion. For such people it was relatively easy to see the point of Christian preaching. On the other hand, most Gentiles spoke a different religious language from that generated by the experience of the Jewish people. For them, Christian talk of a "Messiah," of "Resurrection," and of a God who is actively involved in the course of history made little sense. In their case, consequently, some sort of explanation or translation had to take place, so that they could see what was meant by the proclamation of Christ.

The early Christian preachers and apologists, of course, did not have to address themselves to people who were unfamiliar or uneasy with the word *God*. There is, however, in the history of Christianity, at least one significant attempt to explain—and justify—the Christian way of thinking and speaking about God. This is found in the so-called proofs of the existence of God which were propounded and discussed by medieval philosophers and their successors. From the very beginning, needless to say, these proofs have been the subject of much criticism and debate. None of them is generally accepted as establishing the "fact" of God. From a purely theological point of view, moreover, thinkers have questioned whether the God to whom these arguments point is indeed the God of Christian experience.

Nevertheless, these proofs, like the explanations with which early Christian preachers approached the gentile world, accomplished something important. They connected a central affirmation of Christian faith with a world picture, a way of seeing and experiencing, to which that affirmation was partially strange.

Thus the medieval philosophers would take some aspect of experience—experience common to Christians and non-Christians alike—and then attempt to show that this datum raises the question of an "ultimate." They might point, for example, to the fact of change, and ask how it could be accounted for without positing an original and ultimate Cause of change. Again, they could point to the order and harmony of the world, and ask how that could be accounted for without reference to an ultimate Mind which is its ground. They might point to the experience of differing degrees of goodness in things, and ask how there can be a "better" if there is not an ultimate "best." Even if none of these proofs actually demonstrates what it sets out to demonstrate, it nonetheless performs one essential function. It indicates a focal point in human experience where the question of God can—and must—be asked: and in doing so it teaches people something about what is involved in speaking of God.

From these examples, we can discern a method by which two worlds or world pictures can be brought together in dialogue. The two pictures need not coincide at all points. If they did, they would not be different pictures, and the problem would not exist. But they may be shown to have points of contact. Certain questions which are raised by the world picture of contemporary culture—or questions which are there implicitly, even if they are not usually brought to the level of consciousness—may turn out to be questions which are also raised, perhaps in a different form, in the Christian tradition. In other words, there may exist in modern culture problems or experiences which implicitly ask what we may call "the question of God"; and these can provide starting points for our search.

The Question of Identity

What, then, is a useful or fruitful point at which to apply our method? Clearly an answer to this question involves tactics only, and not principle. It might be fruitful to pursue one or more of the traditional proofs for the existence of God; for not all philosophers have accepted the conclusion that they lack merit as demonstrations. In any case, they might turn out to be useful devices for showing what it *means* to speak of God. On the other hand, as a tactical matter, there may be more central points of contact with the modern world picture than these proofs embody—problems of which people are more distinctly aware and for which they have a more vital concern.

As a matter of fact, one possibility of this sort has already been hinted at in this chapter. In speaking of the relationship with God in Christ which is the foundation of Christian experience and which the recitation of the creeds both expresses and enacts, we have stated it. This relationship, we said, is one which establishes, for individuals and for the community as well, an identity. Now that word has come to play a prominent role in the public language of modern American society. It is a symbol which has caught on because it focuses a range of problems and concerns which people recognize as central for their existence.

It could, of course, be argued that the problem of identity is one which is native to humankind in every age. It is dealt with in a variety of ways—by association with a tribe or clan, or with a particular piece of land, or with a job or profession; but it is always there as an issue to be met in one way or another. Nevertheless, the problem seems to be dealt with more satisfactorily in some times and places than in others. Certainly this is the case if by *satisfactorily* we simply mean "to the satisfaction of the people who face the issue," and do not raise the question whether any solution is ultimately satisfactory.

Our age is having greater difficulty than most in finding an answer which is satisfactory in this limited sense. We live, according to a monotonously long series of commentators, in the midst of an identity crisis. Young people, it is said, are experiencing alienation. They do not discover in the resources of their culture and their society any basis for a secure identity; and so they seek to find or create one for themselves. Housewives and career businessmen alike are disturbed by the question of "who they really are." The settings in which this problem surfaces are many and diverse; but the malaise is the same. Ethnic groups, finding no satisfactory identity in terms of the melting-pot image of American society, are seeking to retain or reestablish their former roots.

These and other possible examples indicate that in the quest for identity we may have a point of contact at which the language of Christian faith and the issues of contemporary culture can be seen to merge into a common focus. For Christian language about God, as the opening phrase of the creeds indicates, is at the same time a language which answers the question "Who am I?" for the believer. Before anything can be said, however, about how the problem of identity may be seen to raise the question of God, we must deal with some preliminary issues. What are the sources, and what is the logic or sense, of this contemporary concern? What are some of the ways in which it shows itself? Why is identity perceived as a problem?

It is easy enough, in an immediate and superficial way, to specify what is ordinarily meant by an identity problem. It consists, apparently, in a *conflict of identities*. On the one hand, people's inner desires and felt needs—their awareness of themselves from the inside—provide each individual with an unarguable sense of being "someone." On the other hand, people are, at the same time, told who they are from the outside, by the demands and expectations of society. These two sorts of identity frequently come into conflict, with the result that the individual feels confused, divided, rebellious, or resigned—but in any case unhappy.

It needs to be observed that while the issue of identity is one which is faced by people in any society whatever, the problem or crisis of identity, as we have just described it, has been discovered by people living under the conditions of a modern, urban, and technological society. In more stable and structured societies, in which both the world and one's place in it are givens, the distinction between the "I" which is experienced internally and the "I" which is defined by one's social role is much less frequently perceived. A visitor from a culture such as ours might well think that personal identity cannot be achieved satisfactorily in a social setting of that sort. Such a visitor would suspect that there is no adequate sense of the individual, and too much conformity of the person to social expectations. The fact remains, however, that persons within such cultures do not find their situation at all stifling or repressive. They do not experience the issue of identity as a problem.

The fact that it does emerge as a problem, and does so rather prominently, in modern western culture, seems therefore to suggest that behind the psychological symptoms of the crisis of identity there lies some more basic factor connected with the way in which people generally learn to see themselves and to conceive their world. What, then, are the conditions which give rise to this sort of perception?

Self and World

It is a commonplace that the physical, social, and economic mobility of our culture has resulted in a severing of people from their roots, and that this circumstance is connected closely with problems of identity. Mobility, however, is only a symptom and not a cause. To appeal to it is not to identify the source of our problems.

On a deeper level of analysis, the very existence of such mobility is expressive of a change in the way human beings are related to their world. This, needless to say, is an utterly basic sort of change; for the way in which people are related to what lies around and outside them determines their internal sense of who they are. It is a truism to observe that the child becomes aware of *self* as it becomes aware of *other*. As it responds to the people around it—as it answers, obeys, rebels, consents—it becomes conscious of being "I," and at the same time wakes to the reality of "you" or "them." Identity and self-awareness, then, are built up through constant interaction with someone or something else. They are built up as people come to themselves by deciding and saying who they are in dialogue with what is not themselves.

This "not themselves," this "other," is in the first instance other people—family, friends, teachers. Other people, however, carry with them a whole world. By *world* is meant not just a neutral set of surroundings, but an environment which is filled with value and meaning because it is the context of action and decision, because it too is part of the "other" in relation to which the individual human being becomes a self. In intercourse with other people, the individual learns to identify, evaluate, and respond to a wide variety of things and events; and these also become, in a certain sense, the individual's interlocutors. They evoke response; and the sort of response they receive expresses the identity of the person who answers them.

From this it can be seen, as we have said, that the way in which people are related to their world—the way in which they see, conceive, and thus respond to it—determines the way in which they see themselves. If it is true that identity emerges in relationship with an "other," then the character of this relationship, the way in which the "I" sees and treats the "other," defines the sort of "I" a person turns out to be. The style of one's relationship to significant others shapes one's identity.

Now western humanity has learned, in the course of the last three centuries or so, to see and treat both the human world and the natural order generally in a special and specialized way—as a collection of things to be understood and controlled. It has learned to value and respond to its world not as something to be contemplated and appreciated, nor yet as the outward expression of some intelligent initiative which evokes personal response, but as something to be looked at, seen through, and dealt with. In part this development is connected with the rise of scientific method, and the latter's encouragement of the attitude of what is called "objectivity." This attitude would have us understand things and people as parts of a scene from which we, as observers and outside manipulators, are excluded. In other words, we understand them not in terms of their relation to us, but solely in terms of their observed relation to one another "out there." They become, then, a group of objects to be watched, handled, and understood. As long as the world of things and people was primarily perceived as calling for personal response or contemplative participation, this attitude was rare. When, however, the "other" becomes "object," the human beings who stand over against it become a different sort of thing themselves. They become both dominant and uninvolved. They initiate changes and adaptations in the world; but they are not much interested in "getting with" it.

Along with the gains which this way of being related to the world has brought in its wake, there have been some indisputable losses as well. To view things objectively means to remove oneself from them, to be dissociated from them. One is not deeply involved with something which is merely the object of one's observations and actions. For example, the modern corporate farmer may have less feeling for the land than did the farmer of earlier times. What was once a part of one's life becomes merely a means of one's livelihood. This change, moreover, involves a clear alteration in the individual's self-understanding. Instead of being a person whose identity is wrapped up with the land on which he or she lives, the individual is now separated from these things and independent of them—even alien to them.

In such a situation, the "I" is not so much "I who am defined by my involvement with this land, trade, craft, family," but rather, "I who am defined by observing, understanding, and using" any and all of these things. "I" have become knower and creator. I must shape my world, and only in that process can I become myself. In short, people's quest for objectivity in their relationship with the world has heightened the issue of identity. I can no longer *receive* an identity; I must *create* one. I can no longer simply *take* my place in the world, but must *make* my place in it.

To live in this way is a very exciting business. It is a heady experience. It marks the transcendence of the human person over all confining circumstances and things. A world which can be understood and controlled implies a self which is capable of going beyond whatever is given, of being forever open to possibilities which are not yet realized. To see oneself—and to *be*—in this role is to have a sense of freedom, creativity, and worth.

But all this comes at a price. Its excitement and its rewards are contingent upon one's success. If I am able to forge for myself an identity as an adequately creative and hence worthwhile individual, I will no doubt find the contemporary world a wondrous place in which to live. I will ascend to heights of personal liberty which few people in previous ages have known.

But there are many factors which combine to make this kind of success difficult to achieve. *First*, the world "out there," which I am expected, by my culture and by myself, to transform, is not always very tractable. It is made up, not only of inert things which I can perhaps push around and rearrange to my liking, but also of social structures and other people who have a reality of their own and who are frequently resistant to my attempts to remake them. Society, whether it be the larger society whose objectivity seems obvious or the smaller and more intimate society of my family and friends, has its own expectations and desires. So I am caught in a world which demands that I be a creative and transforming agent, and yet resists me and my actions. The "big picture"—the cultural symbol system with its high evaluation of objectivity and control—does not guarantee that things will be passive and malleable at the level of the "small picture" which I must daily confront.

Second, to precisely the extent that I try to live up to the image of myself as creative agent and "self-made man," I find myself alienated from the society of my fellow human beings.

If I am to be truly an autonomous person, which is the ideal most obviously entailed by the modern set of expectations, then I am bound to be lonely to a degree rarely matched in prior cultures. In all the ages of history one can find testimony to the loneliness of "the man at the top." Great leaders, shapers of society, have always found friendship and close relationship a rare commodity. Yet how much loneliness is generated when a culture expects such creativity of each of its members! In the world of the self-creative individual, people become indistinguishable from things. They too are to be understood objectively and controlled, with the inevitable result that there seems to be no one to talk to.

Third, and perhaps most frightening of the lot, the world which I have shaped and the identity which I have forged may at some point begin to appear to me as "made up." They may reveal themselves as nothing more than the work of my own hands, and therefore as having no more reality than I have been able to put into them. Then, with this perception, the suspicion begins to emerge that *all* is artifice, invention, and show. World and self alike suddenly look insubstantial and unreal. They look like mere projections: they speak, but their voice is like that of a ventriloquist's dummy, a mere echo of their creator's. In these circumstances—which are, fortunately, usually fleeting, for one puts such thoughts out of mind as quickly as possible—the individual feels a sense of being lost, of lacking contact with solid reality. One is disoriented and "floating"—alone in a truly serious sense. The identity problem has become not simply a matter of frustration and loneliness but of not knowing what is real.

Here is the crux of the modern identity problem. Identity is acquired, as we said earlier, in a relationship; but the terms of the relationship as modern culture understands it are a self who acts and a world which is acted upon. This is no true relationship. It may be an interaction; but not a relationship. A relationship requires at least two persons, each of them able to speak to the other. The lonely self, busily engaged in making and remaking its world, finds no independent voice which talks back to it. It finds resistance, but no confrontation. It can force the world to yield to it, but can evoke no agreement. It meets failure, but no criticism; success, but no congratulation. It is deprived of a significant "other."

And so the modern person typically turns from the public, objective world to seek a private world of personal intimacy. From the superficial and indiscriminate use of first names in the most casual of circumstances to the desperate attempts to establish "meaningful relationships" in carefully constructed "human relations laboratories," the modern age demonstrates its thirst for personal intimacy. The instinct expressed in this is valid. Without personal intimacy, one becomes disoriented, alienated, and afraid. Without someone who cares, the immense challenges of life become unfulfilling.

There has probably never been an age which has valued the private world of personal intimacy as much as this one. The very factors in our mobile, technological culture which threaten the existence of such a world serve also to underscore its necessity. But its crucial shortcoming is seen in the fact that it has of necessity to be merely private. Intimacy is found only by abstracting the personal dimension from all else in life. Only in the gaps between the pressing issues of life "in the real world" can those fleeting experiences of intimacy be found. The presence of a person is only felt when the demands of decision-making and responsible action in the world are relaxed. These moments are precious, but they bear little relation to the greater part of life.

There is, therefore, an unreality about our private moments of intimacy. They occur at the cost of the omission of most of life. They lack substance. The business of life is excluded for the sake of a personal touch, a human word. The results are that the world continues to be dehumanized and personal relations lose real content.

This is not a universal experience, of course. Deep personal friendships can be found among those who are most completely immersed in the tasks of life. Marriages exist in which the personal relationships provide true *re-creation* in the midst of life, instead of merely *recreation* from it. But the culture militates against this. Those who discover such authenticity have laid hold on something for which the rest of the culture longs, but which it cannot often find.

Our world picture asks us to transcend the givens which face us and create a future which is different from the present. It asks us to be sufficiently secure in ourselves to create a world. Yet it provides us with no room for the very relationships we need in order to find this security. It offers us no "other" to speak to us. We can find the "other" only in moments of privacy. The larger world, reduced to raw material for my work of creation, has nothing to say to me on its own. It asks me no question in response to which I can declare my identity and become myself. And the private worlds speak to me only of private things, leaving the rest of me—the person who lives in the public world, unidentified because undeclared.

The Search for an "Other"

Where, then, is a real "other" to be found? People look, as a matter of fact, in a variety of places for an "other" to which they can answer. Some seem to find it in abstractions like "humanity" or "the welfare of society." Others find it in the customs of a particular society, which do indeed, at times, seem to speak—to make demands, and in doing so to shape the lineaments of my identity as a human person. Others again find a significant "other" in some cause in which they can be swept up and through which they can be drawn out of themselves into creative action.

The truth is, however, that none of these can be any more than a substitute, and a temporary one at that, for a significant "other." All of them, in the last resort, are creatures of the very people who turn to them in need. Whether one thinks of the institutions of a given society, or the ideals and hopes which are wrapped up in a particular cause, one realizes in the end that they are products of human creativity and human aspiration. They cannot really answer people back. They cannot take an initiative with people. They can only do and be what people enable them to do and be. None of them, therefore, can qualify as a true "other" for the persons involved with them.

The Transcendent "Other"

Our question still stands, then. Where are we to find the "other" which answers to modern humanity? Where is the "other" which corresponds to a humanity which is forever transcending its world and its own works? To put the question the other way around, to whom do I respond as I make myself and my world? This is the modern form of the question of God. It is the question of a real and transcendent "other" which is the point of reference, the Speaker and the Word, for humankind's self-discovery.

Why do we say, though, that this question about an "other" is a form of the question of God? We say so first of all because it is a question about something which genuinely transcends humanity, something which is not under our control or capable of being shaped by us. It is a question about that which goes beyond humanity in such a way as to be the continuing partner of a humanity which is constantly transcending itself. In the language of traditional theology, it is a question about an "other" which is independent in its own infinite being.

Second, this is the question of God because it concerns something which, while transcendent, is also present with humanity in the most intimate possible way. *God* is not properly the same of an abstraction or an absent absolute. It is a word for a transcendent "other" which gives itself in the most intimate and deep-reaching dialogue with humankind. *God* means not just a transcendence, but a transcendence which speaks.

Third, it is the question of God because it is a question about an "other" which is not only transcendent and present, but also *ultimate*. Self-transcending humanity cannot discover itself and its identity in a dialogue with an "other" which is less than truly final. To put this same thing another way, the meaning of human existence does not appear in any particular historical "jelling" of its identity. It consists in a relationship with God, who pulls it beyond every historical realization of its identity.

Fourth, it is the question of God because the "other"

which is asked about it is a *universal* "other." This "other" does not belong to the private moments of life alone, but speaks through the larger world of things and people which the enclaves of privacy exclude. It is the "other" which allows the world to have a proper and independent reality of its own, and, at the same time, to be a vehicle for people's encounter with the divine.

It must be clear, however, that the question of God is not answered, but merely raised, in this way. The question calls for such an "other," but unless a relationship with it is given to us, the question remains unanswered. Our situation is rather like that of children abandoned by their parents at birth. They can feel the reality of their parents' absence, they can point to their need of them now, they can even infer what they must have been like. None of this, though, will provide them with a loving embrace, a face turned towards them, or the sound of a parent's voice.

All questions about God, then, come to focus on one question: *Has God revealed himself to us?* The Christian theologian maintains that the ultimate questions of human life can be answered only in the self-revelation of God. If God has appeared to humankind in revelation, establishing a relationship with us, then our questions about identity and the meaning of human life are answered in principle. If God continues to appear to us, maintaining his relationship with us, the questions can be answered in our own lives.

· 2 ·

The God
of Scriptural Revelation

One way in which modern people approach the question of God is through their worries about identity: so much, at any rate, we have established. It is true that this is only one of many ways in which one can raise the question. At the same time, though, it is a way which seems characteristic of our own time. To say, however, that the question gets raised is not to say that it gets answered; and so our last chapter ended with a question. Is there, as a matter of fact, an "other"— beyond ourselves and beyond our human and natural worlds—with whom we have a relationship through which our true identity is established? Or, to break that question up: Does the word *God* refer to something real? In what way are people related to this reality? How is God properly described? What happens to people when they accept a conscious, knowing relationship to God?

In this chapter we shall begin to look for answers to these questions by seeing how two particular historical groups learned to talk about God. The groups in question are the people of Israel and that continuing Christian movement which has called itself, among other things, "the New Israel." The story of how they discovered both a reason for speaking of God and a way of understanding God is the burden of the Hebrew and Christian Scriptures—the Bible.

The Witness of Scripture

As we turn to the Scriptures, however, it is important that we understand clearly what sort of help they are going to give us. Plainly there are some sorts of assistance they will not supply. They will not offer arguments of a philosophical sort which are calculated to prove that God exists. Furthermore, they will not answer—or even raise—many of our speculative questions about God's nature and working. The writers of the Bible were not philosophers. They were not even, in the modern sense, teachers of religious doctrine. What they offer is something more basic and, hence, more important than either of these. They offer an account of God's *happening* for people. They tell how it came about that God became real for Israel—and for the New Israel.

Naturally enough, therefore, what the Bible offers us is a story—a history. Its books narrate or reflect upon a long, complex course of events. The reason they focus on events is, moreover, clear. It is that these people discovered God in things that happened to them. They did not find God through philosophical reflection or through self-exploration. They found God as the initiator and the meaning of events which made a difference in their individual and common lives. As a result of these events, they found themselves compelled to speak of God; and thus also to speak of themselves as people who had an identity in relation to God. Consequently, when they want us to understand who God is, what they do is the obvious thing: they tell the story.

But, you will say, there are so many stories in the Bible! At which "story" are we to look? Those which were of greatest interest to the people of biblical times were two in number: the account of the deliverance of the Israelites from slavery in Egypt, and the story of the Resurrection of the crucified Jesus. Why is this? Because the Exodus and the Resurrection narratives are foundation stories. Each of them tells of events which began—instituted, created—a relationship with God.

All the other stories—not to mention the psalms, the pronouncements of the prophets, the letters of the Christian Apostles—function to bring out the meaning, or the effects, or the implications of these foundational events.

The Exodus and Its Background

The series of events which make up the story of the Exodus from Egypt involves a motley crew of people whom the civilized nations of the ancient world called Hebrews. These were, apparently, vagabonds and drifters who belonged to no nation and had no homeland. Egypt had allowed some of them to camp within her borders and eventually found them useful as slave labor in one of Pharaoh's massive building programs. The biblical storytellers make much of the fact that these people were, as we say, nobodies—until the great event.

The great event, of course, was the Exodus itself. Some initiative beyond themselves raised up a leader for them. It called them together under this leader and got them out of Egypt and out of slavery in spite of the opposition of a great world power. In the process, this other power gave them a law and constituted them a people. They were nobodies no longer. They had being, identity, and calling. So, from generation to generation, this newly constituted people told the story of their Exodus. They knew that their character as a people—their values, their aspirations, the way the conducted their common lives—all derived from this mysterious, transforming invasion of their life by an "other" which had called Moses and, through Moses, them. By way of the Exodus, in short, the Hebrews had met God.

Had they, then, been atheists before? Certainly not. The world in which these nobodies lived was thickly populated with divine powers. Some of them were forces of nature. Others were the lords (baals) of a particular territory or a particular people. Above them all stood the dim figure of a supreme God—the source and unity of divine power, and thus the overarching or underlying mystery of things. This supreme God the Hebrews (and others) seem to have called

El, or (in the plural) *Elohim.* No, one cannot say that it was the Exodus which first started the Hebrews thinking religiously about the world or talking about divine powers. What it did do, however, was to change their understanding of who and what God is.

For the typical religions of the Near East—religions with which the Hebrews had been, and continued to be, closely involved—pictured the divine in a way very different from that in which the God of the Exodus had to be understood. The difference can be grasped most easily if we recall that these religions were essentially concerned with the mystery of nature. The supreme God and the lesser gods, by whatever names they were called, represented the power in and behind that given order of things. The divine was the living pattern of nature. It governed and sustained the dependable and regularities of things.

This sort of religion is not hard to understand. What human being has not, from time to time, been overwhelmed by the majesty and mystery of nature: by the sublimity of the heavens on a clear night; by the wonder of recurring seasons; by the miraculous fertility of the dark, rich soil? For agricultural peoples, however, these phenomena are more than just marvels or occasions of insight. They are the primary proofs and evidences of the fact that human beings are dependent on something beyond themselves, something "other." It is logical enough, therefore, that when such peoples think of God, they think of a power which guarantees, because in fact it embodies, the eternal, unchanging design of the natural order.

It was inevitable, moreover, that people whose attention was thus focused on nature and its cyclical regularities, its almost miraculous orderliness, should conceive of human affairs on the model of just such a natural order. Humanity is, after all, a part of nature and throbs to its rhythms. May one not assume, therefore, that the gods who order nature will order human society as well and that they will provide an unchanging design for its right working? Every ancient people thought so; and for this reason, every ancient people saw the divine as the originator and guardian of its political and social set-up. If Pharaoh reigned, he reigned because he was a part of the divine order of things; and if the Hebrews were slaves, they were slaves because of the very "nature" of things.

If that is the case, however, the God of the Exodus clearly did not conform to the normal picture of a God. This deity did not represent the established order of things, natural or social. This God picked out a group of nobodies and made them somebodies. This God changed the order of things. No doubt the Exodus God represented, as all deities represent, the mystery of things. In this case, however, the mystery is the mystery of that which brings about significant change, and not the mystery of that which keeps things in unchanging order. The God of the Exodus was a different sort of God. This God did not give things meaning by keeping them in unalterable order, but by doing something different—by making a difference in the way things were.

Consequently, when the God of the Exodus told Moses his name, it turned out to be a strange name. In the letters of the Hebrew language (which did not originally have signs for vowels) God's name was YHWH. Pious Israelites of later generations would not pronounce this name because it is the name of the ultimate mystery. Whenever it occurred, they said the word for *lord* instead. What is more, the name itself, YHWH, justified their reverence; for it was indeed a name which intimated mystery. It meant something like "I am what I am," or "I will be what I will be." It is, in short, a name which suggests that the one who bears it is no predictable sustainer of things as they are, but one who is *free*, and free to do the unexpected, the new. This God is free even to choose a lot of nobodies for his people.

The Exodus Experience

The point of saying all this is simply to make clear what, in practice, the experience of the Exodus signified. Moses and his companions did not, we may be sure, stop to analyze what they meant by *God*. Nevertheless, when they met YHWH, and when they learned that the God who bore this name, the God who brought them out of Egypt, was the ultimate "other" for them, they had discovered the divine in a new character. No longer was the mystery of life understood simply in terms of the orderly, recurrent courses of nature. The mystery whose name was YHWH had called people to have a history—to grow and change and suffer for the sake of something new which God would bring about.

Just consider the events in the story of the Exodus. God calls Moses from a quiet life in Midian and more or less drives him back to Egypt to lead a lot of slaves into freedom. YHWH then conquers the "divine" powers of Pharaoh: in the words of the ancient song, ". . . the horse and his rider he [YHWH] has thrown into the sea" (Ex. 15:1). So much for the gods of the "natural" order of things! Then the Lord led the people to a mountain where he veiled his fiery glory in the darkness of a cloud while he made a contract—a covenant—with them. In this act, God not only gives an identity to these nobodies by assigning them a law; he also gives them a future to hope for, a "promised land" where they will multiply and prosper.

Each of these events was something utterly new and utterly unexpected in the story of the Hebrew tribes. Who would have dared to think that the divinely established order of Egypt could be challenged and overthrown? Who would have expected that a power which could overthrow the gods of Egypt would then make a covenant with a lot of vagabonds and former slaves? And most of all, who would have supposed for a single minute that such people as these might be promised the future of which the Exodus God assured them?

But just because these events represented something novel and unaccountable, they called for a special kind of response on the part of the people. The people had to want and accept their freedom. They had to recognize and assent to their new identity as YHWH's people by obeying his Law. They had, above all, to take God at his word and travel in pursuit of the future he promised them, leaving all their securities and certainties behind. In a word, they had to renounce the given order of things and follow the God whose word was always: "Behold, I do a new thing!" (Is. 43:19).

The nature of this response is expressed in the language of a ritual vow which has been handed down to us from the distant past:

> Far be it from us that we should forsake the Lord [YHWH] to serve other gods; for it is the Lord our God who brought us and our fathers up from the land of Egypt, out of the house of bondage, and who did those great signs in our sight, and preserved us all the way that we went . . . therefore we also will serve the Lord, for he is our God (Josh. 24:16ff).

The very form of this vow—an ancient counterpart of the Christian's "I believe in God"—shows the kind of identity which YHWH gave his people when he called them. It is the identity of people who do not have an automatic "place" in an eternal order of things, and who must, therefore, responsibly and freely risk themselves for a promised future by committing themselves consciously to God. They will discover who they are, not by "belonging" somewhere in the unchanging structure of things, but by buying into a history in which things change. Their calling from YHWH, the Lord, is a calling to transcend the present order and seek his promise of a "new thing."

The Lord, the God of Israel

In all this, however, we are simply talking about the people of Israel and the quality of their experience and the effect which the Exodus had in their life. What, though, about the God of the Exodus? What do these events say about the nature of the ultimate—the "other"? What is being said about the divine when it is known as YHWH, that is, as "the Lord"?

First and most emphatically, YHWH is the name of ultimate mystery. All gods are mysterious. That is one of the things which make them gods. YHWH, however, is mysterious in a radically different way. The gods of the nations have their fixed roles and can be counted on always to do the correct and expected thing. They always sustain the order whose pattern their lives provide. YHWH, on the other hand, is no part of "the nature of things." He is not even its "eternal dimension," as the phrase goes. He is completely other than the world which humans can understand and predict. He stands apart from it and does new things. The very creation of the world, as Israel's sages came to see, is one of God's new things. YHWH's mysteriousness, then, is not just that of the unknown which may one day be comprehended. No: YHWH is the mystery who is always "beyond" and who says, "My thoughts are not your thoughts; neither are your ways my ways" (Is. 55:8). We might choose to say, therefore, that the God of the Exodus infinitely transcends the world in which he involves himself. He is the *holy* God.

But in the second place, YHWH is actively involved in the very world he transcends. He does not, in his mysteriousness, inhabit or constitute some other world than this, or hide in his inaccessibility waiting to be found out. On the contrary, we are given to understand that this God of mystery calls, covenants, leads, and judges; that, in a word, this "other" is an active agent in the life of Israel. The God who called the Hebrews out of Egypt was "up to something," was, in fact, the very author of the Exodus drama. Though this strange redemption of an insignificant group of slaves was the first inkling the Israelites had of YHWH's activity, it was not long before they were seeing his hand at work wherever they looked. "The heavens," wrote one of their poets, "are telling the glory of God; and the firmament proclaims his handiwork" (Ps. 19:1). By the time, some centuries after the Exodus, that the first chapter of Genesis was written, God was seen to be the initiating agent behind all activity. YHWH is the active, the *living* God.

In the third place, the God of the Exodus is present *for* his people and *with* them. He acts, as we have said; but that is not all. In and by this acting God also speaks—that is, he communicates himself. It is a characteristic of the Bible that it thinks of God and describes God as one who speaks. YHWH *calls* Abraham and Moses; he gives his *word* to the prophets. It is even by speaking that God creates the heavens and the earth. Looked at from one point of view, all that this sort of language shows is that the ancient Hebrews thought of words as intrinsically powerful and effective. From another point of view, however, it testifies to their conviction that God really does communicate with them. The many actions which they saw the Lord doing were not simply things done "out there" which they were meant to gawk and wonder at. Rather, they were genuine words, addressed to the people. They opened up a conversation between the God who did these things and the people who responded to them; and in the conversation YHWH was present, sharing himself with human beings.

Finally, though, if God is that ultimate mystery which communicates itself by what it does, then God is also one who can be known and identified by the character and quality of his activity. And the key word by which the Bible portrays the character of God's acting and speaking is *righteousness*. What YHWH does and says is *right*, both in the sense that it is true and trustworthy, and in the sense that what it brings about is just and good. The God of the Exodus keeps his word. He is a liberator and one who vindicates the oppressed. The Law which God gives to Moses really does set things right when it is kept. The Lord's judgments search the heart and bring truth into the open. In all these ways, YHWH is a righteous God; and he calls the people to be like him in this—to be faithful in their dealing as he is faithful with them.

So the God of the Exodus is the holy, the living, and the righteous God, who nevertheless lives with his people, speaking to them and sharing himself with them. "For thus says the high and lofty One who inhabits eternity, whose name is Holy: 'I dwell in the high and holy place, and also with him who is of a contrite and humble spirit, to revive the spirit of the humble, and to revive the heart of the contrite. For I will not contend for ever, nor will I always be angry; for from me proceeds the spirit, and I have made the breath of life' " (Is. 57:15ff).

The Resurrection

To move from the Exodus to the Resurrection is to cover a great deal of historical ground in one leap. On the other hand, the territory covered is precisely the course of that history of

God with Israel which the Exodus event had begun. We might say that the Resurrection of Jesus brings into focus the very future which the Exodus event had opened up. In other words, the Resurrection occurred as God's word to a people which was searching for the fulfillment of his ancient promise to Moses.

Before it is possible to understand how this is so, however, we must remember that much had happened between YHWH and Israel in the long interval between Moses and Jesus. They had learned a great deal about God; and God had taken them on a strange and difficult path. For one thing, Israel had come to understand that if YHWH was truly the name of the *ultimate*, then YHWH must be the one and only, the universal, God. It was not merely that the people had an obligation to be exclusively loyal to YHWH; more than that, there was no other God to be loyal to. "The Lord has established his throne in the heavens, and his kingdom rules over all" (Ps. 103:19). "He is the great King above all gods" (Ps. 95:3).

> For thus says the Lord,
> who created the heavens
>   (he is God!),
> who formed the earth and made it: . . .
> "I am the Lord and there is no other" (Is. 45:18).

But with this understanding, there necessarily came another. If the gods of Assyria and Babylon, the gods of the nations, were in truth no gods at all; if the peoples of these nations, therefore, had no God but YHWH, then they too must in some sense be his people. YHWH may have called Israel, but his purpose was not for Israel alone. God's salvation was for the ends of the earth. The time would come when

> . . . there shall be neither cold nor frost. And there shall be continuous day, . . . not day and not night, for at evening time there shall be light.
> On that day living waters shall flow out from Jerusalem, half of them to the eastern sea and half of them to the western sea; it shall continue in summer as in winter.

And the Lord will become king over all the earth; on that day
the Lord will be one and his name one (Zech. 14:6–9).

The Lord's "day," the day of promise, will be the day when
all peoples know YHWH and accept his love as their ruler.

None of this learning came easily or without great doubt
and pain. Nevertheless, Israel began to see God's promise to
Moses in a new way. It was not only a promise for Israel, but
a promise which embraced the whole world. It was not just
the promise of a good and fertile land; it was the promise of a
new order of things, in which right should prevail universally. And in view of this "day"—this day of the Lord—Israel
saw its own identity in a new light. The people of God was
the Lord's "servant," called "as a covenant to people, a light
to the nations" (Is. 42:6).

But just as time and suffering brought about this new understanding of God and of the identity of God's people, so it
also brought new problems and doubts. When would God
keep his promises? When would the day of YHWH appear?
Israel, after all, had had a checkered history since the time of
Moses; and while the chroniclers and interpreters of this history might argue that its frequent disasters—conquest, exile,
foreign domination—were all punishments for Israel's sins,
lessons intended to teach her new truths, there were inevitably voices which raised embarrassing questions, and also
voices which demanded that God prove himself, that he do
what is right once and for all. Some people, indeed, questioned whether God would—or could—keep his promises.
Others, however, saw in the disasters which successively
swept over the nation an advancing high tide of evil, in the
face of which God must and would act to set things straight.

But what could such an act be? It could not be one which
involved only Israel. Judgment had come again and again on
Israel, and she had learned to see it as just; it was the prelude
to salvation. But judgment must come on the other nations as
well. Nothing less than universal judgment would suffice, a
judgment which would bring the truth to light in the sight of
all peoples.

Furthermore, it could not, if God is just, be limited to those who were still alive at the time of its coming. YHWH was the God who appeared to Moses, and it had long been recognized that, though not known by name, he had appeared to Abraham, Isaac, and Jacob as well. This God could not leave out all those who had trusted his promises and then gone to their graves without seeing the promises fulfilled. On the Day of the Lord, the graves would be opened and God's people would be raised.

Finally, the Day of the Lord would be a totally new day. It would not be the old order of things cleaned up a little; for in that old order evil was not a superficial wound but a deep-set infection, one which involved earth itself and the angelic realm as well as humanity. The Day of the Lord would bring a new heaven and a new earth, a true Kingdom of God.

Then, in the reign of the Roman emperor Tiberius, Jesus came preaching and teaching and healing in Galilee. And the point of his ministry was that there and then God was beginning to keep his promises to Israel, the promises first made to Moses. "The Kingdom of God is at hand; repent and believe the Gospel." "Today this Scripture has been fulfilled in your hearing." Precisely how Jesus conceived this act of God by which Israel and the world were to be renewed was apparently a matter for misunderstanding and scandal in his own time, even as it is a matter for debate among scholars now. He tried to make himself clear by his actions as well as by his parables and teachings; but many of these seemed mystifying even to the people who remembered them. Two things, however, seem clear. Jesus saw his own work as the beginning of God's action for the redemption of his people: not just an announcement of that action from afar, but a preliminary embodiment of it. Furthermore, this action of God's was, in Jesus' eyes, not something undertaken simply for the vindication of his own name and the rescue of the righteous from an evil world. On the contrary, it was an action which included even sinners in its scope. It was an action of love, which embraced even those whose lives seemed to put them outside God's covenant and beyond the range of his redemption. Jesus proclaimed that such persons could also have a place in the coming new order.

All the more terrible and disappointing, therefore, was his execution at the hands of the Roman authorities. It was as though Israel's history had been repeated in Jesus: much promise, but little clear fulfillment. It is no wonder that his followers on the whole deserted or denied him, or that people mocked him. The disappointment of great hopes seldom evokes generous behavior in the people who have entertained them. Jesus had come pretending to bear God's Kingdom; and the event had proved him wrong.

"But God raised him up, having loosed the pangs of death" (Acts 2:22). This was the proclamation of Easter which grew out of the disciples' experience of the living Christ. He revealed himself to them, constituted them a community, and gave them a mission. In this way they knew that God had acted again, as at the Exodus. YHWH had done a "new thing." He had vindicated the cause of Jesus. He had done so, moreover, in the most dramatic and significant way. "God has made him both Lord and Christ, this Jesus whom you crucified" (Acts 2:36). What this statement and others like it assert is that Jesus' preaching and teaching about God's Kingdom was, after all, true, and that he himself is the one in whom this truth is actualized already. "He is not here: he is risen" means that Jesus is alive and that his is not the life of this age, but the life of the Age to Come. The time of fulfillment has dawned. God has acted for the liberation of his people from the domination of evil and from the destiny of death. In Jesus the new order of things is begun; and those who are with him by faith have started to participate in it already.

The God of Easter

It is easy to see, then, that the Resurrection of Christ proclaims the same God, and presupposes much the same picture of God as does the Exodus. It is, as the New Testament insists, "The God of Abraham and of Isaac and of Jacob, the God of our fathers [who] glorified his servant Jesus" (Acts 3:13). The mysteriousness and ultimacy of God are, if anything, heightened by the message of the Resurrection. The revelation of a new age, a "new creation," a transformed order of things, makes it impossible forever to think of God simply as a power (however great) within the world order, or simply as the divine pattern and guarantor of that order as it exists at present. On the one hand, this God is in the strictest sense ultimate and universal because everything is seen to start and to end with him. What things are and what things mean are shown by the Resurrection to depend in the last resort only on God. At the same time, however, God is sovereign in and over the world and human affairs, and is shown to be so by the fact that in relation to them he is free. The apparent inevitabilities of the world of human experience are not laws for God. In Christ he does a genuinely "new thing," and opens a future which none could have hoped for or conceived. Consequently, God stands not merely as the ultimate, but as the ultimate "other." He is something entirely beyond human calculation or control. The God of the Resurrection is no less a stranger than the God of the Exodus. He too dwells "in unapproachable light" (1 Tim. 6:16).

Yet, just as the proclamation of the Resurrection heightens our sense of the ultimacy and mysteriousness of God, so at the same time it heightens our sense of the active presence of God in and for the world. The holy and living God, mysterious in freedom, draws near to people in the Resurrection of Jesus; for the Easter story is not a mythical symbol of some timeless truth. It talks about something which impinges on the natural and historical order of things and therefore shows God to be actively up to something in our midst. The Easter Gospel proclaims that the mysterious and ultimate "other" offers himself to be the subject of human trust, obedience, and love. God makes himself *our* "other," so that in responding to him we know ourselves and discover who we are. It is for this reason that one New Testament writer characterizes the God whom "no one has ever seen" (1 Jn. 4:12) as "love" (1 Jn. 4:8). God is the mystery who is *for us*.

A Problem Arises

From this look at the two focal events of the Exodus and the Resurrection, then, at least one thing is clear. Considered in the light of their meaning for the people who experienced them, these events bear witness to the reality of an ultimate "other" which enters into relationship with human beings, and in doing so, identifies them—calls them to *be something* in their response to its Word. They show us God as the one who speaks and acts in such a way as to communicate himself to human beings and to let them respond in trustfulness and hope. They are thus revelatory events. They unveil God for us.

But is it possible really to make sense of the God they appear to reveal? It is one thing to see the way in which God is experienced and understood in the biblical history. It is quite another, though, to accept this picture of God as both adequate and coherent. There is, after all, something strange and paradoxical about the Scriptures' way of presenting God to us. On the one hand, we get the impression that YHWH is absolutely "beyond." On the other hand, he is "here," present. In one breath we say that God is indescribable and mysterious and outside the reach of any thoughts of ours; but then in the next breath we say that we know God's "name" or that God speaks to us, or that "God is love," or that God "does" this or that. And the question is: How are both of these ways of talking possible? Can they conceivably refer to one and the same reality?

The problem is not a new one. Christian thinkers of the first four centuries or so were much embarrassed by the fact that the Bible sometimes pictures God as very like a human being—losing his temper, being jealous, changing his mind about things. This reminded them, no doubt, all too vividly of some of the gods of pagan mythology, who seemed to embody many of the worst traits of human nature. In any case, the Church Fathers were sure that language like this had to be taken figuratively. The real truth about God only emerged when he was described as eternal and changeless and perfect. In other words, the language which the Bible uses to characterize God in his mysteriousness, in his "difference" from us, made a great deal of sense to them; but the language it uses to express his nearness, his concern for us, or his activity in our lives tended sometimes to embarrass them.

This attitude is entirely understandable, but it does not come close to solving the problem which the Bible's language about God leaves on our hands. In order to see in what direction such a solution may lie, we must think for a moment about what we mean when we use language about *otherness* or *ultimacy* or *mysteriousness* in speaking of God.

Partly, of course, language of this sort has a very important religious function. It is a perpetual reminder to people against what the Scriptures call idolatry. That word does not just mean making statues or pictures of God. What it really means is any sort of action or talk by which people suggest that they have God all figured out—that they know how to manage him because they know exactly what he is like and how he works. When we say that God is "other" or "mysterious," then, we are saying that he is no tool, no domestic companion, of humanity. Neither God's being nor his will is exhausted by what we know of each; and he is never, therefore, a guarantor of our ideals or beliefs or policies, however enlightened those may seem to us. Nothing that human beings make captures or encapsulates God.

To insist on the mysteriousness of God is also, however, a way of pointing to a philosophical truth, a truth about the character of our knowledge of God. If God cannot be represented visually, or bound to human policies and ideals, neither can he be directly grasped and understood through human words and concepts. All our words and ideas refer originally and properly to something within our world. When we speak of the ultimate, however, or of God, we are speaking of that to which everything in our world is referred for its meaning—that which explains everything besides itself. To suppose, therefore, that any image or idea can give a proper or adequate identification of God is to imagine that he is one of the very things which find their being and meaning in him. It is to reduce the Creator to the level of the creature. Because God is ultimate, then, he falls outside the categories which are used to classify things and events in the world. God stands as that which cannot be classified. He is of a different order.

The Church Fathers, then, were justified in their embarrassment at language which seemed to portray God as no more than an immensely powerful human being. They solved nothing, however, by switching to words for impersonal, nonhuman realities. If it is misleading to speak of God as angry, it is equally so to speak of him as unchanging. Terms of this sort may seem to be more adequate; for they do, after all, portray God as different from the things in this world of ours. The fact is, though, that when you describe God as "different from" something, you are still describing him in terms of that something and by reference to it. And the point is that while things in this world are "alike" and "different" in relation to one another, God stands outside the framework within which they are capable of being compared. "Change-less" and "changing" are equally adequate as descriptions of God—and equally inadequate.

Our conclusion, then, is clear. There is no language of ours which characterizes God literally. When we use words to talk about God, we are not describing but pointing; not grasping but intimating. In short, we are using figurative speech. Our language may sound crude and concrete (as in the case of a word like *angry*); or it may sound sophisticated and abstract (as in the case of a word like *changeless*). If taken literally, though, the most sophisticated language leads to idolatry; and if understood figuratively, the crudest language may point in the direction of truth.

"Person" as a Model for God

And that word *truth* is important here. It may well be the case, as we have said, that no human language about God can be thought to provide a literal description of God's way of being. The Bible itself suggests such a conclusion; for when it talks about God, it invariably uses the language of poetry, myth, or symbol. God is both rock and light; God nourishes and teaches on the one hand, and leads and judges on the other. God is king and lover, warrior and advocate. The very fact that such a wide range of images is used to characterize YHWH suggests that they are being employed, not in the ordinary way, but in a special way—poetically, if you like, or analogically. Nevertheless, the Scriptures suppose that this poetry gets at some fundamental truth, that its language is not just a chance collection of high-sounding terms, but a patterned *way of talking* which intimates and provides access to something real.

What is meant, though, by that phrase *way of talking?* What it refers to is the fact that behind the Bible's rich equipment of symbols and images for God there stands a more general picture of the divine which governs the way in which those images are used and understood. Such a way of talking—or governing rule—can be called a model for God. Just as physicists have constructed models of the atom, or employed wave models and particle models to characterize the behavior of light, so human speech about God tends to work on the basis of some controlling model for the ultimate. The function of such a model is not to describe God (for that, as we have seen, is out of the question); rather its function is to enable people to come to terms with God properly—to relate themselves adequately to the divine, and for this purpose to govern their thinking and speaking about it.

Such a model, moreover, springs out of an experienced relationship with God. In effect, it likens God's relation to the world to some relation which obtains among things within the world; and it does this not arbitrarily, but on the basis of the way in which the ultimate is apprehended or experienced. For example, the Greek philosopher Aristotle used for God the fundamental model of *something which is sought after or aspired to.* For him, the relation between seeker and sought, lover and beloved, is the governing image in terms of which he understands people's relation to God; and God, accordingly, is figured as *that which evokes aspiration.* To God so conceived, many other images can be applied. It makes sense, for example, to speak of God, in the light of this model, as "high and lifted up," as "king," or as "holy." On the other hand, what these images concretely mean or say about God is governed by the general model. God, the ultimate object of aspiration, is king—or exalted or holy—*in a different way* from God modeled as the power of life within things or the designer and architect of things. The same image, in other words, can say different things when it is used within the framework of different general models for God. Needless to say, then, it is important to ask: What is the most useful and adequate model to govern our thinking about God?

In the first place, no model of God can be accepted which does not convey what we have referred to as God's otherness or mystery. As a model, it must accomplish this, not by talking about it but by intimating and manifesting it. In other words, the ultimacy and mysteriousness of God must somehow be communicated simply through the use of the model itself. At the same time, however, there is a second requirement. An adequate model of God must also convey what is meant by speaking of his *presence* and his *activity*. Without the loss of any sense of God's "beyondness," it must make sense of the "other's" character as *that which communicates itself*. Finally, however, there is a third requirement. An adequate model for God must in principle be inclusive: it must be able to encompass and incorporate a variety of understandings and experiences of the ultimate. One might sum this requirement up by saying that an adequate model of God must be "rich."

Now, these are not easy requirements to satisfy. There are and have been, for example, a great many models to shape our understanding of God as mysterious and transcendent. People have sometimes used spatial models (God is "up there" or "out there"). They have also used models which are drawn from logical relations between the qualities of things, and so pictured God's transcendence by portraying him as the contrary or opposite of everything finite (as when he is described as "timeless" or "immutable"). The trouble with such models, however, is that they make God's active presence with us very difficult to affirm. A God who is "away" by his very nature is hard to think of as "here." A God whose way of being is logically inconsistent with that of the world is hard to think of as involved with it. What is more, people who think of the mystery and transcendence of God in such terms as these can only speak of God's active presence by thinking in terms of spatial nearness or by conceiving God as "like" things in the world—even as one of them; and this, too, has its drawbacks as a policy.

Maybe, in the long run, that explains why it is that the dominant biblical model for God is that of "person." Needless to say, we are talking here of a model, not some sort of literal truth. To say that God is a person, as though that description meant exactly what it means when it is used of a human being, is to miss the point entirely. God is *not* a person. God is the ultimate mystery of existence—but a mystery which, in and through such events as the Exodus and the Resurrection of Christ, we learn to trust, to obey, and to love. And in such a relationship, *person* becomes the only adequate way to model this mystery. We are not related to God as we are to an idea, an object in the world, or an ideal. We are related to him as we are to *persons;* and accordingly we model him that way in our thinking.

And the model seems on the whole to work. For one thing, of course, it focuses and gathers up together the various aspects of the biblical experience of God. *Person* refers to what we may call an intentional agent—a center of purposeful activity. This model therefore captures for us the perception of God as "up to something," as the ultimate initiative behind natural and historical events. At the same time, and for just this reason, it also figures for us what is meant when we speak of God as the "cause" or as the "ground" of things. If he is ultimate *person,* God is not a blind force driving or pushing things, nor is he an inert set of conditions which simply determines things. Rather, God is that active purpose which constitutes the setting within which created agents "do their thing" and exercise their own authentic initiative.

In a similar way, the model, person, helps us to grasp God as the ultimate reality which communicates itself. God, modeled as person, is one who addresses us in his actions, establishes us in a responsive relation with himself, and thus reveals himself to us. God modeled as person is a *speaker* and hence a self-giver, one who invites us into his life. For this reason, he can be one whom we love and seek and desire, not as the passive object of our searching, but as an active subject who invites and evokes our trust, love, and responsiveness.

The person model, then, can and does help us to identify and characterize the God of the Exodus and the Resurrection. Above all, however, it assists us to hold together in our understanding of God the apparently opposite truths of his transcendence and his immanence, his being absolutely "other" and his being entirely *with* us.

For clearly that is just the sort of thing a person is. If I know someone as a person, two things are always true in that relationship. The first is that the knowing in question is not just a knowing *about,* as I might know *about* a house that it is made of brick. Where persons are concerned, knowing also involves a certain intimacy, a genuine sharing, which can be expressed by saying that a person and I are *with* each other. Of course there are varying degrees of such intimacy; but to be in the presence of a person is always to have this experience of a very special kind of knowing, which is in fact a sort of participation in a common being. But if this is true, it is also true that another person always is, and always remains, *mysterious* to me. It is true that I can know a person with an intimacy which is entirely absent from my objective knowledge of things. Yet, at the same time, my knowledge of persons is never a mastery of them. They are always beyond me even in being with me. Moreover, there is good reason for this fact. When I know a person, that is always because the person in question *lets* me have such knowledge. The "other" has to reveal itself before I can have a personal relation to it. Consequently, the other person, as a person, is always free of me—always transcends me; and this transcendence is the condition, not the contradiction, of mutual personal presence and therefore of our personal involvement with each other.

When we model God, therefore, as ultimate "person," we are saying just these two things. First, we are saying that God infinitely transcends us in virtue of being "other" and of being "free" with regard to us. Second, we are saying that this otherness is the condition of God's being *with* us and communicating himself to us. In the case of persons, *presence* always means presence of an "other"; and thus it is only the person model for God which makes sense of the seeming paradox of God's being, at one and the same time, both absolutely "other" and entirely with us. It also explains that God's presence with us, and our knowledge of him, is always a matter of the "other's" initiative—a matter, as we say, of revelation. For persons can never be understood or known as such by inspection or by experimental manipulation; they can only be known *as they give themselves to be known*.

Conclusion

In the person model for God, then, we have the most adequate means for understanding the biblical view of God—the picture of God which is implicit in the Exodus experience and the experience of Christ's Resurrection. When a Christian says "I believe in God . . ." therefore, it is not to the ultimate conceived as idea or thing that he refers his life; it is to YHWH, who brought our fathers out of the land of Egypt, to God, who raised Jesus Christ from the dead. In the words of the creeds, Christians put themselves in the presence of one who becomes present for them by acting in their history—that ultimate "other" which speaks to them, and sets them free by calling them out of the present order of things for a new future. This is the fundamental scriptural "model" of God.

· 3 ·

Creation, Redemption,
Sanctification

Who or what is the God of whom the creeds speak? That is
the question we have been trying to answer; and our inquiry
has moved through two stages. First, we attempted to suggest one characteristic way in which the question of God
arises in contemporary western culture. God, we argued, lies
at the far end of people's quest after identity. In Christian
experience, God is known as that ultimate "other" in relation
to which both individual and group identity is worked out.
Then, in the second place, we looked at the picture of God
which underlies the Bible's proclamation of Exodus and Resurrection. These are set forth as events through which a
certain people came to know and to speak of God, and to
understand themselves in relation to him. This proclamation
sees God as the awesome and mysterious Lord who "speaks"
in his historical actions and opens for people the prospect of a
new future in covenant with himself. For this reason, the God
of biblical faith is modeled as "person." God acts and takes
initiative. He speaks and communicates himself. He draws
people into his life and his activity, even while he remains
absolutely "other" and, finally, unfathomable.

All this lies in the background of the creeds. It represents
the historical and traditional matrix out of which they speak.

Their own teaching, however, carries things a step further. Like the Bible—indeed interpreting the Bible—the creeds portray God as one who is known, obeyed, and loved because he communicates himself, and in doing so enables people to come to themselves, to grasp their identity through affirmation of their continuing life with him. The creeds, however, offer an analysis of the relationship of God with human persons. They present it to us as a relationship which has three dimensions. First, God appears as Creator, and human beings as creatures. Then God appears as Redeemer, and human beings as forgiven sinners. Finally, God appears as Sanctifier, and human beings as creatures destined through God's indwelling presence to a new kind of life— "the Life of the Age to Come." Let us, accordingly, look at each of these affirmations and see more exactly what each says about God, and about humanity in the light of its relation to God.

Creation

First of all comes the relation which is spoken of as "creation." This relation is ordinarily explained as meaning that the world—"all things, seen and unseen"—is made or fashioned by God. To understand what such an assertion might mean, however, it is necessary to look at the way in which the idea of creation is used in the Scriptures.

Among the peoples known to the ancient Hebrews, there were many stories current about the creation of things by a god or gods. These myths were primarily interested in the origins of the natural order of things. They portrayed the deity as conquering the forces of evil by turning chaos into order and harmony. The writers of the Bible knew such stories and used or adapted them, but in an odd and interesting way. At least to begin with, they employed the imagery of the creation stories not to picture the way in which the natural order of things got started, but to describe the way in which the people of Israel came to be. In other words, they perceived the Exodus event as a real beginning and thus as a creative act.

What is more, this use of creation imagery is perfectly understandable. The Exodus story assents that YHWH truly conquered the forces of chaos and evil by rescuing a lot of slaves and giving them a common identity as a nation. In doing so, God brought into being what had not before existed and so showed himself as sovereign over history.

Supposing that all this is so, however, one cannot for a minute think that YHWH's presence and activity are confined to the Exodus event itself. If God is Lord of history, his hand must also be seen in everything which went before and led up to that event. It must be the Exodus God who called Abraham and Sarah, Isaac and Rachel, Jacob and Leah, the ancestors of Israel. More than that, it must have been YHWH who saved Noah and his family from the flood. Indeed, if the Lord truly is the one whose initiatives lie behind everything that happens, it must have been he who originally "formed man from the dust of the ground, and breathed into his nostrils the breath of life" (Gen. 2:7).

To speak directly: the conviction that YHWH originally brought humanity into being and gave his commandment to the first of the race (Gen. 2:16) was not something the Israelites learned because they watched it happen. It was something they believed, and expressed in story form, because this was the only possible way of stating a crucial truth: that the Exodus was the definitive clue to the meaning of all of Israel's history from the very beginning. The God who brought Israel out of Egypt and gave it a law was by that act fulfilling his original and universal purpose, the purpose for which Adam was brought out of nonexistence and given a law and a calling, an identity. Thus, the meaning of the Exodus becomes the meaning of all of human history.

But the story could hardly stop there. If the God of the Exodus is the one whose purposes govern all of human history, if it was his will that brought humanity forth in the first place, then the universality of his power requires that this God be seen as the Lord of nature as well. This truth is enunciated eloquently in the hymns of the Jerusalem Temple, where it is said of the Exodus God:

Thou didst set the earth on its foundation
    so that it should never be shaken (Ps. 104:5).

Thine is the day, thine also the night;
    thou hast established the luminaries and
    the sun.
Thou hast fixed all the bounds of the earth;
    thou hast made summer and winter (Ps. 74:16–17).

YHWH indeed is pictured as *calling* the world into existence (quite a different metaphor from that of forming or making):

By the word of the Lord the heavens were made,
    and all their host by the breath of his
    mouth (Ps. 33:6).

And it is this image of creation by God's word which dominates the later account of creation in Genesis: "And God said, 'Let there be light'; and there was light" (1:3).

Thus the story of creation originally said two things. First of all, it said that the God who redeemed Israel from Egypt— that God and no other—is the universal Lord of all things. The righteous love which was revealed in that act of rescue is the purpose which governs all of history and nature. To put the same thing in another way: the *explicit* meaning of Israel's life is the *implicit* meaning of the life of the whole creation.

At the same time, however, the story of creation emphasizes a second conviction. The God of the Exodus is the *absolute* Lord. He is both the *only* Lord ("We believe in *one* God . . ."), and the one who is in final control of *all things* ("the . . . Almighty").

This conviction surfaces in a significant change in the imagery of creation. Nonbiblical creation stories pictured God as struggling with an adversary to produce and maintain order and harmony. Sometimes that adversary was positively malignant—a chaos monster; at other times it was simply a recalcitrant "stuff" or material with which, like any artist or artisan, God had to work as he "fashioned" or "molded" the world. In biblical thinking, however, imagery of this sort tended to be subordinated to another image, one which we have already noticed. According to this later image, the world sprang into being at God's mere word. There was no molding or forming; there was no adversary, active or inert. There was just God. "He spake, and they were created." And the point of such language is clear. It says, in effect, that God's power is final and unique. It is not limited by any opposition; it requires no tools, materials, or other sorts of helpers to be effective. What God says is so.

In later times, around the beginning of the Christian era, there appeared a new way of stating this conviction about the unique absoluteness of the God of creation. Against any idea that creation means God's taking some preexistent stuff or matter and shaping it as best he can to his own ends, the biblical conception of creation was said to entail the belief that God created the world "out of nothing." What this means is that there was nothing at all which God used to make the world. To the question, "What does God make the world out of?" the only possible answer is, "Nothing; he just evokes it." The world exists because of God—and because of nothing else.

Thus the creation of which the creeds speak when they assert that God is the "maker . . . of all things, seen and unseen" is not a process which any human words could conceivably describe; nor is it any part of the world's history. One does not get at what Scripture means by "creation" by speculating about "the first state" of the physical universe, or by asking what there was before the galaxies. Least of all does one get at it by taking the narrative of Genesis 1, for example, as a literal—or even a figurative—description of an actual process which took place "in the beginning." It is very hard to say, after all, what might be meant by the notion of a literal "beginning" of the world. It is not, however, hard to say what is meant by creation as a relation between God and this world. It means quite simply that this world—natural and historical process and the "things" and "events" which constitute it—has its existence in absolute dependence on God; and that this creation, as a totality and in all its parts, is expressive of, or at least open to, his purposes. To say that the world is God's creature is to say that the very structure of its being is such that it stands in a kind of covenant with God, who calls it out (as he did Israel) to "answer to" him.

The Creator God

This idea of creation conforms to the picture of God as person, which underlies the biblical proclamation of the Exodus and the Resurrection. The Creator God is the active initiative behind everything. God summons the world to be itself because in freedom he *chooses* it as something which answers to himself. It is not an automatic overflow of his being; it is a product of his will, his graciousness. God "makes" the world because he sets a value on what it is and on what it can become. Thus he appears as person in the highest sense—as one who loves, and one whose love is creative.

But the doctrine of creation does not merely confirm the model of God as person. That, after all, one would expect. It also draws out, and calls attention to, a basic implication of this model, and one whose consequences are fundamental for a Christian understanding of God. The creation image makes it clear that *there is an absolute distinction between the Creator and what he brings into being.* God is no part of the world he creates. The world is no part of God. God's initiative brings into being something which is *not God;* and it is this *not-God* which he values and loves, and which responds to his love in its turn.

God, then, is the context and source of creaturely being. Yet, at the same time, there is complete discontinuity between God and creatures. The two are not in any way apart from each other; but they are genuinely and radically "other," and this fact has implications.

First of all, it means that God's is the ultimate initiative in and behind everything. All the world depends on him for its being—and at every moment; but God depends on no one and nothing. As someone has put it, the world minus God equals nothing; God minus the world equals God. When we call God "love," we are affirming just this sort of radical and absolute sovereignty.

Second, however, when we say that creatures are not God, we mean that in their dependence on him they have a real being and an authentic identity which is theirs and not his. God does not compete with his creatures, for he is truly "other" than they. Rather, he is the ground both of their being and of their "doing their own thing."

It is wrong, therefore, for people to talk and think as though the activity of God excludes or supersedes the activity of his creatures. It does not. When we say, "God makes the trees grow," do we mean that the trees do not do their own growing? Similarly, when we say that God inspires a person, do we mean that that person is not responsible for his or her thoughts and actions? The answer is No in both cases. God's action does not take the place of ours. It is the context within which ours is possible. The Lord continuously wills our creaturely existence and activity as "not-God," and so establishes us as "others" who can answer him.

So, where there is talk of God's "otherness" or of the "discontinuity" of Creator and creature, what is meant is not that God is absent or uninvolved or inaccessible. What is meant is that God's working is not on the same plane as that of the creature. For that reason, it does not compete with creaturely activity; but for the same reason it intimately supports and grounds creaturely activity at every point. Creation is a way in which God is with us, because in it he *asserts* us. It is also, therefore, a calling to us to assert God in return, to be ourselves by being with him.

Humanity as "Creature"

What, then, does the doctrine of creation say about finite existence and, in particular, about human existence? First, it says that being a creature, being limited and finite, is a good thing in itself because it represents a kind of calling to communion with the "other." Then second, it brings this conviction into sharp focus in the doctrine that humanity is to be understood as "the image of God." We will look at each of these ideas in turn.

What does it mean, then, that "God saw everything that he had made, and behold, it was very good" (Gen. 1:31)? The point of this assertion is not merely that each creature, and all the orders of creation, are valuable in themselves—though it does mean that. The statement also insists that it is a good thing that creatures exist—that being a creature is not something to be unhappy or depressed or resentful about.

To be sure, creatures are not God. There is a discontinuity, as we have said, between God and the world which God calls into being, and this discontinuity marks God out as the sole ultimate. What is more, the Scriptures insist on this point. They denounce as idolatry any elevation of creatures to the level of the divine. Whether it is a question of "dumb images," or of forces of nature, or of human traditions, rites, and institutions, the Scriptures put them all in their place: they are creatures. They are not that transcendent "other" whose word establishes and gives meaning to all that is. To treat them as though they were is to live a dangerous lie. The doctrine of creation thus "de-divinizes" the finite world. Creatures are not God.

Creatures, however, are *something,* even though they are not God. Here we encounter the positive thrust of the Bible's statement about the goodness of the created order. Much human religion has tended to divinize some part or aspect of the natural order, with the inevitable result that it has also tended, by contrast, to denigrate others. If the stars are deities, then the earth is a place of exile from the divine. If mind is God, then matter is anti-God. At best, on this view, the world in its "lower" reaches is a faded or diluted version of the divine. The doctrine of creation, however, insists that the created order is something of its own proper sort and with its own proper value. It is not opposed to God, nor is it an inferior version of something higher. It is something other than himself which God affirms, which answers to him, and which is therefore open to him in all its parts.

The fact is, though, that we have a hard time seeing or accepting this positive side of our creatureliness. All the efforts people make to look especially important (or virtuous or powerful) to themselves and to others bespeak distrust of, and dissatisfaction with, their status as creatures. The doctrine of creation may assure us that we have the dignity of beings valued and affirmed by God; but that, it seems, is not enough.

Much of the reason for this lies in our experience of being limited or finite. We are born, apparently, only to die. Our reach always exceeds our grasp. We can see only a fraction of the things we should like to see, and do only a small part of the things we should like to do. We are confined to a particular bit of time and a particular slice of space—the "now" and the "here"; and even they get broken up into fragments which we can never seem to gather together. Somehow, we can never be all of what we are all at once. We live, therefore, in a state of continual restlessness and frustration.

Frustration is not the whole story, though. There is also anxiety, even fear; for one part of being limited is being forever dependent on things outside ourselves, and that fact induces constant worry. Very little of my life depends solely on me. I am dependent on climate and weather and the availability of food. I am shaped by the culture, language, and values which I inherit and by the social class into which I was born. Above all, I am dependent on other people—on their actions, their words, and their policies. I am what I am only through my relations with others; and this is a situation which can easily seem intolerable. How can I be myself if I am so utterly dependent on them—or on you?

There are certain traditions of mystical religion which regard this limitedness of human existence as the primary evil. They teach people a technique, a "way," whose aim is to attain exemption from finitude, to rise above the limitations of time and space and to achieve interior self-possession and self-sufficiency. By this means, it is thought, the individual can realize identity with the whole of things, thus overcoming the partial nature of ordinary existence, and at the same time achieve freedom from dependence on what lies outside the self.

Whatever the intrinsic merits of this particular sort of mysticism, it does serve to make one thing clear. In human beings, limitedness is not just an objective, given condition of life. It is a condition which people (unlike stones) feel, recognize, and conceptualize. Human beings have their limits; but they peer over them, and they can accept, regret, or try to evade them. Consequently, at one and the same time—in one breath, as it were—it can be said that human beings are limited, and that they can, in imagination, thought, and intention, pierce beyond their limitations. They can reach out for wholeness, though it escapes them; they can pursue the security of perfect self-possession, though they are dependent on others. They have limits; but to some degree, they transcend them.

The doctrine of creation, however, does not regret the creaturely state. It is an affirmation of it—and emphatically so in the case of humanity. It sees neither limitation nor the experience of limitation as evil in itself. It conceives and evaluates these phenomena in a different way altogether. It understands the human, and creaturely, way of being as openness to the "other." Human beings as individuals are incomplete in themselves and dependent on what is not themselves: that is plain enough. What this fact points to, however, is not that people must become "entire in themselves," but that human wholeness is achieved through the transformation of mere dependence into responsive sharing. The human person is inherently directed toward the "other." Its reachings and stretchings beyond its limits, therefore, are not efforts to take everything into itself. They are efforts to find fulfillment in knowing, answering, and loving the "other."

In the first instance, this "other" is discovered in things and persons within the created order. In the last resort, however, people find their fulfillment only in the God who is the ground and source of all created things. "My soul is restless," wrote Augustine of Hippo, "until it rest in thee." In other words, the finitude which Augustine's restlessness betrays points him towards communion with God; and for just that reason, it is no evil, no frustration of his being. On the contrary, it is a necessary component in his, and everyone's, highest good—responsive communion with the ultimate "other."

Thus we come inevitably to our second major point: the assertion that humanity is made "after the image of God." This characterization of humanity is derived from Genesis 1:26–27, the later of the two biblical accounts of the creation of humankind. The earlier account (Gen. 2:5–7) says nothing about this idea of the image; and the remainder of the Hebrew Scriptures knows little of any such notion. The fact is that this conception arrived rather late on the scene in Hebrew tradition, and more is made of it in later Christian thought than in the Bible itself. Nevertheless, as it is set forth in Genesis, the idea summarizes and brings to conscious awareness certain themes which are central to the biblical understanding of humanity.

Of these themes, three seem to be basic. First, Genesis 1:26–27 clearly asserts that human beings have some kind of overall similarity to God, though the nature of the similarity is not fully spelled out. Second, at least one aspect of it is identified for us. It consists in the fact that humankind has dominion over the rest of nature (Gen. 1:26b). But finally, the story dwells on the fact that this dominion has to be exercised in a relationship of responsive obedience to God.

From this account, two matters are quite plain. To begin with, humanity is envisaged as being part of the created order. Adam (and in the passage we are considering, that name does not mean an individual male person, but "humanity") is a creature who exercises control of some sort over other creatures. This fact is symbolically conveyed in the earlier creation narrative by the statement that the first human being named the animals (Gen. 2:20). *Naming* here means recognizing, understanding, and giving expression to the reality of something. Humanity thus appears, in the creation story, as the place where nature achieves self-awareness, and hence as the center from which it controls and directs itself. In this way, humanity exercises a God-like function. It oversees the world of which it nevertheless remains a part. In other words, the human being is that creature in which knowledge, and its inevitable companion, responsibility, explicitly appear. The human being speaks for itself, even as it speaks for its fellow creatures, and in doing so it "images" God.

But to whom is this creature responsible? To whom does it answer? Obviously, to start with, Adam is responsible to the creatures who get named. The one who names something has an obligation to the thing which is named—an obligation to tell the truth about it. The "other" must not be violated by being falsely identified. But then Adam is one of the very creatures over which this human dominion extends. People not only name others; by the character of what they do and say, they name and identify themselves. Consequently, this human being is not only responsible *for* itself, but *to* itself—responsible for living up to its identity and its calling.

True as all this may be, however, it does not lie within the direct scope of the creation story's interest. The narrative in Genesis has its attention focused on something more fundamental. What it insists upon is the fact that all these creatures for whom and to whom humanity is responsible are, in the final analysis, God's creatures. In being responsible to them, humanity is responsible to God; for it is God's will which is expressed in their being and fulfilled in their welfare. Consequently, it is God to whom the human race is ultimately responsible: it is God who commands (Gen. 2:16).

Here then is our final clue to the meaning of the idea that humanity is created after God's image. All creatures exist as "answers" to God's word; but Adam answers to God in a very special sense. A human being's answering is not just an automatic, "natural" affair. It does not consist simply in carrying out some fixed role in the processes of the natural order. Because humanity sets names to things, and thus "sees over" the natural world, it can, within limits, change and control its environment. Consequently, the natural order itself is not, and can never be, the limit of the human horizon. The human being sees beyond the natural order, raises questions about it, and wonders at it. For this reason, the only horizon which humanity knows is that of the Creator of nature, God. It is always God to whom humanity answers. It is God with whom humanity co-responds. In this sense, Adam is "the image of God."

But let us be sure exactly what this means. In the first place, of course, it means that human beings exercise a real moral freedom. We are the creatures who are addressed by God and who answer back to him. In such a relationship, however, freedom emerges, because the very existence of the relationship means that we have to decide about ourselves by the way we answer. Most creatures simply are what they are and do what they do—"by nature," as we say. Human beings, however, because they hear God and must answer back, say for themselves what they will be and do. They have a hand in making, and in remaking, their nature.

In the second place, however, people's possession of moral freedom does not mean that they cease to be limited and dependent like all creatures. Even their freedom is not something which they possess and generate all by themselves. On the contrary. People possess freedom only because they are answerable, and therefore only in relation to the "other" which calls upon them to answer. Freedom is not independence. We still depend for all that we are—including our freedom—on other creatures and ultimately on God.

Finally, in the case of humankind, this dependence nevertheless takes on a special form. The human being is not a puppet, and for this reason its proper way of being dependent is not to be passive in relation to the "other," but to hear, answer, and acknowledge the "other." With humanity, in short, dependence can only take the form of communication and sharing—of being *with* the "other." For this reason, humanity's limitation is also its glory. Adam is fulfilled in, and only in, free affirmation of the "other"—and that is truly a limitation. In affirming the "other," however, this creature reaches out to share the life of God—and that is truly glory.

Redemption

The creeds portray God in the first instance as the Creator of the universe. Then, however, they go on to present him in another role—as the world's redeemer in Christ. This sequence of ideas is significant. It means not only that there is a real connection between creation and redemption, but that the connection is of a particular sort. The doctrine of creation states what has to be true about the world if it is going to be the sort of world in which redemption can occur.

In other words, the doctrine of creation is really the statement of a promise—a promise which is not a matter of words merely, but which is ingrained in the very nature and structure of the world. To say that the universe is created is to say that nature, history, and human existence carry deep within them an orientation to God. They refer to God as their origin—as that "beyond" which confers both being and meaning on them; and consequently they refer to God as the one in whom they are fulfilled. The world's createdness, then, is a pointer. It points to the possibility of the human world's becoming, in an open, explicit, and realized way, what it already is implicitly and in principle: God's world.

On the basis of this understanding of creation, we can begin to see what the word *redemption* means. In Christian parlance, that term refers to happenings in human experience and history through which the promise of creation begins to be actualized—happenings through which the Creator's original purposes begin to find their fulfillment.

To say this, of course, implies that there is, or has been, some obstacle to the realization of creation's promise; and this is true. People talk about redemption, and about the need for redemption, because circumstances in the human world do not correspond with the promise of creation. We may be convinced that the ultimate truth about human beings is that they are made for God and for one another. Nevertheless this truth does not very often or very easily show itself. In fact the very opposite seems to be the case. People are "tied and bound" in relationships and attitudes which make them hostile to God and to one another. To actualize the promise of creation therefore means, necessarily, to put right something which is wrong.

What the nature of that "wrong" is we shall see shortly. For the present, however, our aim is simply to suggest what biblical and Christian tradition has meant by redemption. Literally, of course, the word *redemption* refers to the process of setting free a slave by paying the necessary price. When we say, therefore, that redemption means "happenings . . . through which the promise of creation begins to be actualized," the sort of happenings we have in mind are events through which a people are set free for a new life. In the first instance, of course, such liberation has a negative character. It is a matter of being set free *from* something—from all the obstacles which impede people's realization of their identity in relation to God and to one another. These may be interior obstacles, or exterior obstacles. They may be obstacles rooted in attitudes and habits of the individual or obstacles rooted in the customs and structures of society. Whatever their character, however, the "freeing" which redemption brings with it necessarily involves their neutralization—their overcoming.

This negative side of liberation is, however, only one aspect of the process of redemption. Just as essential is its positive side. To be redeemed is not only to be freed *from* something. It is also to be freed *for* something. It involves a process in which people learn to be themselves in and through their affirmation of the "other"—a process, in other words, in which the human self opens out to God and to fellow creatures. From this point of view, redemption is the occurrence of that which brings people out of themselves into fuller participation both in the life of God and in the life of God's creatures.

How does this kind of redemption happen, though? The creeds assert that it happens through God's action—but God's action in and through the living and dying of Jesus the Christ; and behind this assertion there lies an important principle. Redemption occurs only when, and only as, the ultimate "other" becomes actively present for us in such a way that we meet it as a decisive factor within the field of our own living and acting, and so as something to which we can and must respond directly and personally. God the Creator we can conceive and wonder about and marvel at. Yet this God, this mystery which undergirds and supports all of history and all of nature, is not a specific and particular presence to which we must answer and which affects us as part of the immediate context of our own life. This perhaps explains why biblical faith does not have its historical starting point in a recognition of God as Creator but in an encounter with God as one who speaks in specific and particular terms to Moses and to the people of Israel—and so calls them into fellowship with himself. It is this *speaking* God who redeems: that is, the God who is present for people in their own history as a reality which calls to them, says something to them and about them, and so makes a difference for the character of their lives.

That is why "Word" is a central biblical symbol for God's redemptive action. It is, of course, a symbol. God does not pronounce words in the fashion of a human being. But God's redemptive actions are like human speech in at least three important ways. In the first place, they let us know God is there for us. This is perhaps the first function of human speech—to be a sign of the attentive presence of another person; and God's attentive presence for us is the essential precondition of our redemption. In the second place, however, God's redemptive actions are like words because they are revelatory. They communicate God's purposes and exhibit his character; and in this way they enable us to know God. Finally, a word spoken to a person is something which can, and frequently does, make a difference for the quality of that person's life. A word can do a job and thus change a state of affairs; and in this way, too, God's redemptive action is like a spoken word. It alters human circumstances, and creates new possibilities for people.

To speak of redemption, then, is to speak of the way God acts to fulfill the promise of creation. God does this by becoming present for people as his own Word, and so setting them free for life of a new quality—for a life fulfilled in love.

God the Redeemer

Like the doctrine of creation, then, the doctrine of redemption involves a "picture" of God. The two pictures are not inconsistent with each other. It is the same God who appears in both. Nevertheless, each sees God in a different light, for the obvious reason that people's relation to God as Creator is of a different order from that of their relation to him as Redeemer. The Creator God is the present ground of all actions and events—the infinite horizon or context of creaturely existence. The Redeemer God is present for people in a concrete and specific way, to overcome the evil which infects their lives and to enable their free and personal sharing of their lives with the "other." In redemption, we might say, God the Creator objectifies himself for us, and in so doing alters the quality of our relationship to him. It is no longer a necessary and merely "given" relation. It has become, rather, a relation which involves consciousness and choice, and which therefore involves us in a responsible and personal orientation to God.

For this reason, when the creeds turn from creation to redemption, they call attention to two matters. First they make a theological point. Then they offer an historical recitation. And in doing these two things, they paint the outlines of their picture of God as Redeemer.

The theological point is concerned to say, quite simply, that it is the Creator God and no other who does the work of our redemption. As they turn from creation to redemption, the creeds begin by naming Jesus Christ, and then immediately explain that this person is "the Son of God." The Apostles' Creed does this rather simply. Jesus, it says, is God's "only Son, our Lord." The Nicene Creed is much more elaborate and reflective at this point. It takes great pains to explain who this "Son of God" is, and so to insist that it is indeed *God* who is met in Jesus. It describes the Son of God as "God from God, Light from Light, true God from true God." It says that he is "of one being with the Father." All of this is calculated to emphasize just one thing: that it is the God of creation who meets us as redeemer. It is the same God all over again, now with us as Word.

This Word, however, is incarnate; and this point the creeds make not primarily by saying it straight out, but by referring to a sequence of historical events. They mention Christ's birth, death, and triumph. They even specify a point in time—"under Pontius Pilate." In all this, they identify certain events as happenings in which God makes himself concrete for us, in which the Creator is met as his own Word to us. The Redeemer God is a God who draws near to us by becoming a reality in our world, by making human life his own.

Consequently God the redeemer—God with us as his own Word—is experienced as the God who loves. In making human life his own, in subjecting himself to the evil which human beings do and suffer, in overcoming that evil in his own life—in all these ways, God shows himself as one who reaches out to people in costly love so that they can learn to answer back and share their life with the love which creates them.

Humanity as Sinful

What, though, does the reality of redemption—of God as redeeming Word—tell us about ourselves, that is, about humanity and human nature?

From one point of view, of course, it just confirms and reiterates the fact that humans are creatures, finite beings made to answer God and be with him. At the same time, however, it shows up a new and darker side of humanity. In the presence of God's love, in the presence of his Word, the evil which afflicts and infects humanity becomes palpable. As John's Gospel suggests, the coming of light makes the darkness apparent.

For when they are confronted with God's Word, with his redemptive action and presence, people draw back. In one way or another, they show that they are afraid of God and unwilling to trust him. YHWH brought the Israelites out of Egypt, but their reaction was to grumble, to long for the fleshpots of Egypt, and to ask for gods who would be less demanding and more sympathetic to their felt needs. Jesus, the personal bearer of God's presence, was arrested, tried, mocked, and executed. God's liberating action, it seems, reveals that human beings have a taste for slavery. They are afraid of God's grace. When they encounter God's love, it seems, people at the same time discover that they have a real resistance to love.

And this discovery is the discovery of sin. In the minds of many people today, the word *sin* signifies simply breaking a law or violating rules of behavior established by religious custom. To some extent, moreover, this understanding has been encouraged by the churches. They have led people to think of "God's will" as calling for nothing more than conformity to a particular code of conduct or set of prohibitions.

In fact, however, Jesus' way of interpreting the Old Testament Law should have made it clear how inadequate such an understanding is. To explain the true meaning of the Law, he called attention to two commandments: "Thou shalt love the Lord thy God"; and "Thou shalt love thy neighbor as thyself." These imperatives are not, as Jesus uses them, particular rules or regulations at all. They have a more general function. They are an explanation of what is meant by moral good—and, by implication, its opposite, moral evil.

Goodness for human beings, on this view, consists in affirmation of the "other," and that means both the ultimate "other"—God—and creaturely "others"—the neighbor. Human beings are so constituted that their life, growth, and fulfillment as persons depend on their openness to the "other" which addresses them, makes claims on them, and enables them to "come out of themselves." Consequently, all basic moral values are concerned with maintaining such openness. Social and personal justice, fidelity and loyalty, truthfulness, and respect for life are virtues because existence ceases to be human when the "other" is not affirmed as a condition of one's own freedom and selfhood.

The field of moral action and decision, then, is not people's relation to a code, but *people's relation to other creatures and to God.* The "code mentality" as often as not forgets or suppresses this fact, with unhappy consequences. Especially is this true where an understanding of *sin* is concerned. It is not merely that blind obedience to a legal or customary code sometimes results in violation or denial of the "other"— though that is true enough. More important is the fact that it frequently leads to forgetfulness of the religious—or better, the theological—dimension of sin. For *sin* means moral evil seen and experienced as refusal of the ultimate "other"—God. To put the matter as plainly as possible, sin is violation of God himself. It is not violation of a code of right and wrong which, for some obscure reason, happens to "anger" God. It is closing oneself off from him, and thus denying the ultimate "other" in practice. Adam and Eve's real problem was not that they ate a piece of fruit in contravention of law. It was that they refused to believe, trust, and obey God. They closed themselves to God: they "hid themselves from the presence of the Lord God." And that, at root, is what is meant by "sin."

This is the reason why redemption not only remedies sin but exposes it. Only at the point where God speaks his redeeming Word is sin fully brought out into the open, for sin *is* refusal, fearful repudiation, of grace. It is hiding from God's love.

But who, we might ask, would refuse grace? Who would be so foolish? As a matter of fact, almost anyone. To accept grace is, after all, to admit that one wants and needs it—that one's whole life and being are somehow dependent on the "other's" love and generosity. This is an admission, however, which most people, at least in practice, are afraid and unwilling to make. To make it means that one must learn to live by trusting and loving the "other"; and we are by no means certain that even God (not to mention our neighbor) can really be trusted. We prefer, therefore, as Adam and Eve did, to keep the reins of our lives very firmly in our own hands: to distrust the "other" on principle and to stay in control of our own destinies. In doing this, however, we reject grace; and with it we also reject our status as creatures who are ultimately dependent on God. We close our ears to God's Word and turn in upon ourselves. And that rejection of grace is sin.

The sin, then, which grace brings to light, is not just an act in the present or a series of acts in the past. It is also, and more significantly, a *disposition* which is deeply seated in human life: the disposition to fear dependence, to distrust the "other," and to want to be sure of oneself by achieving perfect control of one's world. This disposition—which is roughly what ancient theology referred to when it spoke of "original sin"—amounts to a compulsion to repudiate creatureliness and to play at being God for the sake of one's own certainty, security, and independence.

It is, as we have said, the rejection of grace which brings human sinfulness to light; but the disposition to sin shows itself in a much wider range of acts and attitudes. In human relations, whether among individuals, among groups, or among nations and classes, it shows itself in a compulsion to dominate or to "do all the talking"—in short, to make sure that other people serve one's own purposes and conform to one's own rules. In our relation to the natural order of which we are a part, sin shows itself in a tendency to exploit and to deny the integrity of the "other"—which in this case cannot answer back. The root of all such behavior, however, remains people's need to be in complete control of their circumstances, and this in its turn grows out of the anxiety and fear which are generated by the claims of the "other" to have a place, an inner integrity, and an initiative of its own.

Furthermore, this disposition—this sinfulness from which sinnings issue—does not affect individuals only. It creates systems of values and patterns of human relations which perpetuate themselves socially and historically. Consequently the Word by which God calls people out of fear and distrust meets not a scattered but an organized opposition from systems which, in different ways and to different degrees, pervert the very logic of human nature. Long before we are old enough to think for ourselves, society teaches us what to expect from life. We therefore find ourselves lured into false needs for self-aggrandizement and self-protection. Our opportunities for trust and mutuality are narrowed. The rejection of creatureliness, of openness to the "other," is made to seem a necessity of existence.

This is the nature of the evil which God's redemptive action brings to light. It is not finitude or creatureliness; it is *sin*—the compulsive inability to affirm the "other" and thus to come out of oneself in trust and love. God's liberating Word, however, does not merely expose this evil; it represents the one basis on which sin can be overcome. When God speaks, he opens himself to humanity. At great cost, he affirms humanity as the "other" which he loves. In doing so, however, he reveals the one foundation on which trust and love can be built—a love, namely, which is stronger, more lasting, and more intense than the anxiety and distrust which oppose it. God's word *reveals* sin in the process of *overcoming* it.

Sanctification

In creation, then, the ultimate "other" is transcendently present as the ground of creaturely being and acting. In redemption, the ultimate "other" is objectively present as its own Word to humanity—the Word which both reveals and overcomes sin, and points to the fulfillment of the promise implied in creation.

The creeds, however, do not stop with mention of creation and redemption. They go on to give an account of yet another dimension in the relation between God and his creatures. They speak of the way in which the promise of creation and the Word of redemption take root in creaturely existence itself and transform it *from the inside*. This is the process customarily referred to as *sanctification*. That term itself means "making holy," and the same Latin root can be seen in the word *saint*, which signifies a holy person.

From the point of view of the Scriptures, it is a strange and rather bold thing to say that a creature, whether a human being or not, can be holy. In the Bible, holiness is properly an attribute of God alone. It is only God's name which is correctly called holy. In the prophet Isaiah's vision, it is "the Lord of hosts" whom the six-winged seraphim describe as "Holy, holy, holy" (Is. 6:3); and what these words express is the awesome otherness of God as that is revealed in his unspeakable majesty and in his unchanging love of what is right and just. Confronted with the glory of God the Holy One, therefore, Isaiah is struck with fear and with a sense of utter unworthiness (Is. 6:5). He is sure, in the presence of the Lord, that he himself, at any rate, is not holy.

How then can we dare speak of the sanctification of human persons? Does not the very idea of a holy person smack of idolatry? Does it not inevitably confuse the creature with the Creator? Certainly human history indicates that this sort of confusion has been made countless times—if not in the case of persons, then certainly in the case of things. Places, buildings, books, and even human customs, have been treated as so "holy" that they cannot be touched by criticism or change. Yet such idolatry contradicts basic Christian belief. "You alone," says the hymn *Gloria in excelsis,* "are the Holy One; you alone are the Lord."

Nevertheless, Christians continue to assert that God sanctifies people, that he makes them holy. How can this be? It is not because any creature matches or even approaches the glory of God. Nevertheless, a created person or thing may be called holy as and when God claims it as his own, as and when it is "set apart" for God.

Notice that this setting apart does not involve any change at all in the nature or character of the creature itself—only in its relation to God. When God calls Israel "a holy nation," that is not because the Israelites have all at once become exceptionally virtuous. It is simply because this nation is his "own possession among all peoples" (Ex. 19:5f). When Paul calls his Corinthian friends "sanctified," he means that they are "called to be holy" and so to belong to God (1 Cor. 1:2), not that they always do or think the right thing.

People who are holy, then, are in the first instance people claimed by God. This means, though, that they are also made open and available to God. God has, as it were, tapped them on the shoulder to get their attention. A conversation has started, and it will be a holy conversation because God has begun it. To be sanctified is to be called to answer God consciously and explicitly, and so to be set apart for God's purposes and his company.

But what happens in this process of sanctification? We might, to continue a metaphor we have already employed, say simply that the conversation which God has started with us becomes one which flows more easily and calls up deeper and deeper levels of our selves. In the presence of his Word to us we experience the disturbance of joy, and we reach out to God by agreeing with his Word, by making it our own Word back to him. Then two things happen. The way we live begins to be shaped from the inside by this internalized Word of God; and the promise of our nature is fulfilled in a sharing of God's life.

It should be clear, then, that sanctification is not something separate or distinct from creation and redemption. The three belong together, as three ways of seeing the same fact—that God loves the world which is his "other." Redemption is the objective historical enactment of the meaning of creation; sanctification is the internal, subjective enactment of redemption. In all three, what is meant is that creatures are open to the ultimate "other," and therefore open to all the rest of the creation God loves.

God the Sanctifier

Nevertheless, when we speak of sanctification, we do in fact acknowledge yet another mode or dimension of our relationship to God—or better, of his presence with us. The mysterious "other" who is with us is not only the power which creates and the Word which affirms our being; it is also the interior presence which forms our response.

Saint Paul, in the closing verse of his Second Letter to the Corinthians, uses language which will do as well as any other to capture this character of God's activity and presence. In a very familiar formula, he speaks of the "grace" of Jesus Christ, of God's redeeming Word to us. He speaks then of the "love of God," the creative love which establishes and sustains the world and which is enacted in Christ for our salvation. Finally, he speaks of the "sharing" or "fellowship" of the Holy Spirit. It is here that we encounter the third mode of God's presence for humanity. Here God is with us, not as the ground of our being, nor yet as the Word which speaks grace to us, but as the Spirit who shares himself as companion, who *stands in with us,* shedding the love of God abroad in our hearts, and thus empowering us to open ourselves to God and to neighbor.

Why do we refer to God in this third mode of his presence as the "Holy Spirit"? And do we say "he," "she," or "it" when speaking of the Spirit? This problem becomes easier when we recall the imagery which suggested the word *spirit* in the first place. In each of the three languages that have influenced our theological vocabulary—Hebrew, Greek, and Latin—the word for *spirit* means "breath" or "wind." Breath is the most easily recognizable sign of life. When a person is breathing, we know he or she is still alive, however few other signs of life there may be. That is why ancient peoples tended to regard breath as life itself, or at least as the power of life—invisible and mysterious, yet obvious in its presence. The wind, too, is a sign of power and vitality. It, too, is invisible and mysterious, and it "blows where it wills" (Jn. 3:8). For ancient peoples, therefore, the wind, like breath, was a power both obvious and mysterious.

So the powerful "wind of God," which manifests God's active and purposeful presence, and the interior breath of life were felt to be akin. *Spirit* is the name both of the divine force which empowered Samson, Gideon, and Moses to fulfill their callings, and of that "breath of life" which God "breathed" into Adam's nostrils to make him a living spirit (Gen. 2:7).

What better word, then, could one find to name the life of God within us as it moves us toward closer fellowship with him? It is only when we try to visualize—to form a mental image of—the Spirit that we get into difficulties. It is, after all, the Word or Son of God who is said to be God's image—that is, the objective manifestation of God's reality. The Spirit, however, is *imageless*, that invisible, powerful life of God whose effects can be seen and whose presence is felt, but of whom no picture, not even a mental picture, can be drawn.

It makes little difference, therefore, which pronoun we use. If, as English speech customarily does, we use "he" for God, this will do for the Spirit also; for the Spirit is God. (The masculine pronoun should not be interpreted as suggesting that God is male. God is beyond sexual differentiation, and both female and male are created after his image because both are *persons* answerable to the ultimate "other.") On the other hand, it makes perfect sense to call the Spirit "she" (the Hebrew word for *spirit* is feminine) or "it" (the Greek word for *spirit* is neuter in gender). The important point to remember is that what all such pronouns refer to is the powerful, life-giving, interior presence of the Lord.

The word *spirit*, then, means God as one who is present in and through human thoughts and actions, bringing people alive and empowering their response to his Word. In that sense, God is one who shares himself, and makes himself the interior companion of humanity in its movement toward God.

Consequently, God as Sanctifier is *one who transforms.* Where his strengthening and vitalizing work is not resisted or perverted, he enables human beings to reorient themselves. In virtue of his presence, we can know ourselves as persons capable of love—capable of affirming the "other"—because we are open to the love of the Creator spoken in his Word. God the Sanctifier is the interior source of a new life—a life of trust in God, and a life which shares in God's holiness.

Humanity "On the Move"

In relation to God the Sanctifier, humanity itself is seen in a third light. We are creatures. We are redeemed sinners. But we are creatures and redeemed sinners in the process of transformation, caught up in the life-giving and strengthening motion of God the Spirit. This is both encouraging and unsettling. It is encouraging—at least in the abstract—because it says that we have a destiny which transcends and exceeds our present state. Whether one speaks of the life of the Age to Come or of the Kingdom of God, or of the resurrection, Christ's and ours, the meaning is fundamentally the same: humanity aims at a life shared with God. It aims at a point where its own authentic life is discovered to lie in absolute openness and availability to God. And this, of course, has an inspiring ring to it.

But it is also disturbing. This destiny is achieved only by way of transformation. The person who moves with the Spirit must indeed *move.* Like the children of Israel as they came out of Egypt, we have a wilderness to cross. Like the Christ as he moved toward the triumph of his Resurrection, we have a dying to accomplish. For the Spirit does not settle us where we are. He always points us beyond, toward the God who draws people out of themselves in love and obedience.

Humanity in the process of sanctification, then, is humanity on the move. Created to answer God, addressed and affirmed by God in his Word, we are free to leave our old selves behind—the ideas, values, and patterns of relationship which bind us not to our future with God, but to our present state of alienation. And this we can accomplish, not in our own strength, but in the strength of the love of God, the grace of the Lord Jesus Christ, and the fellowship of the Holy Spirit.

· 4 ·

God in Three Persons

When people recite the creeds, we have said, they set themselves in a certain relation to God. That relation, however, is a complex one as the creeds picture it. It is, first of all, a relation of creature to Creator. At the same time, it is a relation of sinner to Redeemer. Finally, it is the relation of one in process of transformation to the Power which transforms. This is the threefold way in which Christian faith knows and receives the God of the Exodus and the Resurrection. This is the threefold way in which God makes himself present and enables people to see themselves for who they are—creatures who, in spite of their denial of God, find redemption and hope through his gracious self-giving.

When, therefore, we model God as person, as the ultimate "other" which communicates itself, we inevitably conceive this personal Deity as being, somehow, threefold. In the light of the relationship we have to him, we identify God as Father, as Word, and as Spirit.

The Problem of the Trinity

In this way our examination of the creeds brings us to the doctrine of the Trinity ("threeness" or "threefoldness"). This doctrine often strikes people as strange or farfetched or unnecessary; and certainly it is true that its meaning is not easy

85

to grasp, and that the familiarity of its language often leads to serious misunderstanding of what it says. Nevertheless, this doctrine stands out as the form in which the church through the centuries has sought to explain what is distinctive—or at any rate characteristic—about a Christian understanding of God. Consequently, it deserves to be considered and studied with the utmost seriousness.

It is useless, however, to study the doctrine of the Trinity without considering, with equal seriousness, the doubts and problems which it occasions. The reason for this is not simply that such doubts and problems are, after all, honest, or that they bring genuine issues to light, or even that they may have something to teach us. All this is no doubt true. More important, however, is the fact that the doctrine of the Trinity is itself the historical product of a process of long and heated debate in which just such problems and doubts as ours were aired.

Christians in the first centuries of the church's existence thought and spoke of God—his relation to the world, and his activity—in more than one idiom. They used, for this purpose, a wide range of symbols, and they drew these symbols from an equally wide spectrum of religious traditions and experiences. They did this quite naturally, in an effort to communicate and clarify the meaning of their faith. As they did so, however, they soon realized that different groups of them had begun to say different and inconsistent things about God. Their various symbols and ideas were leading them in different directions, toward differing understandings of God. Consequently, a long series of debates began in which two closely related questions were central. The first was: How do you interpret the formula, "Father, Son, and Holy Spirit"? The second was: What does Christian use of this formula say about the nature of God? The doctrine of the Trinity, therefore, emerged as an answer to both of these questions. It is a statement about the God of Christian faith which grows out of reflection on, and debate over, the threefoldness which the creeds enunciate.

From all this, several points ought to be clear. First, the doctrine of the Trinity is in fact concerned with absolutely basic and essential issues. It is in reality simply a rendering of the Christian understanding of God. Second, this doctrine in its final and established form is the end result of an historical development. It is not given as such either in the Scriptures or in the creeds. Rather, it is a product, achieved after long discussion and argument, which is intended to explain and to state the meaning of scriptural and creedal language about God. Finally, and because this is true, the doctrine has to be understood in the light of the problems which gave rise to it. Since it conveys the heart of Christian faith in the form of a solution to a certain range of questions, its meaning can be appreciated only when these questions are identified and raised.

Trinitarian Language

We will see in a moment what some of the most important of these questions were. Before they can be named, however, there is a preliminary task to be done. A warning must be issued about some of the language associated with the doctrine of the Trinity. Many of the terms—indeed, most of the terms—connected with the doctrine of the Trinity are not, in themselves, technical terms. That is, they do not have precisely delimited significations which assure that they say and mean exactly the same thing every time they are used. On the contrary, the majority of them are rich, and therefore ambiguous, in meaning. In different contexts, they have different sorts of meaning and different sorts of associations. For this reason, it is extremely important to understand exactly how a particular term is used in the context of trinitarian discussion, where its "richness" may have been curtailed for the sake of exactness, or where only one aspect of its meaning may be intended. Much confusion and misunderstanding can be caused by failure to recognize the precise sense in which a certain term is used when it is employed in trinitarian discourse.

One notorious example of this problem is the term *Father*. Jesus employed this word in a distinctive and characteristic way to bring out both his understanding of what God meant to him, and his understanding of God's way with human beings in general. God is "our Father in heaven"—one who loves, nourishes, forgives, and guides. This use of *Father*, needless to say, entered at once into Christian speech and piety, and remains central for them to this day. The same word, however, was also used in another sense. Greek philosophy spoke of "the Father of the universe"; and in this sense *Father* means much the same thing as *creator*. It describes not the way in which God treats people but the way in which he is related to the natural order—as its founder. But finally, in early Christian language, this symbol had a third, and quite distinct use. It referred to God's relation to his "Son"—that is, to the divine Word which "became flesh" (Jn. 1:14) in Jesus. In this case, it is not God's loving care, nor yet his creative activity, which is at the center of attention. In this case, he is called *Father* because he is pictured as reproducing himself in a second divine reality which is "just like" him. And needless to say, it is in this last sense that the word *Father* figures in formal trinitarian discourse. The other senses of the term recede into the background.

A slightly different sort of problem is occasioned for modern Christians by the term *person*. We have seen that this word is used to model God as the self-communicating "other," the one whose active initiative is perceived in creation, redemption, and sanctification. But if this is so, what can possibly be meant by speaking of "one God in three persons"? It looks like a case of sheer self-contradiction to say on the one hand that "person" is the best available model for God in his unity and uniqueness, and then on the other hand to say that God is somehow "three persons." Are there three "ultimate initiatives"? No. For, as a matter of fact, what we confront here is another case of a term which is used in various senses. What the Latin *persona* meant in classical trinitarian discourse, and what *person* means in popular modern parlance, are rather different things. The modern *person* is a center of self-conscious activity and initiative. The trinitarian *person* means something which has concrete, objective reality. "Three persons," whatever it means, does not mean "three personalities."

Elements of the Doctrine

These problems of language, however, are preliminary, and in themselves of secondary importance. The real issues involved in understanding the doctrine of the Trinity only come to light when we begin to identify the questions which originally gave rise to the doctrine. These questions, in turn, have their roots in certain experiences, assumptions, and ideas which we can call the "elements" out of which the doctrine of the Trinity arose.

A TRINITARIAN WAY OF TALKING

The first and most fundamental of these elements can perhaps be described best as a way of talking. The way of talking in question arose in the earliest period of the history of the Christian community. It appeared—certainly it was not consciously invented—as a way of describing or explaining what happened to people when they were baptized, when, through confession of faith and washing with water, they accepted their identity as God's people. Saint Paul, for example, argues that to become one of God's people is to undergo a change in identity. It is to move from being a slave to being a son. And this happens, he argues, because "God has sent the Spirit of his Son into our hearts, crying 'Abba! Father!'" (Gal. 4:6). Christian identity appears, then, at the point when, through the Spirit, people enter into Christ's relation to God. In a similar way the First Letter of Peter describes Christians as "chosen and destined by God the Father and sanctified by the Spirit for obedience to Jesus Christ" (1:2). Again the status or identity of the believer is defined by giving an account of people's relation to the Father, to the Holy Spirit, and to Christ. The same theme and the same way of talking appear in Paul's letter to the Christians at Thessalonica. The Apostle explains:

> God chose you from the beginning to be saved, through sanctification by the Spirit . . . so that you may obtain the glory of our Lord Jesus Christ (2 Th. 2:13f).

In each of these passages, what is being spoken of is the standing—the situation—of those who through Christ have come to trust and obey God; and in each case this standing is described in roughly the same way. The Christian is one who in the power of the Spirit is reconciled to God by being identified in and with Christ. That, in the last resort, is why Saint Matthew's Gospel can say what Baptism is by describing it as an action which registers people under "the name of the Father and of the Son and of the Holy Spirit" (Mt. 28:19). It is also why the scene at Jesus' own Baptism is portrayed by the evangelists as one in which the sonship of Jesus is established by the testimony of the Father and the descent of the Spirit. That scene, after all, does not merely provide a picture of something that happened to Jesus. It also provides a picture of what happens to every believer when he or she is baptized. The Baptism of Jesus is the original and the model of his people's Baptism—the act in which, through the power of the Spirit, they are identified with Christ and thus established as God's children.

From the earliest times, then, a "trinitarian" way of talking sprang up as a means of explaining the character and structure of Christian existence. People's relationship to God, their experience of redemption, was a complex unity. It was not three separate relationships—one to the Father, another to Christ, and another to the Spirit. It was a single, unified reality, a single relationship to the one God *as* Father, established and revealed *in* Christ, and brought home to people *through* the Spirit. God's presence for believers, and their resulting openness to him, took place in just this threefold way.

Needless to say, this way of talking about the meaning of Christian life persisted. From being a way of stating the meaning of Baptism, it became, by the beginning of the second century, the form of the very confession of faith with which candidates were baptized. Converts were taught to profess, as they went down into the waters, their faith in God the Creator, in Jesus Christ his Son, and in the Holy Spirit. By thus agreeing publicly to their calling and identity in Christ, they entered the community of the New Covenant. It was natural and inevitable, therefore, that when the creeds as we know them began to appear (in the course of the third century), their very form should be determined by this threefold baptismal confession, which itself was a product of the way in which Christians met and knew the God of their redemption.

This trinitarian way of talking, however, was not in itself what we call the doctrine of the Trinity. Rather, it is the first and most essential factor in the evolution of the doctrine. It spoke simply and directly of different ways in which the one God is present for people; but it did not explain what this might mean for an understanding of God, or exactly what was denoted by terms like *Son* or *Spirit* or *Christ* or *Father*. Indeed, early Christians had quite a variety of ways of explaining this trinitarian language.

GOD AND GOD'S "POWERS"

The second crucial factor in the development of the doctrine of the Trinity was, in fact, just such a way of understanding or explaining early Christian language about God, Christ, and the Spirit—or "Father, Son, and Holy Spirit."

The world in which Christianity rose and spread believed, and indeed knew, that the supreme Deity was not utterly alone and isolated in his glory. Jewish tradition, for example, knew of angels who lived in God's presence, served him, and acted as his messengers and agents. At the same time, it knew of identifiable Powers—or what we might call derivative manifestations—of God. Such were God's Wisdom (Pr. 8:22–31; Wisd. 7:22–8:1), God's Word (Jn. 1:1–4), and God's Spirit. Through these Powers God did his work and gave his revelation. They were not always carefully distinguished from one another; and Judaism had no systematic theory about exactly what, or how many, they were. Such questions, after all, were not important. What mattered was that God made his will operative in and through these Powers, which were, therefore, both *with him* and *with us,* and so functioned as intermediaries between God and his people.

This portrayal of the divine realm in Judaism (and therefore in Christianity) had a parallel and, in part, a source, in the Greek religious philosophy of the time. The parallel, of course, was far from exact; but it was close enough so that the two could, with some adjustments on either side, be brought together in a more or less unified picture. The Greek tradition, at least in its most widespread form, thought of the supreme Deity as transcendent Being, which brought order and harmony into the visible cosmos by governing the activity of lower divine realities, and in particular, of "the Soul of the World." The World Soul was a divine reality of an inferior grade which acted as an intermediary between the supreme Mind and the physical world. There was, then, on this view, a strict hierarchy of divine beings, ordered under a single, transcendent First Principle. Greek religious philosophy did not originally think of the inferior divine beings as *derived from* the First Principle (as God's Wisdom or Word or Spirit were derived from God in Jewish thought); nor did it conceive of them as bearers of the *presence* of the supreme Deity. Nevertheless, it conceived of a definite plurality of beings in the divine realm, ordered under an ultimate unity.

In such a setting it was natural and inevitable that early Christians should explain and interpret their formula, "Father, Son, and Holy Spirit," by appealing to Jewish and Greek ideas which acknowledged the existence of divine Powers or subordinate divine beings. In the case of the Holy Spirit, this procedure was more or less automatic: indeed, it was virtually required by the traditional meaning of the expression *God's Spirit.*

In the case of the Son, however, the same procedure required a change in the way the phrase *Son of God* was understood. In natively Hebrew thought, *Son of God* and *Christ* properly referred to human beings, not to members of the divine realm. They signified human beings who were called and anointed by God for a particular role or mission. It was in this sense that these terms were originally applied to Jesus. When, however, the human life and ministry of Jesus was acknowledged to be the definitive mode of God's presence with his people, and Jesus himself was therefore seen as humanity incarnating God's Word (Jn. 1:14) or Wisdom (Col.

1:15ff), the meaning of *Son of God* and *Christ* was altered. They came to refer not to Jesus as a human being, but to the divine Power—Word or Wisdom—which had identified itself in and with Jesus. In this way, *Son of God* and *Christ* came, like *Spirit of God*, to refer to a divine reality—a Power in which God expresses and (in some sense) reproduces himself. The sequence "Father, Son, and Holy Spirit," then, is clearly seen to refer to these divine realities: to God reproducing himself as Word and as Spirit.

THE PROBLEM OF INTERMEDIARIES

Behind this way of interpreting the trinitarian formula, however, a crucial problem was concealed: and that problem itself is the third element which goes into the making of the doctrine of the Trinity. It would be entirely correct if we identified this problem as that of God's *unity;* but even though this traditional way of stating the problem is correct, it is not very helpful, because it does not indicate the question which actually stimulated debate. Neither the orthodox Christians nor those who came to be called heretics were deniers of the unity of God. On the contrary, every divergent point of view in the long controversy over the meaning of the trinitarian "way of talking" was seen by its proponents as defending and asserting the unity of God. The differences lay in the divergent ways in which God's unity was defended and asserted; and therefore they lay ultimately in differing conceptions of the meaning of *God.*

What, then, was the root of this problem? The easiest way to grasp it is to reflect on the meaning and possible implications of a word we have already used—the term *intermediary.* When it is used theologically, that term signifies a being which stands between God and the world or God and humanity, and by standing between them, somehow connects them up.

It takes only a little thought, however, to see that this concept carries with it a great deal of theological freight. Suppose, for the sake of argument, that *Father, Son, and Holy Spirit* means "the ultimate God and his two intermediaries."

If this is so, then the doctrine of the Trinity is a doctrine which is essentially concerned with the relation between God and his world. But is it? Again, on the same supposition, it looks as though we were saying that God cannot "get together" with the world—act with reference to it, or be present in and for it—without assistance of some sort from intermediaries. If this is true, however, there must be some kind of inconsistency between God and the created world—something about what they are which keeps them separate. And if that is the case, then God himself must be limited in his very nature—limited by the fact that he excludes the creaturely world and that it excludes him. Finally, moreover, a God who requires or employs intermediaries is not in reality *self*-communicating. He may bestow knowledge or gifts; but he does not bestow himself.

It is just this series of problems which was created when the Christian community's trinitarian language was interpreted by appealing to the idea of "derivative manifestations" of God. This notion had its advantages, obviously. It took seriously the threefoldness of God as people knew him in Christ and through the Spirit. It did so, in fact, by suggesting that God somehow "reproduces himself." On the other hand, there are reproductions and reproductions; and a derivative manifestation may well be a reproduction *on a lower level of reality*—like the image of someone in a mirror. What is more, if people think that God reproduces himself simply for the sake of finding a "mean" between himself and the world, such a conclusion is almost inevitable. For in that case, the "reproduction" is an intermediary in the sense in which we have already explained that term. Understood along these lines, the phrase Father, Son, and Holy Spirit points to a hierarchy of divine realities; and in that hierarchy, Son and Holy Spirit refer to inferior beings and intermediaries.

The Classical Heresies

To see how this problem was worked out, it is necessary, first of all, to look at two solutions which failed, but which nevertheless, even in failing, made a contribution to the development of people's understanding of the faith. These two solutions, known technically as "subordinationism" and "monarchianism," present themselves as polar opposites; and at a certain level, that is just what they are. Nevertheless, as we shall see, they have in common one fundamental assumption which sets both of them apart from the solution which finally prevailed. Each of them, furthermore, is an explanation of the meaning of Father, Son, and Holy Spirit which seeks to defend the absolute unity and uniqueness of God against any attempt to compromise it.

SUBORDINATIONISM

Any teaching which "subordinates" the Son to the Father, and the Spirit to both Father and Son, by treating them as three divine (or quasi-divine) beings which are separate from each other because they exist at different levels of reality is known as subordinationism. In other words, subordinationism is a direct and emphatic assertion that Son and Spirit are intermediaries between God and the world. They are divine; but they are not as divine as the Father. Consequently, they are capable—in a way in which he is not—of being directly related to the finite world. On a map of the structure of reality, they would be "closer" to the visible world than the Father.

This understanding of the trinitarian formula was by no means rare in the second and third centuries of the church's existence. On the contrary, it was more or less commonplace, and even prevalent, though often in ambiguous or tentative forms. Moreover, this subordination of Son and Spirit to Father could be thought of as safeguarding the ultimate unity of God. If Son and Spirit were equal to the Father, then presumably there would be three Gods; but if they are under him and derived from him, then the monarchy (the "rule of one") is preserved.

Yet subordinationism of this sort leaves the status of Word and Spirit highly uncertain. What can it mean to be *divine*, but at the same time not to be, in the fullest and most proper sense, God? What does it mean to be *derived* from God, and yet not to be a creature? What does it mean to be God's reproduction of himself, his very image, and yet not to be divine in the same way that he is? And if questions of this sort do not reveal enough problems, there are still others to notice. For one thing, while this subordinationist outlook may indeed preserve the monarchy of the ultimate God, it nevertheless allows a plurality of divine beings. Then too, it divides up the realm of the divine for the sake of having intermediaries between the Creator and this world; and thus it isolates God from the world. It carefully fences him off from contact with anything finite.

Obviously, then, this prevalent subordinationism needed correction if it was even to make clear and consistent sense; and a correction, accordingly, came along. This correction was, moreover, one which retained the spirit and much of the substance of the prevalent view. It might even be described as an "extreme" or "uncompromising" subordinationism. We refer to the teaching of Arius, which opened the great trinitarian controversy of the fourth century.

Arius, a presbyter from the metropolis of Alexandria in Egypt, was clear—and right—about one thing. The Christian doctrine of creation, he saw, simply did not allow of any middle term between the uncreated and the created. Whatever is not God is creature; and whatever is not creature is God. Consequently, the old subordinationism, which made the Word and the Spirit intermediaries of some sort, had to face the fact that there are in reality only two possibilities: either Son and Spirit are God, or they are creatures—not-God. The question was, which of these alternatives to pick.

To Arius and his serious followers, the answer to this question seemed clear. On the one hand, it was universally admitted that Son and Spirit are *derived* and not *original,* second and not first. If this is so, however, it is obvious which of the alternatives is the correct one. Son and Spirit are creatures. This conclusion, moreover, is confirmed if one considers the consequences of calling them "uncreated," of making them equal to God himself. For, in that case, it seems, there would be three distinct and coequal ultimates, three "firsts"; and that is inconceivable.

Son and Spirit, then, are unequivocally creatures, Arius declared; and his view had certain clear advantages. For one thing, it promised to banish the notion of beings which are neither quite divine nor quite creaturely; and in doing so, it compelled the church to rethink may of its easy and half-conscious assumptions about what might be meant by *God*. Moreover, in accomplishing this useful end, Arius did not have, as he saw it, to surrender the idea that Son and Spirit are intermediaries; for if the "divine" Word is a creature, it is nevertheless the highest and most glorious of creatures, made (as Arius saw it) to function as the medium of God's commerce with other creatures. In this way, Arius contrived to retain much of the spirit of the old subordinationism, even while he revised its content. Above all, however, this position asserted and emphasized the unity of God—the uniqueness and indivisibility of the divine being. God was, for Arius, simply and absolutely *one;* and therefore, by his very nature, segregated from the "manyness" and changeability of the creaturely realm.

For all its plausibility, however, and for all its obvious advantages, Arius's position struck most Christian leaders as both irreverent and idly clever, as pursuing abstract logic at the expense of experienced reality. Most of these leaders, therefore, preferred to reassert the orthodoxy of the old-fashioned sort of subordinationism, which was able to call Son and Spirit divine because it could conceive of grades of divinity. Others, however, saw the seriousness of Arius's basic contention and realized that a choice must in truth be made. Son and Spirit must either be acknowledged unequivocally as God, or else they must be designated creatures. The difference between this last group and Arius lay in the fact that they were sure he had made the wrong choice. Their response to him was to insist that the Word is God in exactly the same sense as the Father.

It was this group—ultimately to be led by Athanasius, who became bishop of Alexandria in A.D. 328—which triumphed at the Council of Nicaea. Their position revolved around two basic points. First, they realized that in the case of the Word and the Spirit, *derivation* did not mean the same thing as *creation,* as Arius had supposed. In the case of the Son or the Spirit, God does not call something different from himself into existence. Rather, he eternally reproduces himself in one who is his true self all over again. Thus the Word is "God from God, Light from Light, true God from true God, *begotten, not made"*; and the Holy Spirit is "worshiped and glorified" in the same way, and for the same reason, as Father and Son. But in the second place, Athanasius and his friends had a reason for saying this which went far beyond any question of the meaning of words like *derive* and *create.* The real question—to be put not only to Arius but also to the older subordinationists—was whether it is indeed *God* who is present to communicate himself in creation, redemption, and sanctification. Put more tersely, the question becomes: Is God, in and of himself, *self-*communicative? Or is it rather the case that he sits, so to speak, at an immense metaphysical distance from creatures, and does his business through middlemen? When the Council of Nicaea asserted that the Word of God is "of one being with the Father," it opted for the first alternative. In creation, in redemption, and in sanctification, it is himself whom God directly communicates. The Son is not something different from the Father; and neither, for that matter, is the Spirit.

MONARCHIANISM

But if this is what one wants to say, why not say it in the simplest and most economical way possible? Why not dispense with any real distinction among Father, Son, and Spirit, and say that it is the one God, the indivisible ultimate, who alone is really divine? This, in essence, was the position of those who are known as "monarchians." These teachers— and their tradition reached back into the second century— would, of course, have agreed with Athanasius in their opposition to any form of subordinationism. They saw no reason, however, to complicate matters by insisting on a real threefoldness in God. Once you have pulled up the rope ladder of subordinate or intermediary "divine" beings, what is left, in effect, is simply the top rung—God, alone in himself.

Moreover, it is only in this way that the unity of God can truly be safeguarded. For all its virtues, the position of people like Athanasius seemed to say that there are three coequal Gods; and Arius was assuredly correct in perceiving the absurdity of that position.

But then what did the monarchians make of the trinitarian formula? How did they explain or interpret expressions like *Father, Son, and Holy Spirit?* Needless to say, they did not want simply to be rid of this way of talking. They merely wished, as we have said, to make sure that it was not taken to refer to any *real* distinctions in God. What they proposed, therefore, was a very simple—and in its way appealing— solution. In one way or another, they all suggested that Father, Son, and Spirit be taken as names for *different ways in which God is seen by us.* This might mean, for example, that they are names for different attributes of God (and thus equivalent to abstract words like *creative* or *self-expressive*); or it might mean that they are names for God's *appearance,* for what he *looks like.*

Now at first glance this position seems both plausible and helpful. It does, after all, give concrete meaning to the trinitarian formula; and at the same time, it asserts in a serious and explicit way the unity of God. A second glance, however, reveals a rather strange thing. Like the subordinationist, the monarchian erects a barrier between God and human beings. In his case, of course, the barrier is not made up of a descending hierarchy of intermediary divine beings. Rather, it is constituted by God's appearance, which for the monarchian takes the place, functionally speaking, of intermediaries. In other words, the monarchian asserts that although God *is* not Father, Son, and Holy Spirit, he nevertheless *looks like* Father, Son, and Holy Spirit. Between what God is in himself, on the one hand, and human beings on the other, there stands this appearance: and again we are confronted with a doctrine which questions the true and active presence of God himself with humanity. On the monarchian view, what we have of God directly is only his appearance, and not also his reality.

It was in order to forestall or correct this rather strange form of the idea of the "intermediary" that most Christian teachers insisted on saying that Father, Son, and Holy Spirit are *hypostases*. This Greek word (which was translated into Latin as *persona,* whence the English *person*) meant simply "something objectively real." When applied to Father, Son, and Holy Spirit, therefore, it was calculated to assert that God does not just *appear* to be threefold; he genuinely *is* threefold. Each of the three names refers to a real something in God. This assertion, moreover, constitutes yet another defense of the conviction that in creation, redemption, and sanctification what is with us is *God*—as he truly is in himself.

Thus, the orthodox position in its basic outlines finally appeared. God is *one* in being. But, at the same time, he is, objectively and in himself, three: "*One God in three hypostases (persons).*" But how can such a thing be said, and what does it mean?

The Divine Trinity

It would be easy, of course, to evade these questions by saying that the doctrine of the Trinity is a mystery, and therefore something which must just be accepted on faith. This policy, however, will not really work; and that is not merely because people have a hard time believing something whose point they cannot see. In Christian faith, a mystery is not something which fails to make sense. It is, rather, something whose sense can be discerned, and even stated, but never mastered or fully comprehended in its richness. The mysterious is such not because of its absurdity or its incoherence, but because of its depth: not because one cannot see or state truth about it, but because the truth as stated is only a bare intimation of the reality to which it points. There can, therefore, be no retreat from the task of asking what it is that the doctrine of the Trinity is saying or pointing to.

In this task, the first thing which must be firmly grasped is the deliberate seriousness with which the doctrine affirms that God is *one*. When it is said that Son and Spirit are God, that they are "of one being" with the Father, this does not mean that they and the Father are three quite separate instances of "Godness." It means, rather, that they are in very truth one and the same God. Each of them is all that God is; and none of them is separated from the others in being God. The persons are not independent individuals: they are, to use classical language, *ways in which God is God.* This suggests, moreover, yet another dimension of God's unity. Because the persons *are* not separate things, they do not *do* things separately, and they do not do *different* things. All of the works of God are works of the Father done in the Son and perfected through the Spirit.

But how is this so? Do we not, in fact, associate creation with the Father, redemption with the Son, and sanctification with the Holy Spirit? The answer to this question is obviously Yes. It needs to be remembered, however, that these three works of God are in reality discovered as "moments" or dimensions of a single relationship. Redemption, we have said, is creation, historically objectified and enacted. Similarly, sanctification *is* redemption, subjectively actualized. What God is and what he does in relation to humankind are *one thing.* What the Word does is what the Father does; and what the Holy Spirit does is what the Word does. All carry out the one work of God, which is, as we have said, always the work *of* the Father, *in* the Son, and *through* the Holy Spirit.

If this is so, however, in what way do the persons differ from one another? How are they distinct?

Here the key word is *relation.* It is worth noticing that every account given of the meaning of the trinitarian formula explains the distinction of the persons in terms of some kind of *relatedness* which is attributed to God. Subordinationism and monarchianism alike focused attention on the relationship of God to the created world as a whole, or to human beings in particular. In other words, the point, as they saw it, of making a distinction of persons was to explain the *how* of God's *relatedness to the finite universe.* That is why the concept of the intermediary played so central a role in their thought. What each of these positions really emphasized, in short, was the distinction between God-in-himself and God-related-to-the-world. Subordinationism identified the Father with

God-in-himself, removed and even isolated from the world. It then explained the Son and the Holy Spirit in their distinction from the Father as God-in-contact-with-the-world—a slightly inferior kind of God. The monarchian, as we have seen, took a somewhat different tack, but worked with essentially the same idea. For him, God-in-himself was the one true God; and God-in-relation-to-the-world was God as he "appeared" in threefold guise.

The orthodox position results from a refusal to make this sort of distinction in God. It wants to say, as we have seen, that God *in himself* is self-communicative and active in relation to the world: that at the very heart of the divine being is a movement of self-bestowal, of sharing, of affirmation of the "other." In other words, the orthodox sought a way of asserting that God-in-himself is not distinct from, but exactly the same as, God-in-relation; and their way of doing this was to say that the distinction of persons is expressive of the fact that relatedness is part of God's own, proper way of being. It is, therefore, not, in the first instance, God's relationship to the world which the doctrine of the Trinity focuses on. Rather, it is the fact that *God stands in a relation to himself*. On this understanding, the language of the trinitarian formula— *Father, Word, Holy Spirit*—says in effect that God truly becomes "other" for himself, that he communicates himself to himself. And this, in turn, means that relatedness to an "other" is not something external or foreign to God, but part of the very logic of his being. The doctrine of the Trinity says what God must be like in himself to be the sort of God who genuinely gives himself—communicates himself—in love. For this reason, it states the presupposition of what we learn about God in considering him as the ultimate "other" who is actively present in creating, redeeming, and sanctifying.

Conclusion

The "mystery" of Trinity-in-unity, then, is the mystery of God's self-communicative nature as that is expressed in his own being. He is his own Word to himself, and his own appropriation of that Word. He genuinely reproduces himself for himself; and yet all these "selves" are clearly *one* in a final and unqualified sense.

Consequently, the doctrine of the Trinity, which is intimated in the very structure of the creeds, states what sort of God it is whose very nature is to affirm, and set himself in relation to, an "other." The creeds, as we use them, enact just such a relation. When they are recited sincerely, they constitute a point at which a created person is seized up in the eternal self-communication of Father, Word, and Holy Spirit; for that is the meaning of creation, of redemption, and of sanctification.

Part Two

· 5 ·

The Story of Jesus
and the Problem of Evil

Up to this point, Christian understanding of God has been the center of our attention. Looking at the trinitarian framework of the creeds, we have asked, in effect, what sort of God it is that must be described in this special and peculiar way—as the Father who through the Word and in the Holy Spirit creates, redeems, and sanctifies humankind. We have answered: the creeds picture God as "person"—that is, as the ultimate mystery which communicates itself and so invites people not only to answer it, but also to share in its life.

History has no doubt shown that this understanding of God can be both appealing and persuasive. No sooner do we examine it, however, than we are bound to ask: How can it possibly be true? The world of human experience does not, after all, seem to encourage faith in such a God. There is no need to be a fanatical pessimist to see that neither nature nor human affairs testify clearly and unambiguously to the reality of a God who is self-communicative and loving. The world as people normally see and experience it is at best a doubtful and ambiguous scene. It contains life and death, honesty and dishonesty, beauty and ugliness, joy and sorrow. It would be pleasant to think that in the last resort it is life and honesty and beauty and joy which triumph; but that does not always, or even normally, seem to be the case. How, then, can a person who prefers truth to mere comfort, reality to sham, put faith in the God whom the creeds portray?

It is important to notice that this is not a question about whether or not God exists. We might all agree to concede (and without being entirely unreasonable) that it is hard to understand the world without openly or secretly presupposing some sort of ultimate, some sort of God. The trouble is, that Christian faith does not rest on a belief that there is "some sort of God." It rests on a belief in a very particular sort of God: the sort of God who brought the children of Israel out of the land of Egypt, and who raised Jesus from the dead. Perhaps there is an ultimate—an ultimate as ambiguous, as wishy-washy, as gray and uncertain, as the world of our daily experience. But that would not be "the God and Father of our Lord Jesus Christ." So the question must stand: How is it possible to believe in the God of Christian faith? Or better: How is it possible to see the Ultimate as one who is *with us*—and therefore *for us?*

The Basis of Faith

This question, which is not a light or easy one, brings us logically to the second great section or division of the creeds: that which sets out not the structure, but what we may call the basis or ground, of Christian faith. After all, if people can and do affirm not only that God is, but also that he is with them as one whom they can trust and love, then it is reasonable to ask how this becomes possible—where such faith comes from. And the creeds, in their brisk and summary style, answer this query by talking about "Jesus Christ . . . conceived by the power of the Holy Spirit . . . born of the Virgin Mary . . . suffered . . . crucified, died, and . . . buried . . . descended to the dead . . . rose again . . . ascended. . . ."

In other words, the basis of Christian faith is Jesus of Nazareth, considered both in what he did and in what happened to him. To indicate or show the basis of faith is to tell the story of Jesus in such a way as to let its proper meaning appear. This is what the creeds do. It is also what the New Testament does in the books called the Gospels. Accordingly, we shall attempt, in this and the next three chapters, to follow their example: to tell the story of Jesus in such a way as to indicate why and how it is possible that people acknowledge him as "God with us," and so discover God as one who evokes trust and love.

In order to do this job adequately, however, we must begin by taking a step backwards to widen our perspective. Our project, we have said, is "to tell the story of Jesus in such a way as to let its proper meaning appear." That means, though, that we must tell his story in the light of the problems and issues which truly belong to it. Its proper meaning, in other words, can only come clear when we understand, in a general way, what it is a story *about*. The story of Admiral Horatio Nelson is, in significant part, a story about naval warfare and its history. The story of Abraham Lincoln is a story about issues in the history of American culture and politics. But what is the story of Jesus about? In what framework do we set it for purposes of interpretation? What kind of significance belongs to it?

Fortunately, it is easy to give a general answer to that query. The Christian community in its Scriptures, its creeds, and its worship sees Jesus and his history as significant, above all, for the relation of humanity to God. It speaks of Jesus as "mediator," as one who makes a certain kind of relationship to God—the relationship of responsive faith and trust—possible. And that judgment clearly defines an overall frame of reference for the interpretation of his story.

But then, what is the problem about people's relationship to God? It is tempting, as we have said, to define this in intellectual terms and to say that the problem is whether or not we can believe that there is such a thing as God. A moment's reflection, however, will show that this is only one— and that not very profound—way of defining the problem. It might be truer to say that the problem is whether people can affirm God as God: that is to say, whether they can let him *be* God in their relationship to him, by trusting and loving him. It is perfectly easy to believe that God is, and still to doubt him. Many of the so-called intellectual difficulties people have about God are really the product of a profound suspicion of him. They may wonder, for example, whether God is not the enemy of human freedom and maturity, or whether one who is ultimately responsible for a world of the sort we experience can rightly be worshiped or trusted.

What this means is that *at the root of the problem of faith lies the problem of evil.* To accept God as God is to see him not merely as "there," but as the one in whom the goodness of things is ultimately grounded and affirmed, in whom the life of all creatures finds fulfillment, and not denial. But is this, in fact, the case? That, from our human point of view, is the problem about people's relationship to God, and hence the problem to which the history of Jesus must be relevant if it is to be good news.

What Is Evil?

But what exactly *is* the problem of evil? It is easy to dash that phrase off—or to read it off—and think that you are clear about what it means, when in fact you have only a vague and very general notion of what it points to. What do we mean by "evil"? How and why does it become a problem? And what qualifies as a solution to this sort of problem?

The first of these questions seems to have an obvious answer. For most of us, *evil* is a word which refers to serious and significant frustration. If I want something, and it cannot be had; if I need something, and it is not there; if something puts an end to the life of someone I love; if I possess some property, and it is taken away from me—these are all situations in which one or another kind of frustration occurs; and they are all situations of the sort people regularly appeal to in order to explain what they mean by *evil* or *wrong.* In ordinary speech, then, evil is a state of affairs in which someone is denied an expected or deserved fulfillment or satisfaction. Life—and not just human life—presses toward fulfillment of some sort; and evil is whatever short-circuits it.

No sooner is this account of the matter stated, however, than a doubt occurs. Why is it necessary, or even appropriate, to describe this phenomenon of frustration by so dramatic a word as *evil*? If all that evil really means is "We don't like it," or "It hurts us," then why not just say as much and let the matter drop there? The reason is, of course, that by evil we do, in fact, mean more than our definition so far allows; and this is proved by the fact that everyone can think of frustrations, or frustrating circumstances, which they would hesitate to describe as evil. Suppose I trip over a curb, rip my trousers, and cut my knee. That is a painful, disturbing, and inhibiting event; but most people would think me overly dramatic if I described it as a manifestation of evil. Tripping and falling are things that just happen, and one must learn to live with them. There is more to evil, then, than the occurrence of frustration or harm.

But what is this something more? Maybe the key to our problem lies in an innocent-looking phrase we used a moment ago—"things that just happen." What this expression calls attention to is the fact that there are things which occur automatically or naturally or by chance. One might think of a storm at sea, for example, or the infection caused by certain strains of virus—or, of course, tripping over a curb—as illustrations of things that just happen. We do, in fact, hesitate to call such natural phenomena evil; and the reason should be plain. Ordinarily we reserve the word *evil* for situations in which frustration or harm is caused by a moral agency; that is, by a person or group of persons who could have acted differently. I may not regard an accidental tripping over a curb as a manifestation of evil; but if someone deliberately trips me up, I will certainly accuse that person of being malicious and of doing wrong.

When we describe something as evil, then, we are not merely saying that it is an event or state of affairs which we find frustrating. We are also saying that in this case the frustration could have been avoided because it did not happen just in the inevitable course of things. It happened because someone did it or caused it to happen. Evil, we can say, speaking loosely, refers to harm or frustration which one can reasonably protest and complain about because some agency is responsible for it: in short, it means responsible wrongdoing. *In a world in which everything happened automatically, it would be inappropriate to speak of evil.*

But if this is true, why is it that people so often complain and protest about events which look as though they have happened automatically and unavoidably? Whose fault is it, after all, that rattlesnakes bite, or that volcanoes erupt, or that viruses infect? Why are phenomena of this sort so often regarded as instances of evil?

The answer seems to be that people are moved to protest such phenomena because, as a matter of fact, consciously or unconsciously, they think that there is someone responsible for them. In certain cases, the "someone" may actually be a human being or a group of human beings. Some disasters of the sort we call natural, such as diseases or floods, are in fact occasioned by human activity or human neglect. But when people complain or protest about nature itself—about the way "the system" works—the only responsible agent they can have in mind is God. God is the someone, the moral agent, who stands behind, and is responsible for, the natural order of things; and it is because people believe this that they can and do protest against what we have called things that just happen—the death of a child, the pain of animals, or the destructive eruption of a volcano.

What Is the Problem of Evil?

In the light of these reflections on what evil means, we can go on to say what the phrase *the problem of evil* refers to.

Philosophers have defined this problem as a strict logical dilemma—that is, as a situation in which people want to maintain two inconsistent beliefs simultaneously. Just consider. It appears, on the one hand, that evil is real. Both in the realm of human actions and in the realm of things that just happen, there are occurrences which justify moral protest or complaint. On the other hand, God is both almighty and benevolent: he is in control of the way things go, and what he wills is good. There, then, is the dilemma; for it looks as though the two statements, "Evil is real," and "God is both almighty and benevolent," are inconsistent. Would not a just and all-powerful God simply abolish evil? Surely he would. Yet apparently he does not. This is the dilemma which is faced by all who ask questions like: "Why did God let our baby die?"

But the full dimensions—and the full depths—of this problem are only revealed when we consider its religious as well as its logical dimension. Experienced religiously, the problem of evil is the situation of a person who is of two minds about God, who really does not know what to think about the character of the ultimate "other." On the one hand, like Job, this person *accuses* God, marking him out as the one who is responsible for evil. On the other hand—and also like Job—he *appeals to* God as the one who stands powerfully on the side of justice and goodness. The question then is, Which of these Gods is real? It could, of course, be the case that both are real, and that the universe is the stage for a colossal struggle between two equal, and therefore equally matched, powers. Whatever the answer may be, though, the position of the individual who experiences the problem of evil is clear. It is the position of one who truly cannot tell whether it is "right" or "wrong" which is throned in heaven.

Strange to say, however, this terrifying doubtfulness is, at a still deeper level, the symptom of a genuine faith. It requires faith, and not just a little, even to put the label "wrong" on things and so protest them. To whom, after all, is such a complaint addressed? If I insist that things have gone thoroughly wrong and cry out to heaven demanding that they be put right, I am assuming that something or someone is there to hear my demand and to care about it. The only person who can seriously protest evil is one who seriously thinks that God is real and that God knows and cares about the difference between right and wrong. It requires an act of faith, then, even to be caught in the problem of evil. A real atheist can grasp the problem in its form as a logical dilemma, and can perceive that believers suffer from the awful doubts which this problem creates. What such a person cannot do, however, is to experience the problem personally; for to do so is to appeal to God—even if the appeal *to* God is, at the same time, an appeal *against* God.

What Is a Solution to the Problem of Evil?

People are not interested, though, in analyses of the character of this problem. What they want is a solution to it. Yet this analysis of the nature of the issue is important; for it helps us to realize that the word *solution* means at least two different things where the problem of evil is concerned. To "solve" the problem of evil can mean either to resolve the logical dilemma or to put things right. The problem can, we might say, have both a theoretical and a practical solution.

What is more, both sorts of solution are necessary, as a moment's thought will convince us. If there can be no resolution of the logical dilemma, if God's power and goodness cannot be reconciled with the existence of evil, then there can be no hope of a practical solution, no hope that things will ever come out truly right. On the other hand, if a theoretical solution is thought to be sufficient, that can only be because we are not taking the concrete reality of evil seriously. We are allowing ourselves to suppose that our solution has, as it were, explained evil away, so that no practical putting of things right is really called for. That, though, would amount to a denial of the proposition "Evil is real."

What this all adds up to is that, in dealing with the problem of evil, we have to speak cautiously, not saying either too much or too little. One says too little, for example, when one "solves" the problem by postulating two ultimate Powers, one good and the other evil, existing in eternal conflict. Such a dualistic solution (as it is called) is in fact no solution at all. All it really accomplishes is to restate the dilemma in a new form. For two contradictory statements one substitutes two contradictory Gods.

On the other hand, it is possible to say a great deal too much in dealing with this issue. That happens when we do too good a job in our task of explanation and "justify the ways of God" by seeming to show that everything in the world is really all right. It is useful to remember that explanations of a successful, or apparently successful, sort often have a curious side effect. They convince us that the thing we have explained is a normal, and therefore presentable, part of our world. Just this sort of thing may happen, moreover, when we have contrived to explain evil to our satisfaction. The explanation can lead us to make ourselves at home with evil, as we either trivialize it by suggesting that it doesn't really create much of a problem, or else resign ourselves to it by arguing that it is simply unavoidable. It is worth recalling, however, that what creates the problem in the first place is our sense that evil is something not to be tolerated, that it calls not so much for explanation as for protest. We must take care not to do too much explaining.

For this reason, the mainstream of Christian tradition has always taken a chancy course which allows full weight to the givenness, and therefore to the reality, of evil. It admits that, in a perfectly proper sense, God is responsible for evil. This is not, however, because God does wrong. It is because he chooses to call into being creatures who can answer him, who can return, and so share, the self-giving love which is his way of being. Such creatures, however, must be moral agents. That is to say, they must be capable of acting responsibly for themselves. If they are, as individuals and as a race, to grow in their capacity for self-communication, if they are to find their fulfillment in free communion with the "other," that fulfillment cannot come about apart from their own freedom and initiative. The human being must find its own way as it responds to God in the setting of his creative and redeeming love; and therefore it must be free to recoil from God, to turn in upon itself, to go wrong. The reality of evil, then, is the measure of the seriousness with which God loves, and asks to be loved by, a creaturely "other."

This does not mean that the wrong which people do to one another and to God is "really all right." Quite the contrary. The argument we have sketched above (in a very incomplete way) does no more, even when thoroughly worked out, than treat the logical side of the problem of evil. It helps us to see how the reality of evil can be consistent with the power and goodness of God, because it suggests that evil *can* be a necessary condition for the fulfillment of God's good purpose.

That, however, is absolutely all it does. It does not show or reveal or demonstrate that God's purpose is good and loving; nor, above all, does it cure the effects and dry up the sources of evil. Arguments will not serve such ends as these. For this kind of solution to the problem of evil, Christians turn to the "good news" of Jesus the Christ, to his ministry, crucifixion, and Resurrection.

The Theme of Jesus' Ministry

So we are back where we started; but by now, perhaps, with a clearer idea of why the story of Jesus is of such central importance for Christians. It is because that story takes up, as it were, just where we have left off in our argument about evil, about the character of God, and about the meaning and the prospects of human existence.

For these questions, real as they are for us, were no less real in the world in which Jesus opened his ministry. In that world, God was *accused;* for people contemplated the wreckage of Israel's hopes under Roman political domination, and asked whether God had forgotten them and gone back on his promises to Moses and David. In that world, God was *appealed to;* for people continually besought his final, powerful intervention to set things right and to redeem the oppressed. In that world, evil was seen and experienced as dominant, and human affairs were judged to be under the sway of malicious or uncaring cosmic Powers. In that same world, however, hope came ever to birth, as people looked for God's anointed representative, his Messiah, to bring in a new age of universal justice. What we have called the problem of evil was not so much studied, analyzed, and explained in Jesus' time and place: it was lived out.

And above all, it was lived out in the ministry, death, and Resurrection of Jesus himself. The question of God's faithfulness and his goodness, the question whether—and how—evil is to be overcome, the question whether God is with his people, and they with him: these are the issues to which Jesus' ministry was addressed; and his story is the story of their working out, not in theory, but in life.

The Kingdom of God

To understand how this is so, it is necessary to look first of all at what we may call the statement of the theme of Jesus' ministry. It is true that we have little knowledge of the exact details of that ministry. What was originally remembered of Jesus' doings and sayings did not include an exact chronology or precise information about the "who" and "where" of his activities. That is the reason why the authors or editors of the Gospels do not always agree about the sequence and location of events in Jesus' life, or even about the identities of some of the people who were involved with him. There is, however, one matter which is perfectly clear from even the most hasty reading of the Gospels; and this is the specific theme or focus of Jesus' doings and sayings. He came upon the stage of history proclaiming "the Kingdom of God."

Saint Mark, for example, describes Jesus as coming to preach "the gospel of God"; and the burden of this Gospel is that "The time is fulfilled, and the Kingdom of God is at hand" (Mk. 1:14f). In Luke's Gospel, Jesus explains that the very purpose for which he was sent is to "preach the good news of the Kingdom of God" (Lk. 4:43). Saint Matthew says exactly the same thing, except that he uses the phrase "Kingdom of heaven" (Mt. 4:17). Since, however, *heaven,* in this phrase, means neither a place nor a state of being, but is simply a more reverent way of saying *God,* the difference of language signifies no difference of thought. All three evangelists are agreed: the theme of all that Jesus did and said was "the Kingdom of God."

But what does that phrase mean? English-speaking people are, as a matter of fact, likely to misunderstand it. In English, the word *kingdom* tends to signify the geographical area over which a king rules. In Greek, however, the word which we translate as *kingdom* has a different basic meaning. Its sense is more truly conveyed by phrases like "the exercise of kingship" or simply "rule." As matter of fact, a more accurate, though not exactly traditional, rendering of the Greek would be "the reign of God" or "the rule of God."

From this we can see the real sense of the passage we have

already quoted from Saint Mark. Jesus came proclaiming a Gospel—good news; and the good news was that the Rule of God was in the process of being asserted. Jesus announced, in effect, that God was about to take a hand in human affairs in a new way: that he was acting to set things right between himself and his people. This implied, in turn, that God was making himself present for redemption. He was setting his people free and reconciling them to himself. He was inaugurating the New Age of promise.

But what did Jesus mean by this *Rule* or *Kingdom* of God? What sort of situation, what state of affairs, did that phrase refer to in his mind? He portrays it as something which is insignificant in its beginnings, but which in the end grows to the point where it encompasses and affects all people (Mk. 4:30–32). It is the one thing worth finding and having (Mt. 13:44–46). The Kingdom is something to which an individual can be close by reason of character or conviction (Mk. 12:34); yet it is far indeed from being something which concerns people merely in their capacity as individuals. Jesus, like the Jewish tradition which formed his thoughts, understood the Kingdom of God as a social—and therefore a public and political—reality. He liked to picture it as a great festivity to which all, "both bad and good" (Mt. 22:10), are summoned, and at which they sit down with the holy people of past ages to share the joy of God's presence (Mt. 8:11). One of the most memorable of the signs which people later remembered his performing was an acted out version of this picture of the Kingdom. Saint Mark even tells the story twice (6:35–44; 8:1–9): vast throngs of hungry people who had followed Jesus were marvelously fed upon mere scraps of food; and when they were done, more was left over than they had started with. The Rule of God, then, means a common feasting of humanity on the infinite generosity of God. Consequently, it touches people in their relations to one another and involves alteration of the social pattern of human relations (Lk. 16:35; cf. Mk. 10:23–26). The Kingdom brings with it a transformation of society as well as of the individual.

This social—even cosmic—dimension of the Reign of God is just as apparent in the personal ideas of the writers of the

New Testament as it is in their reports of the teachings of Jesus. The Kingdom is "the holy city Jerusalem coming down out of heaven from God" (Rev. 21:10), or "the city which has foundations, whose builder and maker is God" (Heb. 11:10). This political reality (the Greek word for *city* is *polis,* from which the English word *political* is derived) is at the same time a new age in the history of humanity. It is the "times of refreshing" which "come from the presence of the Lord" (Acts 3:14), the time when God shall be "everything to everyone" (1 Cor. 15:28).

In brief, what Jesus and his followers were proclaiming was the final revelation of the truth of things—the coming of the moment when God's purposes would be truly known because they would be fulfilled through the reordering of people's lives in their relation to one another and to God.

Interpreters of the New Testament often argue nowadays about whether Jesus (or his disciples) envisaged the Rule of God as something belonging wholly to the future, or whether they saw it as something which, in the ministry of Jesus, had already happened. They also debate at great length the question of whether human beings, by their faithful labors, can realize the fullness of God's Rule. These are complex questions, which require a great deal of study. One or two things seem clear, however. Neither Jesus nor his friends were foolish enough to suppose that the human world as they knew and experienced it embodied the Rule of God. In fact, the reason for their enthusiasm in proclaiming the Rule of God was precisely the fact that they thought the world needed to be put right. Since, moreover, they were announcing *God's* Reign, they can hardly have supposed that it could happen without God's presence and overruling action. On the other hand—and this fact is equally important—they did perceive in worldly happenings and human actions genuine signs and anticipations of God's Kingdom. It is only because they saw, in things that happened in their very midst, preliminary realizations of God's fulfilled Rule that they could believe in and proclaim "the day of the Lord" (2 Thess. 2:2)—the time when things would come right and come right finally, because God would not only show his hand but play out his cards. It is that time and that situation which was, for Jesus and his followers, the true, practical solution of the problem of evil.

The Preaching of the Kingdom

When it is said, however, that Jesus "preached" or "proclaimed" the Kingdom of God, it must not be thought that what he was doing was merely teaching about God's Rule. He was, in fact, doing a great deal more than that. He was making the coming Kingdom of God real for people, both by what he said and by what he did. This is apparent above all in his miracles and his parables.

Jesus, we are told, came healing. He brought sight to the blind, health to the sick, and peace to the frenzied. For many centuries now, people have understood these acts as testimonies that "God can suspend the laws of nature," and so focused attention on the question whether such marvels are really possible. Such an approach, however, leads infallibly to misunderstanding of the New Testament. To the people of Jesus' time, the question was not whether deeds of this sort were possible, or what the mechanism of their occurrence might be. Healers, after all, were not a new thing, even if they were a rare thing. The problem in Jesus' time was to decide what these marvels meant or portended; and that, it appears, was exactly the problem Jesus meant to raise. ". . . if it is by the Spirit of God that I cast out demons," he said, "then the kingdom of God has come upon you" (Mt. 12:28). Jesus' healings were not "miracles" in the modern sense; they were *signs*. People who experienced them were not supposed to arrest their attention at the oddity of what happened, but to ask: "What does this mean?" "Is this a sign of God's presence and power?" The miracles, in short, were not important because they made Jesus out to be a manipulator of divine or quasi-divine powers, but because they were occasions of discernment. They were stimuli which enabled people to see God's Kingdom coming. They were events which said something; and what they said was: "The Kingdom of God is at hand."

And if this is true of Jesus' miracles, it is also true of his parables. We moderns, of course, tend automatically to take the parables as *illustrations* of something—stories intended to provide a concrete example of a general or abstract truth. In interpreting the parables, therefore, we normally try to state the moral or religious "principle" which the story illustrates.

As a matter of fact, however, this does not appear to be the way in which Jesus ordinarily intended his parables to be taken. He was not, in most circumstances, attempting to teach general truths. He was trying to bring about what we have called discernment. That is, he was using stories and figures almost as tools, to trigger awareness of the reality, the nearness, and the character of God's Kingdom. To understand a parable, therefore, is not to grasp a general truth, but to have the meaning of things, as it will be realized in the New Age, unveiled for just a moment. The person who understands a parable sees into the nature of God's rule and is grasped by the good thing which is coming.

The same sort of judgment, moreover, must be made about Jesus' teaching. Consider, for example, the collection of his sayings which underlies the Sermon on the Mount (Mt. 5–7) and the Sermon on the Plain (Lk. 6:17–49). Here Jesus is found commenting on traditional materials: injunctions from the Law of Moses, and established customs of Jewish piety and morality. But what does he do? He does not substitute a new law for the old, or a new piety for the traditional one. Rather, he depicts the overturning of normal human standards which the Kingdom of God will involve. Who are "blessed" in the Kingdom? Not the rich, the fortunate, and the prosperous (as Judaism normally taught), but the poor, the unfortunate, and the hungry are the objects of God's favor. Under God's rule, people forgive their enemies, they "go the second mile," and they "take no thought for the morrow." When he says things like this, Jesus is not laying down laws. He is doing something much more serious than that. He is portraying, and thus anticipating, life in the Kingdom of God. With luck, his words will stimulate people to start rehearsals for the New Age—to try out the sort of life which belongs to it. His teachings have this effect, however, only because they evoke an awareness of what "Kingdom of God" means, and of how it involves a true transformation of human existence, and therefore of human values.

In all these ways, Jesus made the Kingdom of God real for people. He confronted them with its actuality, and made it an issue in their lives—a matter for their choice and decision. In healings, in parables, and in teaching, his word was always the same: "the Kingdom of God is at hand." Consequently, Jesus himself was seen to represent the Kingdom of God. In and through his ministry, the Kingdom approached people. By reason of his presence with them, forgiveness, healing, and hope in God came to people. It was as though, in Jesus' doings, the finger of the Ultimate reached out to touch people; as though, in receiving or rejecting him, they were receiving or rejecting the invitation to God's great feast. Jesus appeared, in a very real sense, as the bearer of the Kingdom whose coming he preached.

Repentance and Sin

But what was people's reaction to this preaching? How did they respond to the power of the Kingdom as that was present in the ministry of Jesus?

One thing, at any rate, is clear. Jesus explained quite openly what their response ought to be. His announcement of the Kingdom in word and deed was always accompanied by a call to repentance. That is, people were summoned to turn to God, to be faithful, from the very heart, to his covenant with them.

The content of Jesus' message, however, meant that in practice the traditional meaning of repentance was altered. Turning to God was normally understood to mean returning to sincere observance of the laws and traditions of Israel. The preaching of the Kingdom, however, revealed that God was not merely calling people back to observance of traditional values: he was calling them forward to a transformed human life. The Rule of God did not require that men and women simply live up to the standards of behavior which they already accepted, whether secretly or openly. Its presence required them to change their very standards. They were not only to behave, but to judge and value, differently. The repentance which Jesus called for, then, was truly a "change of mind," as the Greek word, *metanoia,* suggests.

It is not hard to detect this theme in the Gospels. Jesus clearly made a point of speaking in ways which would suggest that the Kingdom of God truly turns the world upside down. "The first shall be last, and the last, first." "He who would save his life will lose it." "I have not come to call the righteous, but sinners to repentance." "No one puts new wine in old wineskins." In one way or another, each of these sayings evokes a recognition that God's Kingdom is truly something new, and that its newness requires those who would receive it to change their minds: that is, to see things differently, and then to act in accordance with their new vision. For Jesus, this change of mind is a joyous thing. To be sure, it means leaving a great deal behind. It involves deserting a whole way of life. The emphasis, however, is not on this negative side. It is on the wonder which comes with discernment of a new way of being. Repentance, for Jesus, is like accepting an invitation to a party.

Not everyone, however, saw it this way. To many, Jesus seemed a blasphemer, overturning the God-given laws and customs of the Jewish people. To others, he must have seemed a charlatan, or a man deceived by his own dreams. In the face of such rejection, Jesus, we are told, could lament openly: "Would that even today you knew the things that make for peace!" (Lk. 19:41). Of those who could not grasp the reality of the Kingdom signified in the ministry of Jesus, it could only be said that they lacked discernment and were morally blind (Mk. 4:11–12; Mt. 12:25–32). In the last resort, they could not recognize the good when it presented itself to them. For them, God's truth, which comes in love, only served the purpose of judgment, of revealing trees which bear no fruit (Mt. 7:15). From such people, the message of the Kingdom evoked not repentance, but anger or stolid indifference.

Conclusion

Thus, the ministry of Jesus raised a question and created an issue. Was his message true? Did it come from God? Jesus appeared as one bearing not just a word but a reality. He proclaimed that God was acting to overcome evil, and to create a new relationship with people; and his own ministry was intended to show this, to make the beginnings of God's "new thing" visible. If he was right, there was a fresh possibility of faith and hope. If he was right, people's protest against evil and their appeal to God to set things right was ultimately justified.

The trouble was that the good thing which Jesus preached and represented was not necessarily the good thing which most of his contemporaries sought. What he proclaimed as good, they often perceived as violation of God's will. Thus, Jesus' ministry did not settle the problem of faith. It did, however, accomplish two things at least. It raised a question, as we have said: the question of whether Jesus' word was truly God's word. At the same time, though, it clarified the nature of people's problem about evil and God. It showed that human beings may not know or desire the good when they see it. It suggested that the way to faith in God, the way through the problem of evil, must inevitably involve change of mind, because the power of evil has its most obvious base, not in "things," but in the very people who protest it. And this makes evil a problem indeed, as a moment's thought will show. It is one thing for me to sit back, look at the world, and announce that it raises for me the question of whether I can believe in God or not. It is quite another thing, though, for me to realize that the world's evil is something in which I have a part—that, if there is a "problem of evil," I am not just a neutral hunter after its solution, nor a righteous accuser of others, but a part of what needs to be put right. But Jesus' ministry—his preaching and showing of God's Kingdom— makes just this fact clear. The problem of evil is not only—or maybe not even principally—a problem about God. It is a problem about us, who say that we want the good, but who do not always recognize it, love it, or do it when it shows itself.

· 6 ·

Died . . . Rose . . . Ascended

The ministry of Jesus is the beginning of his story; but it is only the beginning. It states the theme of what is to come. It prepares the way for both a development and a climax. But that is all. The Apostles' and Nicene Creeds, therefore, pass over it in silence. They mention his birth; but then they go straight on to his death and triumph. These last are the events in which they see the point of the whole story. His ministry they are prepared to take for granted.

In this respect, needless to say, the creeds are somewhat at variance with the Gospels. Mark, Matthew, Luke, and John may not have had an abundance of information about the ministry of Jesus; but what they have, they pass on. What is more, they take great care that their readers shall understand at least something of the significance of Jesus' ministry. By the way they arrange their materials, and by their own quiet, and often unnoticed, comment, the evangelists try to make sure that people can grasp and understand the issue raised by the ministry of Jesus—the issue of the Kingdom of God.

In spite of all this, however, the Gospels in the end come out in the same camp as the creeds. They too concentrate attention on Jesus' death and triumph. Just consider, for example, the way in which the evangelists apportion space in their books. They assign far more prominence to the events of the last week of Jesus' life than to any other incident or series

125

of incidents in his career. At the same time, they obviously see his death and Resurrection not simply as the conclusion, but as the culmination, of his story. Their books continually point the reader forward to the decisive events reported at the end of their narrative. Strewn as they are with hints of tragedy and victory to come, the Gospels force us to see that only in the last act does the point of the drama become plain.

It is not hard, moreover, to see why this is so. The ministry of Jesus was, as we have seen, the enactment of a promise. It made no claim to be a thing complete in itself. Rather, it was the announcement of a New Age—of something yet to come. The people who followed Jesus believed in what his ministry promised: they accepted the reality of the coming Kingdom of God. Those who rejected him, for whatever reason, either did not want or could not accept what his ministry promised. For both groups, however, it was the future which would be decisive. The future would show whether Jesus had been right or wrong. It would confirm or deny the promise which was the substance of his proclamation.

The central question, therefore, was always: What will the ministry of Jesus come to? What will be its issue, its result? And this question focuses attention at precisely the point where the creeds and the Gospels focus it: on Jesus' death in the first place, and then on his Resurrection. We accordingly will follow the path which they have laid down, and begin by asking what the death of Jesus said—and says—about his ministry.

Approaching the Death of Jesus

This, however, is no easy question; and before trying to interpret the meaning of Jesus' death, we will do well to stop for a moment and ask ourselves how to approach it. What assumptions should one bring to an examination of it? From what point of view should one look at it?

The first thing to be said in answer to these questions is something which is both simple and important. It concerns the meaning of that phrase, "the death of Jesus." When someone dies, there are two ways in which people can look at what has happened. They can approach it, if they choose, from a purely medical and biological point of view, as a doctor or a coroner would. They can attend, that is, to the physical causes and circumstances of the death, and try to understand it in terms of the natural processes which it involves or illustrates. On the other hand, they may, at the same time, approach the death as an event in the moral sphere. They may ask what meaning it has in the context of human life, human decisions, and human values.

And the point to be made is plain. When theology considers the death of Jesus, it considers it primarily as an event in the moral sphere. No doubt Christian language about Jesus' death, when it dwells, as it sometimes does, on blood-shedding and physical suffering, manages to give the impression that what is important about the Cross is simply a set of physical facts—facts which, when added up, happened to spell the biological death of a particular man. This, however, is a false impression. The significance of Jesus' dying lies in the moral sphere. It lies, that is, in the human actions, decisions, and attitudes which brought it about, and in the effect which it had on people's relations to one another and to God. Theology does not look to it to illustrate natural processes. Rather, it looks to the death of Jesus to tell us something about our problems with good and evil, and about the question of our relationship to God. Theological inquiry presupposes that the significance of the death of Jesus has to be measured in moral terms.

Then, in the second place, granted that Jesus' dying was an event in the moral sphere, it is essential that we understand what the issue was which his death raised and focused. What was at stake in the things which happened to him and in his response to them? The answer to this question is not hard to find; and indeed we have already suggested it a number of times. Nevertheless, it is a point which is basic enough to bear repetition. The death of Jesus was an event in which the issue of the Kingdom of God was at stake. That had been the issue in his active ministry; and it was also the issue in his dying. If the crucifixion means anything at all in what we have called the moral sphere, it means and says something about the relation between God and humanity which Jesus himself stood for, proclaimed, and died for.

But then a third question arises. How can we discern and establish what the dying of Jesus means and says about the Kingdom of God? This question is a serious and practical one. Christian piety and Christian theology have, in the course of nineteen centuries, surrounded the Cross with towering structures of explanation and interpretation. This is not a fact to be regretted. In the end, such explanation and interpretation are necessary if people are to enter as fully as possible into the meaning of the event. On the other hand, theological talk about the Cross has been so elaborated and so developed that it is not always easy to see what the connection is between its assertions and the story of Jesus' execution. How does one get from the legal execution of a controversial prophet to the one "full, perfect, and sufficient sacrifice, oblation, and satisfaction for the sins of the whole world"? How does one get from the apparent tragedy with which Jesus' career ended to an event which is said to provide "the double cure" of sin—to quote the words of a popular hymn? What is there about the crucifixion of Jesus which evokes or justifies such language?

This is not to say that such language is not justified. It is, however, to say that we cannot understand it rightly until we see how and why it is justified; and that means that we must start our thinking about the Cross not with traditional explanations and interpretations, but with the event itself. We have to proceed in the direction which history itself took, by beginning with the death of Jesus; and then it may be possible to see how and why this event gave rise to the sorts of interpretation which theology has used to understand it.

For the moment, then, it is essential to renounce the privileges of hindsight. We must try to forget all the meanings which later history and later experience have discovered in Jesus' death, and come at it from the point of view of the men and women who were originally involved in it. In other words, we have to follow the story as it happened; for only when one has climbed a ladder rung by rung can one look back down it from the new perspective of the top. If the death of Jesus is an event in the moral sphere, and one in which the issue of the Kingdom of God is involved, we can only begin to understand it by trying to see what it would have meant to us if we had been part of the immediate world in which it happened.

Why Was Jesus Executed?

The easiest way to do this is to start by asking ourselves why it was that Jesus was taken, tried, and put to death by the civil authority of his time and place. No sooner is this question stated, however, than we come across a confusion which needs to be straightened out if the event of the Cross is to be properly understood. Fortunately, dealing with this confusion does not involve getting off on a sidetrack; on the contrary, it leads directly to the heart of the problem with which we are concerned.

To the question, "Why was Jesus executed?" there has, from almost the earliest times, been a quick—and substantially false—answer given. The death of Jesus has been explained by saying that "the Jews" killed him, whether out of malice or misunderstanding or both. As a matter of fact, this explanation has roots in the Gospels themselves. It is Matthew, for example, who makes the crowd at Jesus' execution cry out, "His blood be on us and on our children!" Similarly, Matthew does everything he can to make it appear that Pontius Pilate, the Roman procurator, was pressured into condemning Jesus by the Jewish mob and its leaders. In John's Gospel, moreover, it is always "the Jews" who are set up as symbols of opposition and hostility to Jesus.

The explanation of this attitude is not hard to find. It is not "anti-Semitism" in the modern sense. It grows out of the historical experience of the earliest Christian communities. At the time when the Gospels were written, Jews and Christians had become alienated from one another. The Christian sect had probably always been a source of irritation to its parent body; but as the new movement took in Gentile believers—and indeed, in most places, came largely to be composed of Gentiles—irritation gave way to hostility. Jews naturally felt that the followers of Jesus had violated the very foundations of Israel's faith; and for this reason, they excluded Christians from the fellowship of the synagogue and often tried to make life difficult for the new movement. Understandably, if not commendably, Christians responded to this attitude with an answering hostility; and they began to interpret what had happened to Jesus as a sort of dress rehearsal for what was happening to them.

In fact, of course, this way of interpreting Jesus' relation to the Jewish community of his time is quite without foundation. It is not only that Jesus was himself a Jew. So were his immediate disciples and the wider circle of those who believed in him or hoped that he might prove to be right. He had his followers, his supporters, and (no doubt) his friendly critics; and these were all Jews. Moreover, Jesus' message was one whose roots were set firmly in Jewish experience and Jewish history. The movement he led was a phenomenon wholly within the life of Israel.

This is not to say that Jesus had no enemies or doubters within the Jewish community, or that there were not some Jews who in one way or another had a hand in his execution or thought it a just deed. It is quite likely, for example, that many folk were disappointed that Jesus did not lead an insurrection against the Roman occupation of Palestine; and such persons, in their frustrated patriotism, may very well have cooperated or consented in his condemnation. Much more certain is the fact that the official religious leaders of Israel thought Jesus a dangerous radical. He was accused of breaking the Sabbath. He called in question the authority of those who were entrusted with the interpretation of the Law of Moses. He openly said that God was on the side of "the sinners" rather than "the righteous," of the poor rather than the rich. No doubt there were many people who ignored Jesus or laughed at him; and some who thought him out of his mind (including, perhaps, his own family [Mk. 3:21]). The authorities, however, were bound to take a more serious view of him. They saw in him a dangerous troublemaker, who corrupted people and led them astray with his promise of a Rule of God which would make "the last first." It was only natural that such men should seek, by one means or another, to silence Jesus.

As a matter of fact, however, it was not the Jewish authorities who executed Jesus. It was the Romans. His trial was before Pontius Pilate, the Roman governor. His death was effected by crucifixion—a method not known to the Jewish law. Moreover, the charge on which he was tried— that he had attempted to make himself "the King of the Jews"—reflects a distinctively Roman perception of Jesus.

For if the Jewish religious establishment saw in Jesus the leader of an ill-conceived religious rebellion, the Romans, for their part, were bound to see him as a political threat. It is true, as far as we know, that Jesus never announced himself as Messiah. Others, however, almost certainly did claim that title for him; and in doing so, they inevitably made him a political issue. For the Romans knew what Messiahs were. They had had to deal with them before. Given the mood of the times in Palestine, every messianic movement was, at least potentially, a rebellion against Roman authority, an attempt to restore the throne of Israel to the House of David. Obviously, then, the Romans would see Jesus and his movement as a threat to peace and to Roman power, and would deal with it accordingly. In fact, that is just what they did. Some Jews, no doubt, had a hand, directly or indirectly, in Jesus' death; but the Romans did it.

And then, what about Jesus himself? When you come right down to it, there is no accounting for the execution of Jesus if you do not take seriously Jesus' own hand in his fate. The Gospels probably exaggerate when they picture Jesus as predicting his death—and indeed, as predicting its circumstances in precise detail. There can, however, be little doubt that Jesus had some premonition, some expectation, of the end to which his ministry would come. There was, after all, a longstanding tradition about what happened to prophets. Yet, we are told, "He set his face to go to Jerusalem" (Lk. 9:51). It was almost as though he meant to bring things to the point of crisis, to trigger whatever destiny was to be his. Needless to say, this was not because he sought death. It was because he had a call and a mission from God, and had to fulfill them no matter what happened. "Father, if thou art willing, remove this cup from me; nevertheless not my will, but thine, be done" (Lk. 22:42).

This resolution, then, and the commitment it expresses also figure among the causes of Jesus' death. Pilate might be determined to maintain the divine commission of the Roman people to bring peace and order to a warring world. The Jewish religious leaders might be determined to maintain the authority of the divinely given Law of Moses. But Jesus was determined too—to let the reality of God's Kingdom become visible and manifest; and to that end he went to whatever fate awaited him, fearing, but trusting God in spite of his fear.

The Fourth Gospel, then, is quite right when it defines the issue in Jesus' trial and condemnation by making Pilate ask the question, "What is truth?" (Jn. 18:38). What killed Jesus was not the Jews—nor even, in any exclusive sense, the Roman government. What killed him was a clash of authorities and commitments, each represented by different parties or groups in the world to which Jesus' proclamation was addressed. "What is truth?" Is it the truth of the righteous followers of Moses' Law? Is it the divine power which Rome appealed to as it struggled to dominate a world apparently bent on disorder and destruction? Or was it the God of Jesus' proclamation, the God who was keeping his promise of a transformed human world? It is not recorded that Jesus ever answered Pilate's question about truth; and for a very good reason. In the circumstances, no answer could be framed in words. The answer had to come through the way things turned out, through what would finally show itself to be the truth. By his silence in the face of Pilate's question, Jesus committed himself to the judgment of events. He waited trustfully for God to demonstrate the truth.

The Cross as a Judgment of God

It is entirely appropriate, then, that the story of Jesus' suffering and death is pictured for us by the Gospels as an extended trial scene. A courtroom is at once an arena of conflict, in which divergent claims and causes struggle to assert their right; and it is a place of judgment, where a verdict is rendered which is intended to declare the truth of the matter in contest. Jesus' last days represent just such a situation: a struggle of conflicting interests and differing values, and one in which a verdict of some sort had to be rendered. The Gospels tell the story with just a touch of solemn irony. The courtroom we are allowed to see is that of Pilate or of the Sanhedrin. All the while, however, we are made aware that this human scene is mere foreground. The case being tried involves a question of ultimate truth—the question of who God is and where he stands; and for just that reason, it is God who will inevitably do the judging. The decision which is declared will be his, not Pilate's. By the way things come out, God will give his verdict and so reveal and identify himself. He will show whether he is or is not the God and Father whom Jesus announced.

And what was the judgment? Well, Jesus died. His cause, as far as anyone could tell, failed. And the significance of that fact was plain to everyone—to Jesus' friends as well as to his foes. It was, after all, unthinkable that God's representative should become the helpless victim of a foreign power. Matthew's Gospel reports that the crowd at Jesus' crucifixion mocked him with very pointed words. "He is the King of Israel; let him come down now from the cross, and we will believe in him. He trusts in God; let God deliver him now, if he desires him!" (Mt. 27:42f). The meaning of these words is plain. They say—in tones of bitter, and perhaps despairing, sarcasm—that God had deserted Jesus; and this could only mean that he had rendered a verdict against him. Jesus was shown by the event of the Cross to have been in the wrong. The God whom he had proclaimed was not the real God.

Thus, in the first instance, from the point of view of those who in one way or another were immediately associated with it, the death of Jesus could only be taken as a proof that everything which his ministry had seemed to promise was a lie. Death, after all, was the penalty assigned in the Law of Moses for "the prophet who presumes to speak a word in my name which I have not commanded him to speak, or who speaks in the name of other gods" (Dt. 18:20). Such, apparently, was Jesus. Consequently, he was treated automatically as one accursed. He was buried on the same day as that of his death. For it stood written: ". . . if a man . . . is put to death, and you hang him on a tree, his body shall not remain all night upon the tree, but you shall bury him the same day, for a hanged man is accursed by God . . ." (Dt. 21:22f).

The Proclamation of the Resurrection

Then, not many days after, certain of Jesus' disciples announced that he had been revealed to them living; and in the light of this experience they proclaimed that God had raised him from the dead. Saint Paul himself had such an encounter with the risen Christ some years later; and he learned gladly from the tradition of the Christian communities at Jerusalem and Damascus that he was not alone in what happened to him. "For," he tells his converts at Corinth, "I delivered to you . . . what I also received, . . . that [Christ] was raised on the third day in accordance with the Scriptures and that he appeared [ōphthē] to Cephas and then to the twelve. Then he appeared to more than five hundred brethren at one time . . . Then he appeared to James, then to all the Apostles" (1 Cor. 15:3–7).

In this earliest written report of the appearances of the risen Jesus, the very language which Paul uses tells something about the nature and meaning of these events. They were not encounters with Jesus as he had been before his death. When he is said to have "appeared" (ōphthē), the very use of that near-technical term indicates that his appearances were experienced as a kind of revelation from beyond. Jesus manifested himself to his disciples as one who now belonged to an order of things different from the world of their ordinary experience. When Saint Paul speaks of his encounter with the risen Christ in his own words, he explicitly calls it a "revelation" (Gal. 1:12); and he goes on to explain that God, "who had set me apart before I was born, and had called me through his grace, was pleased to reveal his Son in me, in order that I might preach among the Gentiles" (Gal. 1:15f). Christ, in fact, had "taken hold [katelēmphthēn]" on Paul (Phil. 3:12), and set his life on a new course—reoriented his existence.

The point of all this is that in meeting or knowing the risen Jesus, the disciples had not just become acquainted with a fact—that Jesus was alive, or that he had not really died. Rather, they had been seized up, if only for a moment, into a new life. Something radical had happened to them. They had seen the Kingdom of God, the New Age of Promise. It was realized and fulfilled in Jesus himself; and in meeting him, they too had a taste of it.

Consequently, these encounters with the risen Jesus were not just startling or amazing incidents. They were events which changed people's lives because they brought a new reality to light. They said, in the first place, that the message of Jesus' ministry had been true after all. Whatever the death of Jesus might seem to have meant, God had not in fact rejected him. On the contrary, he had affirmed Jesus' ministry and fulfilled its promise—in however unexpected and unforeseen a way. The Kingdom of God was not dream but reality. It could be met in the person of the Risen One.

Then, in the second place, this experience made it perfectly clear who Jesus really was. "God has made him both Lord and Christ, this Jesus whom you crucified" (Acts 2:36). The Galilean preacher and healer was indeed God's Christ, the representative and bearer of God's Rule; and the Resurrection made this fact apparent.

Finally, however, these meetings with Christ also said, and said quite plainly, that the new life of God's Kingdom was something in which all human beings could share. It was possible to live with the Christ, and in doing so to have the New Age of promise as one's own inheritance. Consequently, the Resurrection of Jesus was something which had to be proclaimed, to Jew and Gentile alike; for in it was contained the ultimate good news, the essential clue to God's character and to his purposes for humanity.

The Meaning of the Resurrection

From this brief account of the meaning of the Resurrection appearances of Jesus, it should be plain that moderns, whether they are Christian believers or not, need to change the way in which they understand the word *resurrection* as the New Testament uses it to characterize the destiny of Jesus. Time and custom and lack of imagination have seriously eroded its significance and focused attention on questions which in fact miss or evade its intended impact.

For one thing, modern discussions of the Resurrection of Jesus have almost always perceived it, in the spirit of the natural sciences, as a kind of medical miracle. People simply assume that when the disciples preached that God had raised Jesus from the dead, they were asserting that his corpse had been resuscitated or reanimated, that he had, to use the ordinary phrase, "come back to life." For this reason, all attention has centered on the question of what happened—or might have happened—in Jesus' tomb, and on the physical processes which are presumably involved in a resurrection. Debate has raged over whether such revival of a dead person is scientifically conceivable, and over the evidence available that such a thing really happened.

From the point of view of the New Testament, however, all such debate is misleading and irrelevant. It distracts attention from the central point of the idea of resurrection, and hence mistakes the nature of what is being proclaimed. The best evidence of this is the fact that nowhere in the New Testament is there any attempt to characterize, describe, or narrate the process of resurrection. None of the witnesses ever says or tries to say "what happened." There is an old, and very likely accurate, tradition that Jesus' tomb was found empty; but that fact, as everyone knew, was susceptible of more than one explanation; and it stands in the Scriptures not as demonstrative evidence of anything, but simply as the intimation of a mystery. There is, as far as the apostolic witness is concerned, neither a "how" nor a "when" of the Resurrection. God's raising of Jesus is not described. It is simply announced.

Furthermore, there is good reason for this. *Resurrection* in biblical language does not mean revival of the clinically dead or resuscitation. It refers to an event which was understood to mark the dawning of the Kingdom of God, of the Age to Come. Consequently, it is inaccurate, from the perspective of the New Testament, to say that Jesus "came back to life." That is just what he did not do. Rather, it has to be said that he entered upon a new order of life: one which does not and cannot occur as part of the present order of things. The Resurrection is not a here-and-now occurrence—not even a miraculous here-and-now occurrence like the healing of a paralytic. It is the moment in which God's "new thing" begins. That is why Saint Paul says that "flesh and blood cannot inherit the Kingdom of God" (1 Cor. 15:50); for what he means is that resurrection is not something which happens as part of things-as-they-are. It is the juncture, the point of transition, at which the new begins to replace the old. That, and nothing less, is what the New Testament is proclaiming; and that is something more tremendous than any minor medical miracle.

If, however, modern theological discussion has trivialized the Resurrection of Jesus by failing to see the point of its proclamation, modern preaching has trivialized it by dwelling almost exclusively on one possible consequence of it. For reasons which are historically very complicated indeed, the message of the Resurrection has, in the public mind, been boiled down to a promise of individual survival of death. The fact that "God raised Jesus from the dead" is taken as an assurance that the human self somehow, in some form, survives the cessation of biological death.

For all anyone knows, it may be quite true that the human self somehow survives the cessation of bodily life, even if only for a while. Philosophers have debated that issue for centuries; and more recently, parapsychological investigations have addressed themselves to the same problem. Certainly the Old Testament, like the ancient Greeks, knew of the survival of a kind of shadow self in what the Hebrews called "Sheol." The ancients, however, did not assume that such a prolongation of life was necessarily a desirable thing. In fact, the thought of existence in Sheol or Hades was for them a never-ending stimulus to hold on to the real life of the present, even if that were full of misfortune or frustration. What we moderns call "immortality"—the prolongation of individual existence—is, in fact, a prospect which people may or may not look forward to with anticipation. Whether or not one hopes for it depends entirely on what sort of existence it turns out to be.

The message of the Resurrection, however, has, of itself, nothing whatever to say about the question of whether people naturally and automatically survive death. It is not addressed primarily to the problem of survival; it is addressed to the problem of evil. What it says is not that I shall not die; but that God is recreating humanity in Christ, and that I belong to that humanity. It asserts that God is gracious and faithful to his promises, and that he has a new way of being in store for his people. To live again, to be raised from the dead, is not just to continue one's existence under altered circumstances: it is to enter into the Kingdom of God, to share the new life of the Risen Christ. Again, the message of the Resurrection says more than we are quite prepared to hear. It affirms the reality, not of survival, but of the Age to Come; not of my power to hold on to existence, but of God's power to make all things new—even me.

The Evidence of the Resurrection

But what can be evidence for the truth of such a message? Obviously enough, it would not be in the least helpful to demonstrate that Jesus "came back to life." The fact that a particular person revived after a period of being clinically dead would not establish the reality of the Kingdom of God. We have seen, moreover, that "coming back to life" is not exactly what the New Testament has on its mind when it speaks of resurrection. What it is really talking about is conveyed in the language which Saint Luke has taught us to associate with "ascension": namely, the exaltation of Jesus to the new order of life, to life in and with God. And how could that sort of reality be established?

The answer, of course, is that it cannot be established, if *established* means "demonstrated beyond the possibility of rational doubt." The New Testament, in fact, makes no effort to provide proofs. What it provides is simply the witness of persons who encountered the risen Jesus by being caught up in the new life which is his.

This witness is conveyed to us for the most part at second hand. Saint Paul, in his letters, occasionally speaks for himself; but he is reticent, and his statements inevitably seem to us both summary and mysterious. For the rest, what we have are the stories in the Gospels of the appearances of the Risen Lord; and the trouble with these is that, at least on the surface, the different Gospels tell different stories. Saint Mark, of course, gives no accounts of such appearances at all. The closing verses of his Gospel (16:9–20) are from a later hand, and merely summarize materials gathered from the other evangelists. As for the latter, they are manifestly divided in their accounts. They disagree about both minor and major details of Jesus' appearances, as even a hasty comparison of their narratives will reveal.

What sense, then, can be made of these stories? And what authority can they have?

In any attempt to answer these questions, a great deal depends on the way in which we understand what the evangelists were up to. One thing there can be no doubt of whatever: behind these stories there lies an early and reliable tradition of the sort rehearsed by Saint Paul in 1 Corinthians 15:5–7. This tradition, however, was exceedingly matter-of-fact. It confined itself to bare bones—to recording the simple fact that Jesus "appeared" to such-and-such a person or group of persons. The evangelists, however, are not content with such reports. Their accounts of each appearance are much fuller. The stories include details of time, place, and circumstance and take the form of dramatic narratives. Moreover, they appear as parts of consecutive accounts which profess to tell the whole story of Jesus' appearances.

What modern readers of the Gospels need to understand, however, is that the ultimate purpose of the evangelists is simply to bring out the meaning of what happened. Their concern is not primarily to provide factual detail but to convey the significance of encounters with the Risen Lord. In fact, what they provide is more in the nature of theological com-

mentary than it is of journalistic reporting. The trouble is—
from our point of view—that neither the evangelists nor their
sources were in the least concerned with cultivating the virtues valued by modern reporters and historians. They did not
primarily want to report the precise circumstances, or even
the exact subjective "feel," of encounters with the risen
Christ. Their primary objective was to construct a narrative
which would convey the objective meaning of these
appearances—their message, to put it simply.

And the interesting thing is that, when measured by the
standard of their own ultimate aims, the evangelists' accounts show a surprising unanimity. The best way to grasp
this fact, perhaps, is to consider the thrust of three different
versions of a single tradition. Each of the Gospels (except, of
course, Saint Mark's) has an account of a final appearance of
Jesus to his assembled disciples, an appearance which was
clearly part of the earliest tradition. (See Mt. 28:16–20; Lk.
24:36–49; Jn. 20:19–23.) If the three stories are compared, it
can hardly escape anyone's notice that the detail of them
differs vastly: and most notably, perhaps, in the words which
are ascribed to the risen Lord. On the other hand, it is also
clear that the substance of what Jesus is made to say, and of
what is said or implied concerning him, is much the same in
each case.

In each case, for example, the narrative makes it plain that
one meaning of these appearances was the attestation of
Jesus' authority as Lord and Christ, as the representative and
bearer of God's Kingdom. Each evangelist has his own way
of conveying this, but each gets his message across. Furthermore, all of the writers are clear that part of the meaning of
the Resurrection of Jesus is the reality of the forgiveness of
sins—that is, of reconciliation between God and humanity.
John is the most emphatic about this point ("Peace be with
you . . ."; "Whose sins you forgive . . ."); Matthew conveys
it only indirectly through his insistence on Baptism as an
integral part of the church's mission. It is, however, significantly present in all three accounts. Above all, the three versions of this tradition are at one in insisting that the Resurrection of Jesus is a call to mission. The followers of Jesus are to

forgive sins, to make disciples of all nations, to proclaim everywhere the opportunity for repentance.

The testimony of these stories, therefore, must be taken seriously. They convey to their reader the content of authentic experience; and they do so in accounts which, while certainly not circumstantially reliable, are quite unanimous about the essential sense of the events to which they refer. The question, then, is not whether the testimony is honest; nor even whether, on its own terms, it is substantively accurate. The question is whether even honestly conveyed experience can convince people that God truly is the God and Father of Jesus Christ: that the Kingdom of God, reconciliation between God and humanity, the New Age of Promise, has been made real in the Resurrection of Jesus Christ from the dead.

Conclusion

If the testimony is true, however, and the faith evoked by it is therefore justified, it is not just an amazing fact which is acknowledged. Amazing facts, after all, are common enough. What is ultimately startling and, indeed, overwhelming is the possibility that the message of Jesus, his proclamation of God's Kingdom, was in fact the showing in our midst of the final truth about things. That is the fundamental message of the Resurrection; and if it is true, it does not change our view of this or that circumstance in human history. It changes our view of the meaning of human life itself. The burden of the Resurrection story is, therefore, properly and rightly almost impossible to believe—not because it talks about some medical oddity, but because it would persuade us that people really can trust and love God; that they can stand with Jesus and hand themselves over to God, and in thus losing their life, find it.

· 7 ·

"In Christ, God Was Reconciling the World . . ."

At this point in our thinking it becomes necessary to shift gears. Hitherto we have simply been telling the story of Jesus by following out the course of events which is summarized in the creeds, and seeking at the same time to grasp what it meant for the people involved in it. With Jesus' Resurrection, however, the story enters upon a new stage. It now becomes a story focused not so much on Jesus himself as on people's experience of him. It tells how people have understood and entered into the reality which Jesus embodies for them—the reality of God's coming Kingdom.

But what sort of thing happens in this new phase of our story? When we say that people come to understand and enter into the reality which Jesus embodies for them, we are talking about a process which has two sides. On the one hand, it is a process in which people learn to comprehend themselves and what goes on in their world in the light of Jesus and his Resurrection. On the other hand, it is a process in which they come to understand the story of Jesus more deeply in the light of the difference which it has made both in their personal lives and in public history. In other words, what continues the story of Jesus is the history of the appropriation of its meaning and its promise; and in this history

142

that meaning and that promise are shown to have depths and facets which could not have been grasped before.

Thus creative hindsight comes into play, and at this point legitimately. For hindsight means letting new things that happen bring out fresh dimensions of meaning in the events which lead up to them. What it sees is something which was there all the time; but at the same time something which only new developments could bring into focus.

Looking Back on Jesus' Death

Of this process of interpretation, there is no more obvious or more central example than that of people's way of coming to terms with the death of Jesus. We have seen already what the immediate impact—and hence the immediate meaning—of Jesus' execution was. It appeared to signify God's repudiation of Jesus and thus to mark him out as a false prophet. In the most persuasive possible way, it said that what he stood for was not real. The Kingdom of God which he announced was a dream, and so also was the God whom he served.

In the new light of the Resurrection, however, such an understanding of Jesus' death became impossible. Jesus' rising from the dead, his appearance in the lives of his followers as the very embodiment of the Kingdom which he had preached, meant that the true significance of the Cross had yet to be grasped. Later events, in short, set the Cross in an entirely fresh perspective.

Of course certain assumptions about what had happened there had to be retained. For example, there could be no question about the issue which was at stake in Jesus' execution. It was, and had to be, the same issue which his ministry raised and which his resurrection clarified: the issue of the Kingdom of God. In one way or another, Jesus' death signified something about God's overcoming of evil and his giving himself to be with people in a new way. That much, at any rate, was clear.

Furthermore, it was still possible—and, in fact, necessary—to envisage the Cross as an event through which judgment occurred. *Judgment* most fundamentally means "discrimination." A judgment, therefore, is an act or event in which truth is set apart from falsehood, and good from evil; in short, an occurrence in which things are shown up for what they really are. From the very beginning, people thought of Jesus' death in these terms; and they continue to do so. The Cross was the place where God declared himself.

These considerations, however, only bring us back to the original question, which now looks even more puzzling. If the Resurrection indeed represents, as we have said, God's vindication of Jesus, then why did Jesus have to die in the first place? What can his human failure, his victimization and suffering, have to say about the Kingdom of God? And if the Cross was a judgment, what truth did it reveal?

The Cross and the Problem of Evil

A start can be made at answering these questions if we notice, to begin with, that the Resurrection makes at least one thing plain about the death of Jesus. Supposing that his death was a judgment which brought some decisive truth to light, we can say without hesitation that it did not declare Jesus to be in the wrong. The Cross may at first glance look like God's judgment against Jesus; but the Resurrection makes it necessary to revise this initial impression. In his dying, evil was present and at work; but the evil which was there was not of Jesus' making.

Whose then? Maybe the natural and inevitable way of understanding Jesus' execution is to see it as just another tragic illustration of the general wrongness of things—of the fact that goodness is seldom rewarded, and evil is frequently triumphant. Jesus, we might say, is in reality another Job, a man unreasonably afflicted by the indifference or the caprice of an untrustworthy world. To say this, however, is to bring the responsibility for the Cross home to God himself. It is to assert that in truth the judgment which the Cross declares is a judgment against God, who can permit this sort of thing to happen to a man of surpassing goodness and integrity.

But what sense does it make to say that? Why would God first afflict and then vindicate Jesus? Why would he act so as, in effect, to turn against himself? No doubt it is perfectly normal for human beings to conceive of evil as a problem about God rather than as a problem about themselves; but in this case, such a reaction is plainly inappropriate. What God does in the Cross has to be consistent with what he does in the Resurrection; and if that is so, we have to conclude that the judgment which the Cross declares is not a judgment against God.

Whom, then, does it strike, this judgment? The obvious answer is that it lights upon the human beings who betrayed, took, tried, and condemned Jesus. This statement, however, must not be misunderstood. The judgment is not against Pilate and Caiaphas as individuals; and this for at least two good reasons. In the first place, more people were involved in Jesus' death than just the public figures who had official responsibility in it. Their action was empowered and made possible by the attitudes, values, and decisions of a multitude of others, from the Roman Senate itself to the peasantry of Galilee. They did not stand alone. In the second place, moreover, these men did not act simply as individuals. They acted as representatives of the political, cultural, and religious establishments of their time and place. The way in which they saw Jesus and reacted to him was not determined by private or personal considerations. It was determined by his relation to the systems which they represented. Consequently, the evil which afflicted Jesus in his passion and death was not really the doing of this or that individual. It was produced through the spontaneous reaction of a world which could only see God's Rule, the Kingdom which Jesus proclaimed and bore, as a destructive threat to its own values, its own life, and its own hopes.

Considered as an act of judgment, then, what the Cross shows up is the truth about the world in and for which Jesus had proclaimed good news. That world valued and understood things in such a way that the word of God's mercy could scarcely be heard in it. That world was so ordered and governed that God's representative could only appear in it as an unwanted stranger. In short, what the Cross shows up is *the sin of the world:* its helpless estrangement from God and, therefore, from true goodness. The problem of evil as the Cross reveals it is not a problem about God. It is a problem about human beings in the society which they have made, and therefore a problem *for* God, who in Jesus finds himself an outcast and a reject among his own creatures. The problem of evil is revealed in the Cross to be the problem of sin.

The Victory of the Cross

This conclusion, however, suggests an answer only to the second of our questions. It indicates the sense in which the Cross was truly a judgment—a judgment on the world in its sinfulness. What it does not explain is the relation between Jesus' dying and the Kingdom of God which he proclaimed. How do his humiliation and death manifest or realize the Rule of God? How is his dying involved in the appearance of a new relationship between God and his people?

This is a central and pivotal question. From the beginning, it was incomprehensible to almost everyone, including Jesus' disciples, that anyone who represented the cause of God should not merely suffer but die. When Jesus himself intimated such a possibility, Peter—we are told—"began to rebuke him" (Mk. 8:32), presumably because he thought such an eventuality inconceivable. Furthermore, Christians of a later time had exactly the same feelings about the Cross. Paul, whom history acknowledges as the first theologian of the Cross, admits that his Gospel of "Messiah crucified" (1 Cor. 1:23) looks like "foolishness." It is something which evokes the contempt of both Jews and Greeks. It is a "stumbling block"—a fact which the mind can hardly come to terms with, much less explain. How can the failure of God's cause spell its success?

But of course God's cause did not fail: that is the point of the Resurrection. Our question, therefore, must be revised. We have to speak more carefully and ask: How does the suffering and death of God's spokesman point to, or help to bring about, the Kingdom which Jesus proclaimed? And where this question is concerned, we can perhaps see the beginnings of an answer.

The first clue lies in a fact which we have already noticed. Jesus, we have said, died not in consequence of his own sin, but in consequence of the world's sin. The evil which afflicted him was not of his own making. Rather, his death was the point where the world's alienation from God came into focus and showed both its reality and its power. Consequently, it is true to say, morally speaking, that in his passion and execution, Jesus carried the sin of the world. He was associated with his world in its alienation from God; and that sin is the inner meaning of his death. He dies the death of his world.

But God raised him; and this news compels yet a further and more considered look at the Cross. Jesus bore the sin of his world; but that sin did not have its ultimate effect. It did not cut Jesus off from God, or frustrate God's design—the design which Jesus' ministry had proclaimed and expressed. On the contrary, the death of Jesus led to Resurrection. It brought about the opening of the New Age in him. *If his death frustrated anything, then, what it frustrated was sin.* The dying of Jesus seems to have neutralized the effect and the power of his world's estrangement from God. In the light of the Resurrection, the execution of Jesus can only appear as God's way of bringing sin to nothing—of short-circuiting it.

And here the Cross does indeed appear in a new light. It represents not a contradiction of God's design but an essential moment in its realization. The Cross—as the New Testament and the Christian community in every generation have insisted—marks the central point of a great conflict: a conflict between God's Rule and the evil which perverts human existence. In this conflict, however, and in the death which it involved, what happened was not the thing that appears on the surface. It was not sin's victory over God. On the contrary, it was God's victory over sin. Jesus' death was the way in which God drew off the power of sin to make way for the new life of the Resurrection. The Cross itself is, strangely and mysteriously, a scene of triumph.

And what that triumph spells is, in a word, forgiveness. The sin which was borne in Jesus' dying was not—and the point bears repeating—his own sin. It was the sin ingrained in the very life of the world to which he brought good news.

Consequently, the sin which was neutralized and short-circuited in the Cross was just that sin—the world's sin. The dying of Jesus, then, means that the world's sin can no longer stand between it and God. The power of alienation has been conquered. The ground has been cleared for reconciliation between humanity and God. In the death of Jesus sin is forgiven.

The Cross, in summary, marks a triumph; and the triumph it marks is the overcoming of the power which sin has to keep people away from God. From this, however, something else—and something startling—must follow. *The dying of Jesus was not a denial, but an assertion, of God's Rule.* The power of evil was present there, and hard at work. There can be no doubt of that. At first glance, indeed, the power of evil is all that one can discern in the Cross. Beneath the surface of the event, however, God is asserting himself. He too is there, present and active, so bearing the brunt of evil in Jesus' faithful self-giving as to neutralize its power, and thus to set people free from it. The Cross is the world's doing; but in a deeper sense, the Cross is God's doing.

The Idea of Sacrifice

Here, then, is a picture of the Cross as an event which means redemption: an event which first reveals and judges the world's sin, and then neutralizes and forgives it. But how can such an event be understood or explained? With what image or idea can one lay hold on its sense—its inner logic or meaning?

As a matter of fact, the New Testament persistently uses one image to bring out the meaning and the consequences of Jesus' death; and that is the image of sacrifice. This image is employed and developed most formally and most explicitly in Hebrews; but it is not less central in other writings, including the Gospels. When Saint Paul writes of "an expiation by [Jesus'] blood" (Rom. 3:25); when 1 Peter says that the Christ "bore our sins in his body on the tree" (2:24); when 1 John insists that "the body of Jesus his Son cleanses us from all sin" (1:17)—what is being asserted in each case is that Jesus'

dying was a sacrificial event, which for just that reason ex-
piates or atones for sin. And behind this language lies not
merely the age-old sacrificial ritual of the Jerusalem Temple,
but, just as significantly, Isaiah's picture of "the servant of
the Lord," whose sacrifice covered the sin of those who had
held him in contempt.

> Surely he has borne our griefs
> and carried our sorrows;
> Yet we esteemed him stricken,
> smitten by God and afflicted.
> But he was wounded for our transgressions,
> he was bruised for our iniquities;
> Upon him was the chastisement that made us whole,
> and with his stripes we are healed (Is. 53:4–5).

Confronted with the language of sacrifice, however, with
its talk of death and blood, and its use of strange terms like
"expiate" and "atone," contemporary people inevitably
waver somewhere between bafflement and horror. Isaiah's
picture of the Servant is certainly eloquent and inspiring in
its portrayal of a righteous man who bears rejection lovingly
and courageously. But how can we be healed by someone
else's stripes? How can God be called just if he imposes on
one person the suffering which properly belongs to others?
And besides, think of the slaughter of animals which accompanied ancient rituals of sacrifice. Was not that cruel as well
as superstitious?

Yet, in spite of all these questions and problems which the
ancient practice of sacrifice creates for us, we know that sacrifice has a central role in all relations among persons. If a
person gives something up for the sake of a cause; or surren-
ders time, money, or effort to help someone else; or suffers
serious inconvenience in order to maintain and deepen a valued friendship: these are all situations in which sacrifice occurs, and we find nothing strange or immoral in them. To
give oneself or one's possessions for others is commonly
counted a noble thing; and indeed, apart from such sacrifice,
the web of human relations could never survive the strains

which we place on it. Where people are alienated from one another, it is only a costly gesture of sacrifice—of self-giving—which brings reconciliation, or, to use traditional language, "makes atonement."

Sacrifice, then, means giving oneself to or for another; and understood in this sense, it is not only essential to human relations, but also to the relationship of people to God. That relation too is constituted by self-giving: by the creature's opening itself to God even as God gives himself to be present with the creature. Sacrifice, the gesture of handing oneself over to the other, is therefore part and parcel of all religion.

One may, of course, object to the way in which sacrifice was institutionalized or ritualized in the Old Testament world. We may prefer the ritual of the United Thank Offering to a ritual in which the flesh of an animal is shared between God and his worshipers. In expressing such a preference, however, we need to be aware that the ancients regarded animals as more valuable, because they were more essential to life, than money. That is why they thought one should not slaughter an animal at all without making acknowledgment to God, and also why animals were used to symbolize truly costly self-giving. The real problem, perhaps, lies in the fact of ritualization itself; for sacrifice is a moral reality, and when it is formalized, whether in United Thank Offerings or in whole burnt offerings, its moral substance can be forgotten or ignored. True self-giving is always costly. It always, as the ancients knew, involves a kind of dying, a handing over and sharing of life.

Moreover, it is for just this reason that sacrifice is closely tied up with expiation and making atonement. When persons are estranged from one another, when responsive trust gives place to hostility and fear, sin—which we have defined as denial or refusal of the "other"—is actively present. But how is sin dealt with? How is reconciliation, or atonement, effected? The answer is that sacrifice must be made. Each party to the relationship must bear the hurt of the other. Then, and only then, does forgiveness occur. Then, and only then, do the two stand together once again. They are enabled to share a common life again by first sharing a common death, by taking up the burden of each other's pain.

And this exactly is the meaning of what the Scriptures call expiatory or atoning sacrifice. Such a sacrifice is not an attempt by human beings to appease or placate an angry God. Nor is it an action in which God punishes some people (or one person) so that others can get off the hook. These interpretations of expiatory sacrifice—widespread though they have been—simply miss the point. Expiatory sacrifice is a single gesture or action in which two things happen together: God in his love takes upon himself the burden of human guilt and estrangement, while his people takes upon itself God's judgment of its sin. Mercy on the one hand, and the acceptance of judgment on the other; divine action and human action: these are the two constitutive factors in expiatory sacrifice, the sacrifice which covers sin. And it is just this sort of event which the early Christians saw in the death of Christ.

The Atoning Sacrifice

But exactly how does this image of atoning sacrifice fit the case of Jesus' death? Where is the correspondence between the idea of expiation and the moral meaning of the Cross?

In the first place, Jesus' dying was, like his life and ministry, a gesture of self-giving to God. Simply as a human reality, the Cross represents the final and voluntary commitment of a human life into the hands of its Creator. Moreover, this self-offering was and remains an act in which Jesus handed himself over for judgment; and in what happened to him, judgment was in fact passed.

In the second place, however, the judgment which Jesus thus accepted was not a judgment on himself, but on his world. He stands with God through his act of self-giving; but at the same time, he stands with those who sought to reject him. It is their estrangement and their sin which he takes upon himself, and whose judgment he accepts. Thus Jesus' act of sacrifice has two sides. He gives himself to God; and he gives himself for his fellows, whose estrangement he carries and shares. In receiving judgment, he represents the very people who are denying him.

In the third place, this human action is one in which God is asserting his Rule. In and through what Jesus does, God is active. It is God's love which is the basis of Jesus' self-offering. It is God's love, furthermore, which in Jesus bears, suffers, and overcomes the world's estrangement. The event of the Cross, then, is in very truth the point at which human self-giving and divine self-giving coincide and become one. It is the very occurrence of reconciliation, therefore; for in such an act the power of sin and estrangement meets its match.

Finally, it is in this way, and in no other, that the Cross covers or neutralizes sin and makes the promise of forgiveness real. The Cross is no technical wonder which does away with sin automatically. Neither is it a kind of cash transaction in which one thing (Jesus' life) is exacted in payment for another (forgiveness). The Cross makes atonement because it is an event of the moral order. In it, divine love and human self-offering flow together into one action—an action in which the hurt of sin is borne and healed and the New Age begins to dawn.

Conclusion

What is true of Jesus' ministry and true of his Resurrection is therefore true also of his death. In each of these events, the Kingdom of God is signified. It is not signified, however, merely by being pointed out and named. It is signified by being realized. In his ministry Jesus made the Kingdom real for people by his effective proclamation of it in word and deed. In his sacrificial dying he realizes that reconciliation of God and humanity which sets people free for a new life. In his Resurrection the New Age begins to dawn. The final point of the story of Jesus, then, is this: that in him the "new thing" which God has promised effectively comes to pass. In him God and humanity are at one, and God is seen to be truly with us.

· 8 ·

Divine and Human

No one can think about the story of Jesus without realizing that it raises a final and crucial question about Jesus himself. As a matter of fact, this problem was stated and puzzled over by many people even in the course of Jesus' ministry. We are told that when Jesus asked, "Who do men say that I am?" his disciples answered: "Some say John the Baptist, others Elijah, others one of the prophets" (Mk. 8:27–28). Clearly enough, the folk who heard Jesus' preaching and discerned its import realized that if his claim was true, he must himself be a figure of extraordinary importance. On the other hand, they were uncertain precisely what role or office to assign him, or how to say who he was. Jesus himself, as the Gospels make abundantly plain, was not in the business of supplying an answer to this question. What was important to him was not his own status, but the proclamation of the Kingdom of God. Nevertheless, the question was bound to be asked; and people tried to answer it, even though they had little to go on.

What was merely a natural question for those who originally experienced the impact of Jesus' ministry became a necessary question for those who grasped the meaning of his death and the reality of his Resurrection. Here was a person in whom God's Rule was not merely announced, but effected and actualized. Here was one who, by what he was and what he did, made the thing he talked about come true. Because of

Jesus, a new relationship between God and humanity had come into being. In him a New Covenant had been made between God and God's people. Who—or what—was he, then? What sense can be made of Jesus himself, given the meaning of his ministry, death, and Resurrection in the lives of those who knew him?

This question defines the area of inquiry which theologians technically call "Christology." The word itself, of course, means simply "the doctrine about Messiah." In Christian usage, however, that does not mean a teaching about messiahship in general, or a history of claimants to the messianic title. It means, quite specifically, teaching about the person of Jesus; for it is assumed that in the last resort it is he who defines the meaning of messiahship, and not *vice versa*. Jesus is the bearer of God's Kingdom.

But, someone might ask, what need is there for inquiry and discussion? Do not the New Testament and the creeds answer the question for us? Do they not tell us that Jesus is Messiah and Lord? Do they not insist clearly that he is Son of God, and indeed the Word of God made flesh? Do not these assertions provide all the answers we need?

It is certainly true that these answers are supplied us; but it is not so certainly true that they are all the answers we need. The christological question cannot be settled, and people's desire to understand Christian faith cannot be satisfied, merely by sticking honorific labels on Jesus. Such a procedure too easily ignores the question of what people mean, or think that they mean, when they use such labels. It also ignores the question of what the same labels meant when they were originally used in the New Testament and the creeds; for there may very well be a difference, say, between what "Word of God" meant to Saint John and what it suggests to a contemporary reader of the Bible. There is, therefore, no way of avoiding the question of what the church's traditional christological language means, what exactly it intends to say about Jesus, and what it intends not to say.

Such clarification, however, is not enough. Once we understand, at least in general terms, what this language means, it becomes necessary to ask why it is used, why this account, and not some other, is given of the person of Christ. The task of "understanding the faith" is not complete until it is possible to point to the reasons which underlie it. Why, in fact, have people wanted to speak about Jesus as "God made man"? What sorts of experiences and ideas have gone into the making of such a faith? What kinds of arguments have been employed to explain and ground it? Does it really make sense of what Jesus was and what he did? Only by answering such questions as these can we find out what sense the church's traditional language about Jesus makes, and how it is possible for us to find the language and ideas in which to make that sense clear in the present day.

The Starting Point

Where, then, does christological reflection start? This question has two possible meanings, and both of them raise important issues. In the first place, the question can mean: What gives rise to christological reflection? The answer to that is simple enough, but absolutely basic for everything else we shall say. Christological reflection is occasioned by the new relation between God and humanity which Jesus proclaimed and brought with him. There are all sorts of inquiries that people can make about Jesus. They can wonder what he looked like, or try to reconstruct the events of his life, or set about assessing the effects of his career on the later history of the Roman Empire. Such investigations are not only legitimate; they may be important. They are not, however, christological inquiries. The form of the christological question is always roughly this: What does it mean about Jesus that he is the bearer of God's Kingdom, and hence of God's salvation?

Our question can also have a second, and perhaps more obvious, meaning. It may simply be asking when it was that people began to engage in what we have called christological inquiry. And here again the answer, while simple enough, is of central importance. Christological inquiry began with the preaching of the earliest Christian community—a preaching which is reflected and partly set down in the books of the New Testament. The first business of the earliest Christians was to proclaim the good news of the Resurrection; and this meant that their first business was to explain the significance of Jesus and of what happened to him. When, accordingly, their preaching began to take literary shape—in Saint Paul's letters first of all, but then in the Gospels and other writings of the New Testament—what it produced was a series of writings whose whole purpose was ultimately christological. The Books of the New Testament talk about all sorts of things, to be sure; but the basic purpose of each one of them is to say—to one audience or another, in one set of circumstances or another—what Jesus did and who he was.

Needless to say, what this means is that the New Testament writers came up with a great variety of ways of assessing the significance of Jesus. It also means that over the period which is covered by the writing of the books of the New Testament, people's ideas about Jesus developed and changed, and not always in the same direction. Insights were deepened; images and ideas which had originally been prominent in the church's understanding of Jesus were forgotten or played down; new ways of conceiving and explaining his significance were developed. The New Testament, in fact, represents only the beginning of a long historical process of christological inquiry, which indeed continues in the present day.

This beginning, however, is not just a start; it is a foundation. The New Testament descriptions of Jesus—as "Son of Man" or "Second Adam," as the new Moses or the eternal High Priest, as the Messiah who would come at the end, and as the Messiah who had already come, as the heavenly Lord who bends the course of the world's history to the will of God, as the Wisdom of God, as the Word of God enfleshed— each of these ways of accounting for Jesus and for what he accomplished embodies a fundamental testimony of Christian experience. Each of them, therefore, must be interpreted and incorporated in any contemporary statement of what it means to say that Jesus is the one in and through whom God's Rule is actualized.

The problem, then, is to pick one's way among these images and descriptions of Jesus in such a way as to see where they point: or better, perhaps, what direction they lead us in as we pursue our own christological inquiry. It would be extremely easy, in trying to deal with so rich and varied a set of ideas, to miss the forest entirely for the sake of the trees. In order to avoid any such result, therefore, we will take care to look at this body of material with three questions constantly in mind. These three questions are derived from our earlier formulation of the basic christological problem: "What does it mean about Jesus that he is the bearer of God's Kingdom, and hence of God's salvation?" For in reality, there are three questions contained in this one. There is, first of all, a question about Jesus' function or role. How do we describe *what he does* as the bearer of God's Kingdom? Then, in the second place, there is a question about Jesus' relation to God. What does it mean to say of him that he is, in himself, the bearer of God's Rule? Finally, there is a question about Jesus as a human being. What is involved in asserting that *it is a man*, one human person among others, who is the bearer of God's Kingdom?

Prophet, Priest, King

In the New Testament it is the first of these questions—the one about Jesus' function or role—which is the starting point of christological inquiry; and therefore it had best be ours as well. But how can we organize the abundant materials which the New Testament provides on this subject?

There is, as a matter of fact, lying right to hand, a useful scheme of classification which we can employ for this purpose. This scheme arose much later in history than the writings of the New Testament, and for that reason it runs the risk of imposing on the biblical materials a logic which is not original to them. Nevertheless, it has the advantage of taking off from certain basic biblical ideas, and using them as heads under which New Testament portrayals of Jesus can be sorted out. What the scheme does, in effect, is very simple. It notes that the terms *Messiah* and *Christ* both mean "anointed one." Then it observes that in the biblical tradition generally, the offices or roles for which people were solemnly anointed are three in number. Or, to put it another way, there are in the Bible three "messianic" offices: those of prophet, priest, and king. Not unexpectedly, therefore, much of what is said about Jesus in the New Testament portrays him in one or another of these roles.

Take first of all the prophetic office. Where this role is concerned, the center of attention is always Jesus as the one who conveys God's Word to his people. It needs to be understood, of course, that the reference here is not merely to Jesus as the preacher or teacher. The Word of God may indeed be conveyed by human words; but it can also be conveyed by actions and events. It can be something that happens. Consequently, it is not merely in the image of Jesus as the new Moses (which underlies Saint Matthew's "Sermon on the Mount"), or in portrayals of him as a true prophet (Acts 3:22), that one looks for indications of his prophetic office. Insofar as his whole ministry—as well as his death and Resurrection—communicate God's judgment and forgiveness, Jesus was prophet in all that he did and in his response to everything that happened to him. It is this fact to which the Fourth Gospel calls attention when it teaches us to envisage Jesus as the very presence, the embodiment, of God's Word. The ordinary prophet hears God's Word and then speaks or enacts it. In the case of Jesus, however, prophecy is raised to a new height. He does not receive God's Word and then speak it. He simply *is* the Word of God in all that he does. He *is* what God has to say to humanity about itself; and for that reason, he is not a prophet, but the definitive Word of prophecy.

A very similar logic governs the New Testament's portrayal of Jesus as priest. We have already had occasion to notice how often, when speaking of the significance of Jesus' death, New Testament writers will use the image of sacrifice, and particularly of expiatory sacrifice, which covers sin and makes reconciliation possible. In the tradition of Israel, however, such a sacrifice required the service of a priest, who stood before God as the people's representative, and presented to God the symbol of their self-offering. Inevitably, therefore, it occurred to people to picture Jesus as the definitive priest. His self-offering was the ground of the New Covenant between God and humanity. He was, therefore, the one in whom the priestly vocation was finally fulfilled. Like a priest, he represented his people. Like a priest, he did this in the act of surrendering life to God. In his case, however, the priestly action is carried out in a unique way. Jesus did not offer a mere symbol of his own or his people's life. He offered that life itself. He was the priest who gave *himself* to God; and in doing so he brought with him those with whom he was identified in his life and death. In this way, he made peace where before there had been only alienation. This idea, spelled out elaborately and mysteriously in the Epistle to the Hebrews, makes Jesus the ultimate agent of forgiveness and reconciliation.

Most familiar of all, however, is the New Testament's portrayal of Jesus as King—that is, as Messianic Ruler. It is this image which underlies the most frequently repeated biblical language about Jesus. When Saint Peter proclaims, "God made him both Lord and Messiah, this Jesus whom you crucified" (Acts 2:36, my translation), the reader is face to face with the same idea which Saint Paul expresses in slightly different language when he says that Jesus was "designated Son of God . . . by his resurrection from the dead" (Rom. 1:4). The three titles used here are in origin messianic titles: "Son of God," "Lord," and of course "Messiah" (= "Christ") itself. They refer to a status or role to which Jesus was called by God. In the phrase from the Acts, it is by his resurrection that he is "made" Messiah. In Paul's thought, the Resurrection simply declares or manifests a status which had belonged to Jesus before his Resurrection. In spite of this difference, however, the fundamental idea is the same. Jesus is the one who exercises God's Rule over his people—and, indeed, over all of time and history. He brings and asserts that rule by his ministry, death, and Resurrection; and in his risen and exalted state he carries it on in the present, preparing for the time when "God will be all in all."

It should be clear that none of these basic images—those of Prophet, Priest, and Messianic King—and none of the titles associated with them, wants to say anything in one way or another about what we call the "divinity" of Christ. *Son of*

God, in its original meaning, is not a title of divinity; and neither, in the strictest sense, is the title *Lord,* which seems to have come into Christian use as a way of expressing in Greek the implications of the title *Christ.* What all of these ways of characterizing Jesus look to is not his relationship to God, but the nature of what his living and dying accomplished. He is Messiah, Prophet, and Priest because he actualizes a new relationship—a New Covenant—between God and humanity.

Nevertheless, the use of such images was bound to push thought about Jesus a step or two further. For one thing, it was impossible to describe Jesus in such terms without realizing that his whole story must, in the end, be understood as manifesting the purposes of God. If by his resurrection he is definitively accorded status as the Son of God, that can only be because in the counsels of God he was set apart as Messiah from the very beginning. Things like that do not happen apart from God's providence and foreknowledge. Moreover, if Jesus is the one who simply is God's Word to us, whose sacrifice reconciles, not this or that person but the world to God, and whose rule encompasses not just the church but all of humanity, then his living and dying must have incorporated and revealed something truly ultimate. The question then becomes how to express this truth adequately and correctly.

Back to the Beginning

The most natural way, perhaps, of pushing further in the understanding of Jesus was to make it clear that his status as Messiah belonged to him from the very beginning. But then what is the beginning of his story?

Was it his Baptism? The Gospels lay great emphasis on the Baptism of Jesus; and part (though only part) of the reason for this is that by doing so they make Jesus' role as Son of God commence not with his resurrection, but with his ministry itself. At the Baptism by John, Jesus is discovered, to himself and others, as the promised Messiah: he assumes his office as the bearer of God's Kingdom.

Even the Baptism, however, was not in the end accepted as the true beginning of God's work in Jesus. It could not be. For that, one must go back at least to his birth—even to his conception. It had to be the case that Jesus was born to be, and therefore born as, Messiah.

It is this conviction which Saint Luke's account of Jesus' miraculous conception sets forth in graphic form. Since most scholars believe that the preface which Luke gave his Gospel is partly or wholly legendary, it would be irresponsible for theologians to treat this account as though it represented literal truth. But then mere historical fact is not what the story wants to convey anyhow. Through the elaborate, contrapuntal narrative of two miraculous births—John the Baptist's and Jesus'—the evangelist is setting forth a theological understanding of the Christ. For him and his readers, the whole of Jesus' life, from the very moment of his conception, is a manifestation of God's active will to save his people. The man Jesus is God's direct gift to humanity: that is what the story says. The beginning of redemption is the effective purpose of God, who calls Mary, and in Mary her son, in order to bring his Kingdom to pass.

Christ the Wisdom of God

But is it not necessary to carry the story back even further than Jesus' conception and birth? The purposes of God are eternal. What he wills for humanity he wills from the ultimate beginning—from before the worlds. If this is so, however, to acknowledge Jesus as "Lord and Christ" is to say that he is the very embodiment of what God intends for humanity from all ages. What his ministry, death, and Resurrection accomplish is God's unchanging design. They actualize in human experience what is in fact the final reality of things—the way things ultimately are. Not only grace but truth "came through Jesus Christ" (Jn. 1:17).

To express this idea—the idea that Jesus in his birth, ministry, and triumph is the embodiment of God's eternal design—the New Testament resorts to two closely related images. The earliest of these to appear is that of Jesus as the embodiment, the presence among human beings, of the divine Wisdom (1 Cor. 1:30). Wisdom is that power of God in which God's plan for things, his mind, as it were, is expressed as a living force which forms and governs the created order. This Wisdom, therefore, is two things at once. On the one hand, Wisdom images God, because she is the perfect expression of who he is and what he wants. On the other hand, and at the same time, she is the "original" of which the created order is meant to be a copy; since what God wills and intends is the model for what he does and for what he makes.

If, then, the Messiah is the one in and through whom God and humanity are brought together in such a way that the ultimate purpose of God is revealed and effected, there is nothing one can say about him except that he *is* the Wisdom of God. He is God's purpose for humanity embodied in a human life. So Saint Paul tells us that "Christ . . . is the likeness of God" (2 Cor. 4:4); or, in another place, that

> . . . in him all things were created in heaven and on earth, visible and invisible . . . all things were created through him and for him. He is before all things, and in him all things hold together (Col. 1:16–17).

In both of these statements, what Paul is saying is that Jesus, in virtue of the fact that he is Christ and Lord, is the very presence in the world of the eternal Wisdom of God. The Christ's "beginning" is not found at his Baptism, nor even in his birth of Mary: it is found only in God himself.

So the Fourth Gospel, taking up this same theme in another form, starts its account of Jesus not with the story of his birth, but in eternity, in that same unlocated "beginning" with which Genesis starts. "In the beginning was the Word"—the eternal self-expression of God's being and will; "and the Word became flesh and dwelt among us . . . and we have beheld his glory." John's "Word" and Paul's "Wisdom" indicate what is essentially the same reality; and both are trying to express the same fundamental idea. What happens for us in Jesus the Messiah is that the eternal reality in which God expresses himself—his Wisdom or Word—becomes effectively present for human beings; and this effective presence of the Word spells itself out in the historical, human work of Jesus' ministry, death, and Resurrection.

Incarnation and Preexistence

It is at this point in the development of christological inquiry that we encounter the idea of incarnation ("enfleshing"). In order to understand what it really means to say that Jesus is the messianic Prophet, Priest, and King, that he brings and realizes God's Rule, the New Testament writers envisage him as the very embodiment of the eternal Wisdom of God. This means that in Jesus' person, and in what he did and suffered, the ultimate inner logic of things shows through and takes effective form. It also means, however, that in order to give a true account of Jesus, it is not enough to tell his story simply as a human story. One must also tell it as a story about God. The coming of Jesus is the coming of God to be with us. The ministry of Jesus is God's taking a hand in human affairs. The dying of Jesus is God's way of loving and forgiving sinners. The triumph of Jesus is the "happening" in which God begins his new creation. And this is precisely what the New Testament and the creeds say. They speak of God's Son— meaning, in this context, the Word or Wisdom in which God reproduces himself (Heb. 1:2–3)—and then they tell of how he "came down from heaven, and was incarnate and was made human." (Cf. Phil. 2:5ff.)

Needless to say, such language is symbolic or analogical. God has no "up" from which to "come down"; and he does not change what he is and become something else. The point of this language is not to say that the divine Word "turned into" a human being. Rather, it is to say, in a direct and pictorial way, that in Jesus there is a complete coincidence of divine and human being and action. What Jesus does is the work of God in his Word; and what God does is the work of Jesus in his human ministry. There is, in that sense, a true "en-fleshing" of God's eternal Wisdom.

If that is so, however, it must be true to say that the reality which people encountered in Jesus somehow preexisted the career of Jesus himself. It is this notion, as a matter of fact, which is the real content of the statement that the Son of God "came down" and "was incarnate." The "grace and truth" which are met in Jesus did not come to birth with his appearance on the stage of human history. They are always with God, from eternity to eternity, as his Wisdom or Word. They are what God is for himself, now in Jesus made present and effective in human existence: made "incarnate."

Much criticism is currently directed at this concept of the preexistence of Christ. From one point of view, moreover, the criticism is entirely justified. People often talk as though they thought Jesus preexisted his own historical career. Such a notion, however, misses the whole point of the doctrine of the Incarnation. What preexists the historical career of Jesus is not that human person himself, but the Word of God which becomes actively present in him. And once this point is perfectly clear, the real significance both of the idea of incarnation and of the concept of preexistence emerge. What both assert is that the human person and activity of Jesus are the point in our history and experience where the ultimate truth of things appears as grace, as the personal presence of God in his Word, being and doing what he always is and what he always purposes.

The Two Natures of Christ

No matter how appropriate this account of Jesus may seem, however, it creates problems; and the history of Christianity is strewn with the controversies and conflicts occasioned by these problems. The most obvious issue it raises, of course, is the simple one of how we are to conceive or understand what it means to say that the story of Jesus really does have God the Word—God the Son, to use the language of the Nicene Creed—as its ultimate subject. The story, after all, is a very human story. It centers in a man who was born and who died; who in the course of his career of teaching, preaching, and healing made friends and enemies; who had family problems; who knew fear and trouble and doubt. How can the story of such a person have God in his Word as its ultimate subject? How can it be, in short, a story about God?

It does not help much, in the face of this question, to pull out traditional phrases like "the divinity of Christ," or a statement like "Jesus is God." These are familiar enough; but they really do little more than phrase the problem, or make it seem even more acute and difficult. What could a statement like "Jesus is God" possibly mean, after all? We have already said, and said emphatically, that God as Christians know him is radically "other" than any created being. How, then, can a human being be called God? It makes no sense. It seems, in fact, to verge on blasphemy.

The truth is that this way of talking—which first appears around the beginning of the second century—has always been carefully qualified, or at any rate carefully explained in a certain sense. Christian teachers were quite clear that they were not saying either that Jesus was not human, or that God had somehow ceased to be God by getting himself turned into something else. What they wanted to say was that there are, somehow, two sides to everything that Jesus did and was. From one point of view, Jesus is God-with-us. From another and equally legitimate point of view, he is us-with-God. And he is both of these things at the same time: humanity revealed in God, and God revealed through humanity.

This understanding was summed up in the classical doctrine that there are "two natures" in Christ—a divine nature and a human nature. Even this formula, however, scarcely solves the problem. To be sure, it prevents people from thinking that Christians assert the simple identity in Jesus of Deity and humanity. It says quite clearly that God and humanity are not one and the same thing, but two different things, even though in Jesus they are at one in a unique way. But then what is this unique way in which God and humanity are brought together in Jesus? The formula of two natures solves one problem only by raising another.

This second problem, moreover, is an extremely difficult one. People's temptation, in dealing with it, was to use analogies from the natural order and then to take the analogies much too seriously. They would look for some way in which, in their own ordinary experience, they saw two different sorts of things combining in one, and then talk about the Incarnation as though it were one particular example of such a combination. For instance, there was a time when the analogy of a chemical mixture—in which two elements are fused in some sort of compound—was frequently appealed to as an explanation of the Incarnation. Jesus, so understood, was a kind of compound of Deity and humanity, just as water is a compound of hydrogen and oxygen. Again, some ancient teachers thought that the best analogy was that of the way in which soul and body are united in human beings to form a single organism. On this view, God in his Word is conceived as the "soul" of Jesus' humanity. The possible dangers of this analogy appeared when someone asked whether, on that assumption, it was not best to deny that Jesus had a human soul at all. After all, if the Word of God is Jesus' soul, what use could he have for an ordinary, human kind of soul? On the other hand, though, if he did not have a soul like other people's, what was the point of calling him human in the first place?

The trouble with debates of this sort, however, is not just that they invariably produce understandings of Jesus which cannot in the end be supported. More than this, they are occasioned by a way of thinking about Jesus which looks, on closer examination, to be simply absurd. For they all make one basic mistake. They all treat God as though he could figure as one factor among others in some sort of natural relationship: as though he could be the soul of a particular body; or one element out of two in a quasi-chemical compound; or, in general, one kind of thing which gets attached or related to another kind of thing. God, however, is no "kind of thing": he is the reason why there are different kinds of things in the first place.

Thus there is a basic difficulty in the doctrine of the two natures; or rather, there is a basic ambiguity in the doctrine of the two natures. If that doctrine is taken to assert that there is a real difference between being God and being human, and that this difference is not abolished in Jesus, then it must be affirmed. On the other hand, if it is taken to mean that "God" is the name of a particular sort of thing which can be compared, contrasted, and related to other sorts of things on the same level, then it is mistaken. I may cross an orange with a grapefruit, compare the color of a sunset with the melodic feel of a piece of music, or take two parts of hydrogen to one of oxygen and get water. All these things, different as they are, stand inside a framework of some sort which allows them to be connected with one another in a variety of ways. But God does not stand inside this framework. He supplies—indeed, in a certain sense, he *is*—the framework. So Deity is not a "nature" in a list of natures which can be compared and differentiated from one another. Least of all is God a "nature" which can be put side by side with human nature as a different sort of thing on the same plane.

The Chalcedonian Definition of Faith

What solution is there, then, to our problem? The solution which the early church finally produced was an odd, but in the last resort perhaps a wise, one. It came in the form of a "Definition of Faith" issued by the Council of Chalcedon in A.D. 451. This council had been confronted with a series of points of view about how Christians should understand the person of Jesus. All of these points of view were debatable. In fact, all of them had, in one or another extreme form, been criticized and rejected as false or misleading. Confronted with a demand to clarify this situation and to set down the outlines of an adequate formulation of the faith, the council produced a brief "Definition" which dealt with the problems raised by the doctrine of the two natures, and did so in a fairly surprising way.

What is surprising about the "Definition" is the fact that it does not dwell upon any of the analogies which had regularly been used by believers to explain how God and humanity are at one in Jesus. It speaks much more formally and abstractly. In fact, what it offers is not so much a picture of Jesus' make-up (which is what most Christologies had tried to do), as a statement of what it thinks is the right way to talk about Jesus.

The first thing it says and insists upon is that everything which Jesus was and did has a single ultimate source—God in his Word. Jesus' person and his career are ways in which the Word or Son of God is actively present in human affairs. Consequently, when Christians speak of Jesus, they do so in the awareness that what in the last resort they are talking about is the Word of God.

The second thing which the "Definition" says is that everything which Jesus was and did is a genuinely human reality. Just as the Word of God is completely and perfectly God, so the human being in which he is "with us" is completely and perfectly human. This means that one not only can but must talk about Jesus as one would about any other human being. The Incarnation is not an abolition but an affirmation of creaturely human existence.

The third thing which the "Definition" says is that these two ways of talking about Jesus really are *different* ways of talking. They do not say the same things about Jesus. Each relates him to a different order of reality, sets him, as it were, in a different framework of understanding. The "natures" are genuinely distinct.

Finally, however, the "Definition" asserts in effect that both of these ways of talking—that which refers everything about Jesus to the Word of God, and that which sees everything about him as an authentic human reality—belong together. One sees and understands Jesus adequately only when one realizes that both ways of talking are necessary in order to make sense of what he was and did. In him, the divine and the human coincide.

This last point is the one which most clearly defines the problem of the Incarnation for us. The problem is not to come up with a picture of how a single "thing" can be partly divine and partly human. The problem is to understand how the same events and the same person can only be understood properly by being accounted for in two quite different ways at the same time.

This sort of problem, though, is not, when you think about it, an unfamiliar one. We encounter it in more ordinary— though equally puzzling—forms every day. Consider, for example, a commonplace human action like waving one's hand. If I choose, I can explain this motion solely and completely in terms of a chain of physical causes: electrical and chemical reactions which produce "waving" as their final effect. On the other hand, and with equal plausibility, I can explain the same motion by reference to personal intention and choice. I can say, "Smith is waving goodbye to his children"; and that accounts for the action. It is true, of course, that people often feel compelled to exclude one of these sorts of explanation and opt for the other. That is the issue in many modern debates about determinism and free will. Yet the truth of the matter is that everyone in fact uses both sorts of explanation, or at least assumes in practice that both are valid. The advocate of determinism does not in practice stop describing human actions in terms of purpose; and the advocate of free will does not in practice suppose that hand-waving cannot be explained in terms of physical-chemical reactions. The trouble is that they cannot see how the two sorts of explanation can be consistent with each other.

And that is the true form of the classical problem about the Incarnation. We really tend to think, even if we do not articulate the thought, that being God and being human are mutually inconsistent things. To look at the story of one human life and say first: "This is the story of the man Jesus," and then say, "This is the story of God in his Word," seems to us virtually self-contradictory. *But is it?* It is true that being God and being human are utterly different. But are they *inconsistent* because they are *different*? That is the basic question.

The doctrine of the Incarnation asserts that what really separates God and human beings is not their different "natures"; for God is not a "nature" at all in the sense that humanity is. God is the power that makes humanity human. What separates God and human beings is sin. For this reason, it can make sense to say that God in his Word identifies himself for us in and as this human person Jesus. At the same time it makes sense to say that, as a result, this human person discovers himself—and therefore humanity—in God's Word. It also makes sense to say that it takes just this event to make the Kingdom of God happen.

Part Three

· 9 ·

The Work of the Holy Spirit

How, though, does the Kingdom of God happen for us, for the writer and the readers of this book? We say that it has happened, and is therefore real, in Christ. We say that with Christ the New Age of God's promise has been inaugurated. But we still want to know what enables people like us to get involved in God's work. We also want to know what form our involvement takes.

In a very general way, we already know at least part of an answer to these questions. Saint Paul suggests it to us when he says that people "put on" Christ (Gal. 3:27). By this strange-sounding expression he means that they get "clothed" or even "dressed up" in Christ. They discover and take on a new identity for themselves, an identity which is defined by the pattern of Christ's life and destiny as a human being. They share his relationship to God. They share his relationship to other people. They have as their own future the hope to which his Resurrection has given substance. *To be involved in God's work, then, means to be part of what Christ is and what he does.*

But what does that mean in plain, concrete terms? If such participation in God's work is to be real for ordinary people, then it has to take what we can loosely call normal human shape. It has to get embodied and expressed in the ordinary stuff of human existence. It must, for example, have some sort

173

of social and institutional expression; for otherwise it can be no significant part of the world of human life and action. At the same time, it must take shape in people's personal, interior existence as they "grow up . . . into Christ" (Eph. 4:15). And, needless to say, it must also come alive in the way people act and, by acting, change their world. It is not enough, therefore, simply to repeat Paul's language about putting on Christ, or being in Christ, or having Christ in us. Such language has to be cashed into the common currency of our social and personal life.

And that, in effect, is what the creeds try to accomplish in their very last lines. They try to tell us what is most basically involved in this new identity in Christ of which Paul speaks. Somehow, they insist, "church" and "Baptism" and "forgiveness of sins" and "the life of the Age to Come" are involved. They do not say, or even attempt to say, why or how these different sorts of phenomena are fundamental to the life in Christ. They leave the explanations to us. Nevertheless, they point firmly to the things which determine or express identity in Christ; and if we want to understand what it means to be involved, to have a conscious part in God's work, we must pursue the hints they supply.

The Holy Spirit and Identity in Christ

Before it is possible to follow out these hints in detail, however, we must stop and notice one all-important fact. When the creeds give their shorthand sketches of the shape of life in Christ, they do so within a particular framework. They give their description of the way in which people participate in God's work under the head of faith in the Holy Spirit; and by doing this they make an essential point clear. The fact that people have a share in God's work, the fact that they can appropriate their given identity in Christ, depends upon the activity of God as Holy Spirit. It is in and through the Spirit, and in no other way, that God accomplishes his will in human beings, that he pulls them, so to speak, into the powerful flow of his purpose in Christ.

This means, however, that anyone who talks about life in

Christ is also, and necessarily, talking about life "in the Spirit." Neither of these is independent of the other. Neither happens without the other. Both the identity of the Christian community collectively, and the identity of the individual person within it, are shaped, if the creeds speak truly, by a kind of divine pincer movement. People's identity and their hope are objectively set forth as the Word of God in the person and the doings of Jesus the Christ. The same identity and the same hope are brought home inwardly to them by the Spirit of God. That is the picture.

Can we understand it? It takes only a moment's reflection on this picture to see that it occasions all sorts of questions. For example, why is there this close connection between the Holy Spirit and the work of God in Christ? Does not the Holy Spirit have his own thing to do? And in any case—just to take another example—why is it necessary to appeal to the Holy Spirit at all? Is it not, in the last resort, our own human spirit which grasps and appropriates identity in Christ? These questions and others like them must be thought through before we can even begin to follow up the creeds' portrayal of life in Christ.

Spirit and Messiah

To get at our first question—about the connection between the Holy Spirit and God's work in Christ—it is first necessary to look at some of the ways in which the Scriptures understand the Spirit or "breath" of God.

In the Old Testament the Spirit of God is a dynamic and all but impersonal force, whose manifestations are always powerful and sometimes unpredictable. There are two general areas in which the Holy Spirit's work is observed. One of these is the realm of nature. Here God's Spirit is a creative force, closely associated with the Word of God (see Psalm 33:6). The "moving" of the Spirit over the face of the waters (Gen. 1:2) betokens the activity of God bringing order out of confusion and life out of its opposite. It is when God "breathes" into Adam's nostrils that mere clay becomes "a living being" (Gen. 2:7). The Spirit, we might say, is the way in which God bestows upon his creatures an interiority and a selfhood of their own—the power to be something in themselves and to act as themselves.

More noticeable, however, and hence more frequently recalled, is the activity of the Holy Spirit as a strange force from God which seizes people up and sets them about a particular (and often temporary) activity. The Spirit of the Lord "took possession of" Gideon (Jg. 6:34) and whirled him up into leadership of the people against the Midianites and the Amalekites. In the same way, "the Spirit of the Lord came mightily upon" Samson so that he was able to tear a lion into pieces (Jg. 14:6), or to kill and spoil the Amalekites (Jg. 14:19). The Spirit of God, which is the abiding interior power of life in humanity and in other creatures, is also the power which comes upon men and women from time to time and enables them to rise above themselves to new heights of heroism and dedication.

It is not only heroes and military leaders, though, whom the Holy Spirit inspires. With Moses, the Holy Spirit was an abiding presence (Num. 11:17). It enabled him to lead and judge Israel; and he could even share it with the elders whom he appointed. When Samuel anointed David, "the Spirit of the Lord came mightily upon" the young man "from that day forward" (1 Sam. 16:13): it was the Spirit of God in whose power David rescued and established and ruled Israel. With some individuals, the Holy Spirit settles in to enable them to carry out, not temporary and extraordinary feats, but the duties of a lifelong calling. Above all, perhaps, this is true of the prophets. It is the Spirit of God who sends the prophets (Is. 48:16), entering them (Ezek. 2:2) and indeed filling them (Hos. 9:7, in the ancient Greek text). But it also inspires artists (Ex. 31:3), as it inspired David to write hymns. Whenever people's deeds rise to a level of excellence or grandeur which reflects some aspect of the glory and the majesty of God, the Holy Spirit is at work.

The Spirit, then, which is called "Holy" because it is God's Spirit, is a way in which God touches people and gives himself to be with them. God is said to have "put in the midst of them his Holy Spirit" (Is. 63:11); and this means that he himself dwelt among them in his power. In the end, the Spirit is not just God's gift to unusual people or to people with an unusual vocation. The Holy Spirit is the power of God which enables all human beings to live for God and in the presence of God.

That is why, as the later prophets look forward to an age when Israel, and indeed all humanity, will know and love and serve God, they can describe this Coming Age by speaking of an outpouring of the Spirit of God on everyone. "And it shall come to pass afterward," says Joel, "that I will pour out my spirit on all flesh; . . . Even upon the menservants and maidservants in those days, I will pour out my spirit" (Jl. 2:28f). Jeremiah earlier had spoken of a "new covenant," which would come about when God's will for his people would no longer be a law imposed from outside, but a law "within them," one which was a part of their own interior being and hence written "upon their hearts" (Jer. 31:31–34). It is hopes such as these which explain why the dawning of the New Age was always associated with the gift of the Spirit—the gift of God's interior, enabling, and transforming presence.

There could, therefore, be no separation of the coming of the Messiah from the gift of the Spirit. In fact, merely to call someone "Messiah" was to say two things at once. It meant, of course, that this person was the bearer of the New Age— the New Covenant. It also meant, however, that this person was the bearer and bestower of God's Holy Spirit. The Christ and the Holy Spirit were the two agencies through which God's inauguration of his Kingdom would be carried through.

The New Testament, moreover, is perfectly clear about all this. From the very beginning, Jesus is companioned by the Spirit of God. The Holy Spirit presides over his conception and birth. The beginning of his ministry, his Baptism, is marked by an event which distinguishes him as one to whom the Holy Spirit is given. To be sure, it is not until Jesus is "glorified"—exalted to the New Age—that the Holy Spirit is poured out on God's people in fulfillment of Joel's prophecy (Jn. 16:5–11); but this is because the universal gift of the Holy

Spirit waits for the clear revelation of Jesus as God's universal Messiah. "Being . . . exalted at the right hand of God, and having received from the Father the promise of the Holy Spirit, he has poured out this which you see and hear" (Acts 2:33). That is, *the gift of the Holy Spirit at Pentecost is simply the other side of Jesus' Resurrection.* The new life in Christ is, as the creeds insist, life "in the Spirit." The two can be distinguished; but they cannot be separated.

The Holy Spirit and Christian Life

In the New Testament, therefore, there is no getting the Holy Spirit and the work of God in Christ apart from each other. The Holy Spirit—the true Spirit of God—is always "the Spirit of Jesus" (Acts 16:7). Where it is at work, three things happen, at the very least. In the first place, missionary witness is borne to the Good News of what God has done in Jesus Christ. This is the theme of Saint Luke's story of Pentecost, in which the phenomenon of speaking in tongues is carefully and deliberately reinterpreted. For Luke, the real speaking in tongues which Christians do in the power of the Spirit is not ecstatic and unintelligible utterance. It means "telling . . . the mighty works of God" in every known tongue (Acts 2:11).

In the second place, the Holy Spirit manifests himself as "the Spirit of truth," who "dwells in you" (Jn. 14:17). This is, of course, a theme which is most prominent in the Fourth Gospel; and what the writer means by it is that the Holy Spirit "will teach you all things, and bring to your remembrance all that I have said to you" (Jn. 14:26). The truth which the Holy Spirit conveys is none other than the truth which Christ himself taught and embodied (Jn. 1:17). The Spirit, indeed, is the mode in which the risen Christ is present with his disciples. Through its inspiration, people who were never with Jesus in his earthly existence can understand and enter into his life in ever new and deeper ways. They may even come to know Jesus in a more profound and proportioned way than those who accompanied him on his earthly journeys. Nevertheless, the Holy Spirit teaches, the Holy Spirit actualizes for us, only one thing—Christ. ". . . he will bear witness to me" (Jn. 15:26).

This truth—that the Holy Spirit is not just "power" in general, but quite specifically the power of the new life in Christ—is brought out in yet a third dimension by Saint Paul. Scholars have sometimes remarked that in Paul's letters it is not always easy to differentiate between the work of Christ and the work of the Holy Spirit; and they have wondered, on the basis of this observation, whether Paul did not somehow confuse the two. The answer seems to be that in a sense he did. Paul saw no difference between what Christ does and what the Holy Spirit does; he only saw a difference in the ways in which each carries out the same divine work. For him, the Holy Spirit which dwells in the hearts of believers is the "earnest"—the down payment—which guarantees the fulfillment of those "promises of God" which already have their "Yes" in the risen Christ (1 Cor. 1:20–22). To be baptized, in Paul's eyes, was to be "washed . . . sanctified . . . justified in the name of the Lord Jesus Christ and in the Spirit of our God" (1 Cor. 6:11). The work of Christ and the work of the Holy Spirit are two sides of the same coin.

In Saint Paul's mind, accordingly, there were at least two important truths to be recognized about the work of the Holy Spirit. In the first place, the Holy Spirit is *not* the peculiar possession of certain people with special gifts. The Spirit is the life of Christ dwelling in and informing the whole community of believers, and at the same time showing itself in differing ways in different individuals. In some people, the power of the Holy Spirit might show itself in ecstasy or prophecy. In others, though, it shows itself in other ways: in the ability to heal, to teach, or to give sound advice. "There are varieties of gifts, but the same Spirit" (1 Cor. 12:4).

But, in the second place, Saint Paul went further than this. He claimed that there was, in the last resort, only one sure sign of the work of the Spirit. That was the love which held people together in Christ by making them a true community: that is, a community where the "other" is affirmed by men and women who are patient and kind with one another; who make allowances and are not vengeful or mean; who look for the best and not the worst in their fellows (1 Cor. 13). The work of the Holy Spirit is most clearly seen where the kind of life which Christ himself lived comes to expression in the doings of his people.

And that, of course, is the point of the whole New Testament witness to the work of the Holy Spirit. There is no Spirit of God which is not also the Spirit of Christ, which does not focus attention on Christ, draw people to interior understanding of the new life in Christ, and enable that new life to get expressed in their own varied ways of living. In a word, the Holy Spirit in the New Testament is the principle, the motive force, which enables human beings to acknowledge and live out their identity in the crucified and risen Word of God.

The Holy Spirit Is God

Once all this is said, moreover, the point of the creeds' language about the Holy Spirit becomes much plainer. The Spirit is described as "life-giver"; and this means both that he is the power of life in all creatures, and that his activity, wherever it is found, conforms human beings to the new life in Christ. Such a description, however, makes no sense at all unless it is recognized that to talk about the Holy Spirit is, quite simply, to talk about God. To say "Holy Spirit" is to name one of the ways in which God is what he is for himself. Therefore, it is also to name one of the ways in which he gives himself for what he is to creatures.

What, after all, does it take to involve people in the work of God? Who or what could bring such an enterprise off? Who can make it possible not only for us to live in God's presence, but to get caught up in what he is doing, in the New Covenant which he has brought about in Christ? The answer to these questions is simply "God himself"; and that answer explains what the church means when it speaks of the Holy Spirit. It means that the God who does his business of bringing forgiveness and creating new life in Christ adds to this what is, if possible, an even more startling work. He does not simply do this business of his *for* us or *at* us. He insists upon doing it *in* us and *with* us. That is, he makes people part of his work of redemption. He lets them in on it.

Consequently, the Nicene Creed, in one of the most cautious and careful understatements in all of Christian history, acknowledges that the Holy Spirit, the life-giver, "is worshiped and glorified" together with the Father and the Son. When it uses that expression, of course, the Creed is referring to something quite specific. It wants us to recall formulas like "Glory be to the Father and to the Son and to the Holy Spirit," formulas in which people give a single and undivided praise to God as they name the three different ways in which he exists and communicates himself. God identifies himself for himself in his Word; and then he communicates that Word to human beings in Jesus as the secret of their own identity. By the same token, God knows and appropriates himself through his Spirit; and then, by that same Spirit, he makes himself the power through which human beings appropriate their identity in him.

So it is all one thing. The Holy Spirit, as the New Testament insists, is the life of Christ within people. But the life of Christ within people is the power of God's life, as he lets human beings in on what he is and on what he is doing. If there is reconciliation between God and humanity, if there is indeed a New Covenant, that can be so because what God does for us in Christ he also does with us and in us as Holy Spirit.

The Idea of Grace

And so, inevitably, we come to the question of what Christians call *grace;* for what that word normally denotes is one of two things. Either it means the active work of the Holy Spirit, enlivening people and helping them to grow into their identity in Christ; or else it means the results—what we can call the fruits—in the lives of human beings, of what the Holy Spirit does.

We say "normally denotes" here, because the term *grace* does have a broader and more general meaning than this. To speak of grace in this more general sense is to speak of any attitude or activity in which one person shows favor to another. Such an attitude or activity is called gracious because it stems from uncompelled generosity and love. Grace is never automatic, and consequently it is never earned or deserved. When my employer pays me my monthly wage, that is not grace. It is a matter of contract and of obligation. If, on the other hand, the same employer helps me on the side with a problem or makes a friend of me, that, at the human level, is grace. In the same way, if two people love each other and treat each other lovingly, that is a matter of grace on both sides; for love is always free and never deserved.

When, therefore, Christians speak of God's grace, what they mean, in general, is that love—uncompelled, free, and spontaneous—which comes to light in God's communication of himself to creatures. God is gracious in creation, because he communicates being to what, apart from him, has no being. God is gracious in redemption, because he lifts up the life which he has created to a new fulfillment in communion with his own. Each of these activities is, properly speaking, a matter of grace.

Nevertheless, as we have said, there is a narrower and more technical meaning of *grace*, according to which the word refers simply to the work of the Holy Spirit within us. In other words, the doctrine of grace is concerned with one particular form of God's free communication of himself. It signifies the way in which, as the Holy Spirit, he becomes the interior power through which people learn to know themselves in Christ and are strengthened to grow up into his life.

And this points, as we have already suggested, to another, derivative, sense of the term *grace*. We meet this secondary use of the word when people talk about the "gifts" or "graces" or "charisms" which mark the lives of individual persons. What is in question here is not the actual presence and activity of the Holy Spirit, but the effects of his activity: the results which it produces in human lives.

The thing most people think of when one mentions "gifts of the Spirit" are very particular and individual gifts— "special" graces, as the expression goes. This is the sort of thing of which Saint Paul is speaking when he writes: "To each is given the manifestation of the Spirit for the common good. To one is given through the Spirit the utterance of wisdom, to another the utterance of knowledge according to the same Spirit, to another faith by the same Spirit, to another gifts of healing by the one Spirit . . ." (1 Cor. 12:7–9). In other words, the work of the Holy Spirit shows itself in different lives in different ways. These showings or manifestations of the Spirit, however, are not for the benefit of the individual concerned. They are given for the sake of the community, for the sake of service to others. They may be quite dramatic charisms; and they may be the sort of thing which other people depend on but never really notice. In either case, however, they are called gifts of the Holy Spirit because they are ways in which people can exhibit the mutual love and dependence which mark them out as persons who share in the life of Christ.

Such special graces, therefore, are not the sole—nor even the most fundamental—effect of the Holy Spirit's activity. The most basic result of the Spirit's activity is not special at all. It is the same for everyone. It is what we have called involvement in God's work, or sharing the identity of Christ. "The free gift of God," says Saint Paul, "is eternal life in Christ Jesus our Lord" (Rom. 6:23). To have that gift is what it means to be "under grace" (Rom. 6:24); and the form in which this gift is given is that of a sharing in the very life of Christ, in his death to sin, and therefore in the new life which he is bringing (Rom. 6:4–5). What the Holy Spirit does, therefore, is to fix in people the yeast of a new mode of existence. Paul calls it "the law of the Spirit" (Rom. 8:2), as though it were a principle of some sort which structures and restructures people's way of seeing and acting; and this "law of the Spirit" is "life in Christ Jesus." That is the primary and essential effect of the Holy Spirit's operation.

Grace, then, is both the activity of the Holy Spirit and the effects of that activity (Rom. 5:5). What grace is not, though, is a "something," a special kind of stuff or substance, which God confers on people. Christians have ways of talking which seem to suggest this sort of thing: as, for example, when people speak of "having grace," or "being given grace," or "praying for grace." Such language seems to imply that there really is a kind of spiritual medicine called "grace," which is not unlike a vitamin, and which God injects into people to brace them up or keep them going. To conceive of the matter in this way, however, is simply to be led astray by the ambiguities of words. Grace is not something other than God which he prescribes for us as a moral tonic. Grace is nothing more or less than God himself communicating himself to creatures. More specifically, it is God himself dwelling within people as the Holy Spirit and working in them their identity in Christ.

Who Needs Grace?

This point, moreover, is a very important one to keep in mind when the inevitable question arises about why human beings need grace. People often raise this question explicitly. Even more often they ponder it silently. Why, after all, is it not possible for men and women to get on without grace, to please God without putting themselves in the undignified position of being the recipients of a favor? Why can they not stand on their own two feet? Who *needs* favors?

The customary answer to this question, to state it very baldly, is that grace is necessary because, apart from God's help freely given, human beings cannot keep God's commandments; and if they do not keep his commandments, he cannot fairly reward them. Grace, in other words, is the remedy for people's inability to live up to the high standards of behavior which God requires of them if they are to win eternal life.

There is, though, something very unsatisfactory and even incoherent about this answer, traditional though it be. It intends to explain why grace is necessary; yet behind it there lies a picture of the relation between God and human beings which makes the whole idea of grace—that is, the whole idea of God's giving himself in any way at all to be "with us"—seem either irrelevant or immoral.

Look at this picture more closely. Notice first of all how it portrays God. He is lawgiver and judge, the administrator of a moral or legal system. What is more, he is strictly confined to this role. The human beings in this picture have a good deal of respect for God and may even be afraid of him; but they certainly do not desire his presence. He is nothing more than rule-setter and referee, and therefore not at all the sort of person whose company anyone would choose to keep. What people ask of God is not himself or any relation to him, but something quite other than himself—the reward he gives. Thus the picture suggests that people's relation to God is rather like that of a student to an examiner. Human beings stand before God as candidates for a sort of diploma; and their business is to prove, under the rules of the system, that they qualify for heaven.

To those who operate with this picture of God and of people's relation to him, the idea of grace cannot possibly make sense. Everyone knows that it is not the business of judges and examiners to show favor or to be helpful to people. It is their business to do strict, impersonal justice within the terms of the law. They must act without prejudice and without caring for the persons involved. God so conceived, then, can only show favor—that is, act graciously—at the cost of being thought to act immorally.

But then, in the second place, look at this same picture from the point of view of the human beings involved in it. What are they like? They are seekers of a reward which is strictly proportioned to their accomplishment. But can I say that I have truly deserved the reward I seek if I get outside help in meeting the conditions of it? Grace, in such a setting, is bound to look like cheating, not only cheating on the part of the person who gives help but also on the part of the person who accepts it. In the circumstances presupposed by this picture of things, simple honesty demands that grace be ignored and, indeed, rejected if it is offered. It is out of place.

But then a question arises. Is this picture the right one? Does it tell the truth about the relation between God and God's creatures? Certainly it is widely accepted. Most people seem simply to assume that this picture describes the normal Christian way of seeing things. Yet even a moment's thought will show that it does not correspond to the imagery which the Scriptures use to portray people's relation to God.

It is true that the Bible frequently and deliberately pictures God as judge. He turns out, however, if we look closely at what Scripture says, to be a judge of a very improper sort. He is not the cool, objective administrator of a legal system. Far from it. He cares about his creatures and loves them. He wants to be their God, and he wants them to be his people. What he asks and desires for them is not so much that they keep a certain code, as that they accept and return his love; and in order to bring this about he lavishes love upon them. He liberates them from slavery. He dwells among them (Jn. 1:14). He gets his own Son "reckoned with transgressors" (Lk. 22:37; cf. 2 Cor. 5:21; Lk. 7:34) for their sake. He reveals their sin, condemns it, and forgives it. His judgment, when it comes, therefore, is not that of an impersonal assessor of merit points. It is far too serious a thing to be viewed in that light. God's judgment is much more like that which is passed on us by a friend's pain or a lover's hurt. It is the judgment of one who is involved with us, one to whom we matter. That is the real reason why the image of God as angry or wrathful appears so often in the Scriptures; for, unlike proper judges, God loves us too much not to get frustrated sometimes at our response to his love.

Now of course all this is picture language, as we have suggested. Where questions about God are concerned, however, the pictures which underlie and inform our ideas are crucially important; and the fact is that this biblical picture of God and of people's relationship to him is incomprehensible apart from the reality of grace. In fact, that states the case too modestly. The point is not that grace is *necessary* in the scriptural way of seeing things. The point is that where the Scriptures are concerned, *grace is the name of the game.*

The reason for this, moreover, should be clear. In the biblical understanding, human beings are not out to qualify for some reward from God; and God is not out to make people jump through hoops so that he can enjoy the pleasures of judging. In the Bible picture, God wants his creatures—and those creatures find their fulfillment in knowing and loving

God. That sort of thing, however, can only come about through self-giving and self-communication. Whether it is a question of knowing God, or of having faith in him, or of loving and hoping in him, or of obeying him, all of these ways of being "with" God depend finally on the love with which he gives himself to us, and on the answering love which that evokes in us. And the love with which he gives himself to us is grace.

Grace, then, may indeed be, as tradition tells us, the only possible remedy for sin; but it is not only a remedy for sin. On the contrary, it is the word we use to denote the very pattern and logic of God's way of dealing with people. For God to be truly "with us" is *grace*; for us to come into God's company is the result of *grace*. And that is why grace is necessary.

Conclusion

That is also why the creeds open their account of the nature of Christian existence with a statement of faith in the Holy Spirit. Whether they talk about the church, or about the forgiveness of sins, or about Baptism, or about Christian hope, they are talking about the ways in which people get involved in God's life by coming to themselves in Christ; and such involvement occurs because God allows it to happen by being with people as the Holy Spirit. Grace is not one factor in our relationship to God through Christ. It is what constitutes that relationship.

· 10 ·

The Church

No sooner do the creeds teach us to confess faith in the Holy Spirit than they summon us, with our very next breath, to acknowledge something called *church*. The Apostles' Creed explains what this word means by going on to use the expression "communion of saints." The church, it suggests, is a society of some sort, a "fellowship of holy persons," which the Nicene Creed further qualifies as "one, holy, catholic, and apostolic."

The basic idea which the creeds are trying to convey in these phrases is obvious enough. They are saying that when God sets about involving people with his work in Christ, he does so in such a way as to involve them at the very same time with one another. The first effect of grace, the first work of the Holy Spirit, is the creation of a society or community; and it is in their capacity as members of this society that people have a conscious share in the new life which the risen Christ embodies.

Why a Society?

To many people nowadays, this whole idea—that conscious involvement with the work of God in Christ takes the form of membership in a soceity—seems strange and even outrageous. After all, we tell ourselves, religious faith is a personal, individual, and even private matter. Is it not possible, then, for someone to practice a faith sincerely without belonging to a religious organization? And if the answer to this question is Yes, why does Christian tradition insist so dogmatically upon the necessity of membership in the church?

In the long run, the only satisfactory answer to these questions, and others like them, lies in a fuller understanding of what Christian tradition really means when it uses the word *church*, and also of what the term *membership* signifies when it is employed in this connection. It may be, for example, that "religious organization" is not the right expression to describe what the New Testament and the creeds mean when they say church; and by the same token, it may be the case that membership as Christians use it denotes something different from mere association with the business of an organized group. In order to see how this might be the case, however, we must begin by looking closely at some of the assumptions which underlie our questions; and, in particular, we need to look skeptically at the belief that religion is a purely personal and individual matter.

There can be no doubt, of course, that religious faith is personal and individual. At the same time, though, it always has a social as well as an individual dimension; and that for at least two good reasons. In the first place, the religious ideas and values which individuals make their own are transmitted to them—made both available and plausible—through the social network in which their lives are set. No one simply invents or originates a personal religious faith. Like the language in which we express ourselves, and like our picture of how the world "works," our religious perceptions and commitments derive from the social and cultural matrix within which we grow to mature individuality. The person who does not belong to a religious organization is nonetheless dependent, though often unconsciously, on the religious tradition of his or her culture.

To say this much, however, is still to see only half of the picture. There is another reason why religious faith is not, and cannot be, a private or merely individual matter: which is simply that such faith is a way of being engaged with realities which concern not me alone but everyone. If *God* were simply the name of an idea in my mind, I might legitimately keep that idea to myself and nurse it as something private and personal. But "the maker . . . of all things, seen and unseen" is the mystery whose purposes are the ultimate ground of all existence. To know God and to respond to him, therefore, is to be engaged with a reality which concerns other people as well as myself. What is more, since God's purposes include these other people, I cannot be related consciously to him without having my relationship to other human beings altered in the process. Religious faith always has social consequences, and it always seeks social expression.

Nowhere, perhaps, is this fact made clearer than in Jesus' use of the symbol, "Kingdom of God," to denote human life perfected and fulfilled. What this symbol conveys is precisely the idea of a society. It says that when people are related to God in the right way, they are also related to one another in the right way. Jesus himself, when he tried to explain what the Kingdom of God is, regularly compared it to a feast, a social gathering for the celebration of some great joy. The redemption, therefore, which Christianity proclaims and for which it hopes, is never a merely individual redemption; it is a redemption of human beings in their relationships to one another. For that reason, it can only adequately be represented by a social image.

If this is true, though, it is not hard to see why God's involvement of people in the work of Christ entails the appearance in human history of the social reality which we call the church. One might, of course, explain the phenomenon of the church in a more elementary way. One might say that it appears on the stage of human affairs because people who share in the hope which Christ brings them just naturally band together; and that, of course, is true enough. It is not the whole truth, however; for the hope which Christ brings is a hope for a new sort of human community under God, and such hope can only be lived out, can only find expression, in the life of a real society. To have a share in the new life which the Resurrection of Jesus promises is to live as part of a society, a society which anticipates, by the very shape of its life and activity, the Kingdom of God.

What Sort of Society?

But what sort of society can this be? Clearly it will be a visible human group or association of some sort. Clearly, too, it will have some sort of organization and be marked by characteristic institutions and activities. There are, however, many different sorts of human groups, which function in different ways and pursue different sorts of goals. There are what we call "natural" groups, like the family. There are groups based on common interests, or simply on the fact that a certain set of persons live in proximity to one another. There are elaborate organizations which serve the needs of government, and others which provide goods and services. So what sort of group or society is the church? How are we to understand it? What is the basis and aim of its existence?

For the most part, people understand the church and deal with it by likening it in their minds to other, more ordinary and more familiar, sorts of human associations. In other words, they take some particular type of society or organization, one with which they regularly have dealings, and make it their model for the church. Most often, of course, this is an unconscious process. People do not explicitly ask themselves what sort of body the church is. Rather, they automatically see it as another example of a type of group with which they are already acquainted, and they then treat it and think of it accordingly.

This way of identifying and understanding the church is admirably illustrated by the contemporary custom of describing the church as "organized religion" or "institutionalized religion." When people use such phrases they are likening the church to an association which is consciously and voluntarily formed for the pursuit of common interests, ideals, or goals. The idea is that a group of individuals band themselves together because they find that they have convictions, needs, or aims of a similar, if not identical, sort; and they are prepared to cooperate in the cultivation of their shared purposes. The religious community, then, is a society created by human enterprise and designed to serve particular human ends. It is constituted by the agreement of a number of individual persons who presumably define the terms of their association and its goals.

Within the framework of this very general model, the church can be understood—and, indeed, is understood—in a variety of specific ways. It is not unusual, for example, to find people who picture and treat the church as though it were essentially a club. Seen in this light, the church appears as a voluntary association of individuals who get together and organize themselves for the pursuit of a specific interest or avocation. In the special case of the church, of course, the interest in question is religious. Nevertheless, the structure and functioning of this body is basically similar to that of, say, an association of people loyal to certain political ideals, or of people interested in chess. In both cases, there is a national organization (or even an international organization) with local chapters, all sharing a common set of principles or aims. People join the association because they are interested in what it does and because they assent to its principles. This is one example of what one might mean by "organized religion" or "institutionalized religion."

But there is another and equally important example. Frequently people who use the word *church* have in mind the picture, not of a club but of a large corporation which maintains itself by offering a certain service to the public. On this view, the church is rather like General Motors or American Telephone and Telegraph. It has a product, and a useful one, which it wants to sell, and which, accordingly, it markets in the most attractive possible form. It is not like a club, of course; for it is not constituted by general agreement of its members. Indeed, in the strictest sense, it has no members. Rather, it has stockholders, directors, officers, employees, and customers. This may seem, when set out in this explicit way, a very strange model for the church; but strange or not, it is one which operates quite pervasively in contemporary American society. How many church members in fact cast themselves mentally in the role of satisfied or dissatisfied customers? How many church "executives" (bishops, for example, and other clergy, not to mention lay employees of the church) cast themselves mentally in the role of people who have to maintain the prosperity of their "corporation" by assuring good public relations and an appealing product?

The question is not, then, whether these models of the church as "organized religion" are or are not influential. They are. The question is whether they are useful or helpful models, whether when they are put to work, they really do bring out the true nature of the society which the creeds call church. If people habitually perceive the church as—and treat it as—a club or a corporation, and if, as a result of this fact, the church begins to behave like a club or a corporation, or perhaps like a little bit of both, what will be the result? Will the church, under those circumstances, fulfill its calling as a "fellowship of holy persons" which is living out—and living up to—its sure hope of the new life in Christ? And if the answer to this question is, on the whole, No, is there an alternative model for the church? Is there a model which does clarify for us the constitution and the purpose of this particular society?

The "Ekklesia" of God

In fact, there is such a model; and it is supplied by the New Testament. Unfortunately, modern Christians are for the most part simply unaware of it. It is hidden from them by a barrier of language. The model in question is intimated by the Greek word *ekklesia*. This is the word which English versions of the Bible translate by the term *church;* but *church,* as a matter of fact, conveys almost none of the Greek word's meaning. Consequently, readers of English Bibles miss most of the point of what the Scriptures have to say about the church.

What does *ekklesia* mean? It is a term which, even when the writers of the New Testament used it, had a long history, and therefore a fairly clear set of associations. It is a compound noun, which is formed from a particle meaning "out" or "from," and a root meaning "to call." What it refers to, therefore, is a gathering of people who have been "called out," summoned, to be something and to do something together. The ancient Greeks often employed the term to describe what we might call a town meeting. When the Old Testament was first translated from Hebrew into Greek, well before the birth of Jesus, the translators used *ekklesia* to refer to the "assembly" of Israel; that is, to the gathering of the covenant community. Quite naturally, therefore, early Christians used it to describe their own assembly. Church means, not corporation and not club, but a collection of people who have been *called out together* by a voice or a word or a summons which comes to them from outside.

Now this is an important fact in itself, because it suggests the way in which the early Christians perceived themselves as a society. They were not the organizers of a religion. They had not set up a society or an association to pursue their own religious aims, or to purvey their own religious product. Far from it. The fact that they assembled together, and worked and prayed and lived together, was not the result of their own designs at all. It was the result of a call or summons which came from beyond themselves and gathered them together. Consequently, this group did not have much basis in the natural affinity of its members for one another. To begin with, of course, it was almost entirely Jewish in its make-up; but that state of affairs did not last long. The call came to others than Jews; and it was not only in ethnic background that its membership was varied. The church included people of different religious backgrounds and both women and men. It included people of differing language and social class. This, no doubt, explains why the early church was so full of tension and disagreement: different kinds of people saw different kinds of meaning in the Gospel of Jesus and his Resurrection. It also serves, however, to make another fact clear. The basis of this group, the sole ground of its existence, was found in the call which assembled it. What its members had essentially in common was nothing which any of them brought to its life. What they had in common was the call itself, which not only assembled them but also put them in a new set of relationships, relationships which they did not always have an easy time handling.

But where did this call come from? On that score, the early

Christians were quite clear. They habitually described their *ekklesia*, their grouping or assembly, as "the *ekklesia* of God" (e.g., 1 Cor. 10:32; Gal. 1:13; 1 Tim. 3:15). This phrase means that the Christian assembly is distinguished from others by the fact that what establishes it is a certain relationship with God; or, to put the matter in a more exact way, that it is founded by "the calling of God" (Phil. 3:14; cf. 1 Cor. 1:9). It is an initiative from God's side which accounts for the visible existence of this group, this "people." The church, then, is not created by its members as they organize to cultivate their interests, religious or other. It is created by the fact that God does something, speaks a word, which brings it together. It exists, therefore, and continues to exist, only by the grace of God, only in virtue of his call and in virtue of the power which his Spirit gives people to respond to that call obediently. From moment to moment, the church exists in dependence on the one who summons it.

Does this mean that the church is "divinely instituted"? Yes, it does. But that phrase must not be misunderstood. Sometimes it is taken to mean just the opposite of what the New Testament intends when it describes the church as the "*ekklesia* of God." Not infrequently Christians have thought that "divinely instituted" meant that the church is itself divine, a kind of superhuman or supernatural institution which is not ultimately subject either to the limitations of human nature or to the effects of human sin. Such a picture, however, is very far from the one which the New Testament gives us. In Scripture, the church frequently portrays both itself as a whole and its leaders in particular as going wrong in one way or another. Its divinity, then, does not lie in its own powers or its own inherent character. In itself and in its own right, the *ekklesia* is a very human society indeed. What the phrase *divinely instituted* means, therefore, is that the church does not make itself, or depend on itself, or pretend to be anything "special" in its own right. It exists, and is what it is, because it is focused not on itself but on the "other," on God and on God's call. It is a people which exists by always looking and pointing beyond itself and by being responsive to the word of its call.

The best model, therefore, for this Christian society is not that of an institution, divine or otherwise. No doubt this people must, and inevitably will, have its characteristic institutions; just as it must, and inevitably will, be organized in some fashion. Nevertheless, the only adequate model for it is that of a covenant community, a gathering like that of the tribes of ancient Israel. Those tribes knew that their identity as a people depended on their fidelity to the God who had called them out of Egypt and who, in doing so, had given them their very being. They are, in fact, the first *ekklesia* of God, whose history the Christian *ekklesia* shares and continues. That is why the New Testament itself models the church on the covenant community of Israel. Both Saint Paul and the author of 1 Peter appeal to some words of the prophet Hosea (Hos. 1:10, 2:23) to argue that the Christian *ekklesia*, including its non-Jewish members, is "the people of God" (Rom. 9:25f.; 1 Pet. 2:9f.), created simply by the grace of God's call. More specifically, the church is the people of the New Covenant (Mk. 14:24; Heb. 12:24). *Church*, then, means "covenant people, assembled by the call or word or summons of God."

Called in Christ Jesus

But what is the *word* by which God assembles his church? This may sound like a strange, or even artificial, question; but in fact it goes to the heart of our problem about the nature of the Christian society. A covenant community, like any other, has to have a constitution of some sort. There must be some principle or principles which define its identity and thus govern and direct its life. In the case of most human societies, such a constitution is provided by the people who figure as their founders. The founders formulate basic laws, or guiding ideals, which then become the distinguishing marks of the community's continuing identity. The Christian *ekklesia*, however, has its foundation, and hence its constitution, in the word or call by which God assembles it. To know what that word is, then, means to know what the church essentially is.

Does it seem odd or paradoxical to say that a community can find its constitution, its identity, in the word which calls

it together? At first glance, perhaps it does. It is worth re-
membering, however, that a word or address always involves
an identification of the person or persons it calls. Suppose
that someone calls me, and I answer positively. In doing so, I
agree implicitly to what that call makes me out to be. By my
action or word of response, I accept the identity it proposes
for me. If someone addresses and summons me as "Smith,"
by a title such as "Colonel," or by a class name such as "fellow
Republicans," and I answer, then I have been identified, and
I have agreed to the identification by my answer. In the same
fashion, we might say, God's word identifies people as it
summons them; and by their response they accept his identification. They recognize themselves in what he calls them;
and this identity constitutes them a community, while at the
same time it provides them with their fundamental "constitution."

With what word, then, does God summon the church?
Saint John's Gospel supplies the answer to that question
when it points to Jesus as that Word of God in which both
"grace and truth" come to light for us (Jn. 1:14). Similarly,
Saint Paul speaks of "the calling of God in Christ Jesus"
(Phil. 3:14)—as though "Christ Jesus" were precisely the
Word by which God summons people. So we have to say that
the Word which constitutes the Christian *ekklesia* is Jesus, the
incarnate Word of God. He is (to use Saint John's language)
"grace," because he is the Word through whom people are
reconciled to God. He is also "truth," because in him people
discover who they really are. He is God's identification of
human beings to themselves. Christ, in short, is the name by
which God calls us, all of us; and when we answer, accepting
that name as somehow our own, we find ourselves "called
into the fellowship of his Son" (1 Cor. 1:9)—the church. The
Christian *ekklesia,* we might say, is the assembly which God
summons to exhibit to the world what *he* means by "human
being"; and what he means by it is conveyed in his Word to
us—Jesus the Christ.

And to what lengths the New Testament goes to get this
idea across to people! Think, for example, of the figure which
the Fourth Gospel employs in its fifteenth chapter. There

Jesus says—for us a bit mysteriously—"I am the true vine" (Jn. 15:1). The key to an understanding of these words lies in the fact that *vine* was an accepted symbol for Israel; that is, for the covenant community, the people of God. (See Ps. 80:8–13; Is. 5:1–7; and Hos. 10:1.) What this statement means, therefore, is that Jesus is the person who sums up in himself the identity of the covenant community. He is the representative core of the people of God. To belong to that people, then, is to stand in with Jesus, to share his life and his identity before God. "I am the vine, you are the branches . . ." (Jn. 15:5). The *ekklesia* of the New Covenant is called by, and has its constitution in, Jesus the Christ.

The Body of Christ

The same fundamental idea comes across to us through the writings of Saint Paul. For example, Paul explains or describes Christian existence by saying that it means sharing in the death of Jesus and thus being able to look forward to participation in his Resurrection life (Rom. 6:4–5). Alternatively, Paul can refer to the *ekklesia* as a group of people who are "sanctified," dedicated to God, "in Christ Jesus" (1 Cor. 1:2). What such dedication to God might involve he tries to explain by saying: ". . . in Christ Jesus you are all sons of God through faith" (Gal. 3:26). In other words, when people answer God's call with the Yes of faith, and so accept the name God puts to them, they assume the identity of Christ himself: they become children of God. Our "life is hid with Christ in God" (Col. 3:3).

In all these figures and turns of phrase, Saint Paul is circling around the same basic idea. He is attempting to say that the *ekklesia* is an assembly which exists because it has Christ as the basic principle of its life, and in that sense as its identity. None of these figures, however, has spoken so eloquently to people—or been so widely used and misused—as another which occurs in several forms in his letters: the image of the *ekklesia* as the "body of Christ."

This well-known figure has its origin in a perfectly commonplace analogy. Paul was trying to explain to his converts at Corinth that differences among the people who belong to the church should not, and indeed do not, destroy its basic unity. Christians do not all have to be alike, or to have the same talents, tastes, and gifts, in order to be at one together. In order to make this point clear, he seizes upon a widely used metaphor. He compares the *ekklesia* with a body, a living organism. He says that just as a body has many parts and limbs (*members*, in old-fashioned English), which all look different and function differently but still constitute a single body, so the church has a variety of "members" which all belong and contribute to its one life. In the process of working this analogy out, Paul is caught by a new idea. The one life of this Christian body, it dawns on him, is Christ; and so at one crucial point he simply writes "Christ" when he might have said "the *ekklesia*" (1 Cor. 12:12). What has occurred to him is the thought that the church, as a social "body," can be called by the name of the one whose life and identity it shares, and that this manner of speech will serve better than any other to express the church's essential unity. The *ekklesia*, in some sense, is Christ.

But in what sense? Are they simply identical, simply the same thing? Paul has qualms about taking his idea to such an extreme as that; so he turns his image in a slightly different direction. Instead of saying that the church as a social body simply *is* Christ, he begins to say that it is the body *of* Christ (1 Cor. 12:27), or that the *ekklesia* is one body *in* Christ (Rom. 12:5). Both of these formulas qualify the earlier one: that is, they establish a certain distance between the church and the Lord in whom its identity is given. The church shares the identity of Christ; but it does not fully embody or express that identity.

These second thoughts are later summed up in yet another use of the "body" image, according to which Christ is the "head" of the church, his body (Eph. 4:15; Col. 1:18). What this metaphor means is that the *ekklesia* participates in Christ because he is the source of its life. It also means, however, that the church falls far short of the life thus conferred on it. It must still "grow up in every way . . . into Christ" (Eph. 4:15). Its perfection is found not in itself, but outside itself in

Christ, in the Word by which it is established and in which it finds its identity.

The Church and the Kingdom of God

It begins slowly to come clear, then, what the New Testament means when it speaks of the church or (better) *ekklesia*. It means a covenant people constituted by God's call. It means a covenant people whose identity is determined by Christ because he is the call by which God assembles it, and his is the name which God puts to it. Consequently, the church is a people given life, unity, and vocation through its real, though partial and imperfect, participation in Christ, its "head."

What this means, though, if you think about it, is that the church is pointed toward, and is, in fact, a pointer to, the Kingdom of God. For what, after all, do we mean when we speak of the "life of Christ," or the "identity of Christ"? We mean, to be sure, the life and identity of the incarnate and risen Word of God. That life, however, and the identity which it defines, is the life of the New Age—the life of the coming Kingdom of God, now embodied and realized in Jesus himself. It is the same reality which Jesus came proclaiming in Galilee. It is the same reality which his sacrificial dying established and his Resurrection actualized. The church, then, through its participation in Christ, its head, is a people whose life is rooted in the coming Kingdom of God. It lives, we might say, by being focused on what lies ahead of it. United with Christ by the power of the Spirit, it is the here-and-now sign of that transformed world which God has promised in Christ. One might describe the church as a kind of dress rehearsal—clumsy, no doubt, and ill-conducted—for the Kingdom.

The Kingdom of God, however, is not promised only to the church. It is promised to the world. It is the "whole creation" which is waiting for "the revelation of the sons of God" (Rom. 8:19,22). It is not the church alone, but "all things" which God purposes to "sum up . . . in Christ" (Eph. 1:10). God's salvation, in short, is not intended simply for his *ekklesia.* It is intended for the world whose sin Jesus bore and overcame. What the church is rehearsing is not just its own future, but the future of the world in which it is set.

And it is this fact which provides the essential clue to the meaning and purpose of the church's existence. The church is not called by God in Christ simply for its own sake, or for the sake of the spiritual comfort and salvation of its individual members. If, through the power of the Holy Spirit, God involves people consciously in the work of Christ, the reason is that their participation in that work is part of God's purpose for the world which he created and which he loves (Jn. 3:16). The *ekklesia* is called out and called together to be a sign of what God is up to, to be an intimation within the present order of things of the destiny which God intends for humanity in Christ. If the church is the body of Christ, if it bears the identity of Christ, that is for the sake of the world as well as for the sake of the church itself. The business of the church is to manifest the grace of God in Christ, and by doing so to let the truth about humanity, the truth which is called the Kingdom of God, show clearly.

How does this happen? The first thing which comes to mind in this connection is, of course, the church's proclamation of redemption in Christ. The church preaches the Word of God: that is, it announces Christ to the world as the one in whom God's love and humanity's fulfillment are both contained. The church's proclamation of Christ, however, is not a matter of words and speech alone. The church signifies Christ and points to him by all its activities. It is a sign of God's Kingdom in its worship; for in its worship it serves and praises God as a body which shares Christ's relationship to the Father. It is a sign of God's Kingdom by its devotion to justice and mercy in the affairs of the world; for by standing with the oppressed and showing God's love for those whom society despises and casts aside, the church acts as a body which shares Christ's mission to human beings.

In short, the church, which is the people of God and the body of Christ, has a vocation, a calling which stems from the identity which God gives to it in Christ. It is hardly necessary to point out that the church does not always fulfill this calling

very eagerly or very skillfully. It sometimes forgets its identity in Christ. It sometimes acts in ways which contradict that
identity, just as individual human beings will often act in
ways that seem to deny their known character. Nevertheless,
through God's operation in the Spirit, the *ekklesia* really does
have this identity and the calling which goes with it. It really
is a pointer to the Christ in whom humanity's destiny is
revealed, though sometimes it points to Christ only by its
shortcomings.

One, Holy, Catholic, and Apostolic

This way of understanding the church's identity and vocation
helps us to comprehend the Nicene Creed's description of the
church as "one, holy, catholic, and apostolic." These four
adjectives seem to claim a great deal. In fact, they seem to say
things about the church which are plainly untrue (as, for
example, that it is completely united, or that the common life
of its members is uniformly a holy life). The fact is, though,
that these adjectives are applied to the church, not for what it
is in itself but for what it is in Christ. He is the one to whom
unity, holiness, and catholicity primarily belong. He is also
the one who is the heart and substance of the apostolic
preaching and teaching. The church is "one, holy, catholic,
and apostolic" because it shares in, and grows up into, the
life and the identity of Christ, and because by doing so it is a
sign to the world of the destiny which God has in store for
humankind. In other words, these adjectives portray the
church not as a "perfect society," but as a pointer to the life in
Christ as that will be fulfilled for humanity in the Kingdom of
God. Let us look at each of these terms with that principle in
mind.

In the first place, then, the Creed instructs us to believe that
the church is *one* through its sharing in the life of Christ. This
description of the *ekklesia* does not mean that the divisions
among Christians—or the sin and self-will which create
them—are unreal. No more does it mean that among the
many Christian bodies it is possible to identify a "true"
church which always has been, and is now, perfectly one.

What it means is that insofar as the church exists at all, divided or not, it does so because, and only because, it shares in the one life of Christ. It exists because of him and in him (1 Cor. 3:11). In spite, therefore, of the myriad—alternately tragic and laughable—ways in which its members busy themselves with dividing what is indivisible (1 Cor. 1:13), the church has its being in the one Christ, and is called to reflect that fact in its own life. For just this reason, however, the church in its human brokenness stands as a sign that humanity too, with all its divisions, is one. God has put the name of his Son to all of us, sinners though we be, by giving Jesus to die and rise again for the world; and in that fact is the seed of the perfected unity which belongs to the Kingdom of God—to a church fulfilled in a world redeemed.

Then, further, the Creed instructs us to believe that the church is *holy* through its sharing in the life of Christ. This description too is open to misunderstanding. It is often taken to suggest that the church is a society whose members live up fully to their identity in Christ, and thus invariably exhibit exceptional moral qualities. From time to time, no doubt, individuals and groups within the church come close to doing just that. We have all known singularly saintly people whose lives reflect something of the awesome goodness of God. More often, however, Christians seem to think, live, and act much like everyone else.

To notice and state this fact, however, is not to deny what the Creed means when it speaks of the holiness of the church; for that holiness is not a simple matter of undeviating and unchanging moral excellence. Holiness in human beings means being set apart, being dedicated, for the service of God; and what we mean by describing the church as "holy" is that it really does belong to God because he has called it together in Christ. In thus belonging, or being dedicated, to God, however, the church is once again a sign, a pointer. It is a sign to all people that humanity's fulfillment lies in fellowship with God himself, and that such holiness is not just a hope or an ideal, but, in Christ, a reality.

It is along much the same lines that one must interpret the *catholicity* of the church. The word *catholic,* of course, has two slightly different shades of meaning. On the one hand, it is synonymous with "universal" or "inclusive." On the other hand, it means "whole" or "integral." To see how these descriptions apply to the church, one must first of all understand how they apply to Christ; for he is, as we have said, the one to whom catholicity primarily belongs. To begin with, he is the universal Redeemer. The truth which comes to light in him is the truth for everyone and about everyone. In him, God's purpose for all of humanity is both revealed and accomplished. This means, however, that in Christ the wholeness of humanity is achieved. To know Christ is to know what it is to be an integral, fulfilled human being: it is to find oneself in God.

How is the church catholic, then? It is catholic just as it is one and holy—through its sharing in the identity of Christ. In this case, such sharing means that the church is essentially inclusive. It is not the affair of any particular race or nation or class. It is not for men as distinct from women, or young as distinct from old. The life by which it lives is one which can be, and to a significant extent truly is, shared by all sorts and conditions of people. At the same time, however, this catholicity is only possible and only real because the church's life reflects the wholeness of Christ. By its teaching and proclamation, by its life of worship, by the way in which it orders itself and its activities, the church reflects, and thus points to, the wholeness of humanity in Christ—or better, to Christ as the wholeness of humanity; and this is the root of its catholicity. The catholic church is the church as it points all people, and relates all people, to their own completeness in Christ.

So it is right and inevitable that the Creed should end its description of the church by using the adjective *apostolic*. For if what we have said is correct, the church is one, holy, and catholic only because it keeps itself focused on the Word of God, the Christ, in whom its identity is given. It does not look to itself, or proclaim itself, or offer itself to people as the solution to all their problems. Rather, it does what the Apostles did. It points itself and everyone else to the truth which appears in the ministry, death, and Resurrection of Jesus: to the unity, holiness, and wholeness which God gives people in Christ. That is its apostolic function. Consequently, the church is bound by the apostolic message. It repeats, in its words and in its life, the good news which the Apostles brought to the world in their preaching of the risen Lord. As it does this—and only as it does this—the Church itself becomes a true sign of the Kingdom of God, as the Apostles were.

Conclusion

Not a club nor a corporation, but a covenant people called out to share in the new life of the Risen Christ, and by doing so to point the world to the Kingdom of God—that is the church. In all aspects of its life, it is an utterly human society. It is human in the way it functions, in the sins and limitations of the people who make it up, and in its own constant need of the grace and forgiveness of God. That grace and forgiveness, however, it possesses in Christ, in the Word by which God calls, nourishes, and sends it. Through that Word, the *ekklesia* participates in the life of the coming Kingdom and points the world to its fulfillment in God.

· 11 ·

Word and Sacrament

The first effect of the Holy Spirit's working is the calling together of a society, the church. This society stands before the world as a sign of God's love in Christ and therefore as a sign of the world's transformation and redemption. Through this society individuals have a conscious share in Christ and in God's "new thing."

Such a body, though, if it is not to appear for just a moment in history and then fade away, must have a visible social shape. For one thing, it needs places where its members meet and where its activities are carried on. For another, it needs regular times when its members gather in these places. Then, too, it must have organized ways of doing its business. Above all, however, every society of whatever sort must have certain characteristic activities which both express and renew its fundamental identity. A group devoted to the cause of bowling or poker or the study of French will surely meet to "do its thing"; and in the process it will not only show the world what it stands for, but also maintain the commitment which constitutes the group. Even a vast political society like the United States of America has need of activities of this sort: for example, national elections, ceremonial inaugurations of newly elected presidents, meetings of the people's representatives in Congress. In such activities the society enacts its identity. It explains itself out loud by doing the thing which makes it what it is; and in this way it renews itself.

The church is just such a society, though. What, then, does the church do when it is "doing its thing"? What are the activities which are essential and fundamental to the church's life? One can think off-hand of a whole multitude of things which this particular society does. For example, it maintains hospitals and schools. Its members lead social and political movements in their nations or neighborhoods. It breeds and nourishes associations of various sorts, from communities of monastics to charitable organizations. What is more, it would be hard to imagine the church existing apart from this wide range of activity.

Nevertheless, these are not activities in which the church discovers and renews its identity, even though they certainly are activities in which that identity is expressed. There is, moreover, a reason why this is so. As we have already seen, to talk about the identity of the church is to talk about something which depends on people's relationship to God in Christ. Unlike a poker club—and unlike the United States of America which is constituted by "we, the people"—the church lives from outside itself, through a life conferred on it as a gift. For this reason, the regular activities which maintain and renew its identity are bound to be of a specific sort. They have to be activities through which its life and hence its identity are communicated to it from beyond itself.

To say the same thing in other words, the activities and institutions which are absolutely fundamental to the life of the church are those through which God communicates Christ to it as the source of its life. To ask what the church's characteristic and essential activities are is the same thing as to ask how—by what means—it is, and knows itself to be, "in Christ."

The Church Assembled

What are these activities? The best way to answer that question is to look at what the *ekklesia* typically does when it assembles. To be sure, Christians assemble in all sorts of circumstances. Sometimes they assemble in small groups just to pray or talk together. Again, they may assemble as committees or commissions, or in legislative bodies such as conventions. Most typically, however, and most regularly, they assemble on the Lord's Day to celebrate the Resurrection of Jesus. So typical, and so regular, is this sort of assembling that people nowadays refer to it simply as "going to church."

What happens at such a meeting? The pattern of events varies, of course; but not so much that it is impossible to discern the regular presence of certain normal activities. In fact, the general outline of what is done at such assemblies has not varied a great deal since the first centuries of the church's existence.

In the first place, such assemblies are the places where the Scriptures of the Old and New Testaments are read and expounded. Psalms and hymns are interspersed with these acts of reading and preaching, and quite naturally: what the Scriptures and their proclamation in a sermon convey is the word of salvation—the word of "God with us"; and that message unavoidably evokes the response of thanksgiving and song.

In the second place, such assemblies frequently involve a ritual of washing or "baptism." Through this ritual individual persons are acknowledged—and acknowledge themselves—to belong to Christ and thus to the life of his *ekklesia*. Here, then, we have a ritual of initiation, one in which people are joined to Christ, and in which, for just that reason, the church celebrates the very basis of its existence as a community.

In the third place, such assemblies even more frequently—and in most cases invariably—involve a ritual meal. In this meal, bread and wine are taken. Thanks is given over them to God both for his creation of the world and for its redemption in the death and Resurrection of Jesus. The people then share the consecrated bread and wine, and in doing so understand that they share both in what Christ does and in what he is; for these ordinary things are signs which convey Christ's actual presence for them. Here again, in a ritual deed, the church seems to enact its own identity; for it enacts the life of Christ as its own life.

It is not our business at just this point to talk extensively about the significance of these three activities. Rather, we need simply to note a character which they all share. Whether one thinks of the reading and expounding of the Gospel message contained in the Scriptures, of the Baptism of new Christians, or of the celebration of the Eucharist, one is bound to note a similar logic about each of them. They are activities in which the church connects itself with the source of its life and identity; that is, with the Christ in whom God calls it together. They are, therefore, activities in which, in an absolutely fundamental way, the church identifies itself and becomes itself.

These activities, then, either are, or involve, just the sort of institutions for which we are looking. The fact that this is so is enshrined in an idea handed down in the theological tradition. This is the idea that "Word and Sacrament" are the twin bases of the church's life, the two human realities through which God's call in Christ is heard and made effective. In the preaching of the Gospel on the one hand, and in the sacramental (symbolic) enactment of its meaning on the other, the church is reached and touched by God in his Spirit and involved in the work of Christ. These, then, are the characteristic activities and institutions of the church's common life, whose meaning we must now explore further.

The Scriptures Taught and Preached

We must look more closely, therefore, into the meaning of this phrase "Word and Sacrament"; and we can begin by asking what is signified when we speak of "the Word of God."

That is not an unfamiliar question. More than once in the course of this book we have used, and tried to explain, the expression "Word of God"; and even a brief and hasty attempt at recollection will serve to remind us how many and how various its shades of meaning are. For all that, however, there is a single idea in which all the meanings of "Word of God" have their center and their focus: and what we must do now is to identify that idea.

Basically, what "Word of God" means is whatever God does to communicate himself. In the Old Testament, it can refer either to things that God does or to things that God says; but in both cases it signifies moments in human experience where the presence and activity of God are recognized and where, in consequence, people come into communication with him. The Word of God is God making himself known to people and being with them.

It may seem a bit strange, once this is said, to go on and speak of the Word of God as God's Son—that is, as the second member of the Trinity. The strangeness wears off quickly, though, when we recall what it is that the doctrine of the Trinity is trying to say: that God really is, for himself and in himself, what he is for us. What he communicates to us, what he "says" to us, is the same thing he says to himself. "Word of God," therefore, does indeed mean "God showing himself"; but it means that in a twofold way. It means both that God has a Word for himself in which he knows himself—his eternal Son—and that this very Word is also his Word to us. He communicates his very self to people by communicating his Son.

This happens, moreover, in a definitive way in the life, death, and Resurrection of Jesus. The whole point of the doctrine of the Incarnation is to say that the human life of Jesus is the historical expression of what God is for himself in his eternal Son. In the Christ we meet God's Word—a Word which means the simultaneous judgment and forgiveness of humanity; a Word which embodies and conveys the new life of the Resurrection; a Word, in short, which is "God with us."

But how is this Word conveyed to people now? What are the human media by which the truth of "God with us" is communicated to people in the present? In short, how does the Word of God happen for us?

The answer to this question comes in two stages. The first stage, of course, is the Scriptures themselves. These books, as everyone knows, are regularly described as "Word of God." That description does not mean that the Scriptures are identical with Christ himself. It does mean, however, that for us they are an essential medium of the Word of God: they communicate to us the grace and the truth which are found in the Word of God made flesh. Being in this way the vehicle of God's Word, they too, in a secondary sense, are "God showing himself."

In themselves, however, the Scriptures are no more than words printed on a page. To come alive, to function as God's Word for us, they have to be interpreted. What they say has to be seen and grasped for what it is. In short (for this is what *interpretation* means) what the Scriptures say has to take form in the thoughts and words of their readers and hearers. Their Word has to pass through our minds and come out as something which *we* say.

So there is a second stage in the answer to our question about the way in which God's Word gets communicated to people. It gets to them through the Scriptures —but that only happens when the Bible's message is taken up, understood, and set out in living thought and speech. It is not the Scriptures in themselves, as they just lie about in a bookcase or on a table or a lectern, but the Scriptures comprehended and expounded which are the vehicles of God's Word. For this reason, it is not simply the Bible, but the Bible taught and proclaimed which is the medium of people's contact with what God does and says in Christ.

But how are the Scriptures interpreted and proclaimed to us? In many ways. There is the continuing work of people who devote themselves to scholarly study of the Bible. There is the regular private study of Scripture which is carried out constantly by ordinary Christians. Both of these bear fruit in the public life of the church. In addition to these activities, however, there are two institutions through which the message of the Scriptures is regularly interpreted to us.

The first of these is the church's creeds. The creeds are, in fact, summaries of what Christian experience through the ages has seen to be the heart of what the Bible proclaims. They are the community's shared and traditional identification of the central theme of the Bible: which is a new relationship to God based on his communication of himself to men and women in Christ and in the work of the Holy Spirit. The

creeds are, then, the church's public guides to the understanding of the scriptural message.

The second of these institutions is the activity of preaching.
The creeds are a pointer to the basic message of the Scriptures. Preaching is the proclamation of that message for a
particular group of people in a particular time and place. It is
the way in which the grace and truth of God's Word incarnate
are brought home to people through living human words
which interpret the Scriptures. The importance of preaching
lies in the fact that it lets God's Word get spoken as part of a
real human conversation. People are always talking, to themselves and to others, about the problems of life, the events of
their time, the meaning of what they do and of what happens
to them. Preaching lets Christ, God's Word, be heard as a
word in that ongoing conversation; and for that reason it is an
essential medium of the scriptural message.

In the first instance, then, the church is reached and
touched by God and involved in the work of Christ by the
scriptural Word, taught and proclaimed. When that message
is heard and understood and received with appropriate response, people find themselves in the presence of God, with a
new awareness of his will for them and his calling to them.
Furthermore, this proclamation of the scriptural Word is, in
the strictest sense, part of the very constitution of the church.
It is the way in which God's summons to his people, his call
to them in Christ, actually reaches them. Apart from the
Scriptures proclaimed, the church—the assembly of
believers—would not exist.

Sacrament: The Word Enacted

God's Word is addressed to people's understanding so that it
may be acknowledged, believed, and followed. To say the
same thing in another way, Christ—who is God's Word—is
set forth for men and women as the truth about themselves,
as the embodiment of the new life for which they are destined. This truth, however, is not just something to be
affirmed, as one might affirm the statement "Australia is
south of China." It is a truth which is meant to be taken in,

absorbed, and made a part of the person who knows it. It is a truth, in short, which has to be lived out. It has to get inside of people; or maybe it would be better to vary the metaphor and say that they have to get inside of it, so as to be in tune with it and live in accord with its rhythms.

How does this happen? It happens when, in the most profound sense, people *agree* to God's Word. "Agree," however, must be understood in this case to mean more than it usually does. For example, it must obviously mean assent to the truth of God's Gospel. Further, though, in this special case it means trust in that Word and obedience to it. Further still, however, it means that our word back to God becomes the same as his Word to us. We agree to God's Word when, and only when, it is also ours.

This is not a difficult point to understand. When one person truly agrees with another, such agreement cannot be expressed by mere mental or verbal assent. It reveals itself only in a real unity both of thought and of action. It takes shape only when the word which you speak to me and the word which I speak back to you are one and the same. Then, and only then, is the truth which each speaks to the other genuinely internalized. Then, and only then, do I "get in tune with" the word you address to me.

To say, then, that the Word of God must become a part of people, that it must get inside them and shape their being and acting, is much the same thing as to say that their answer to God must be a repetition of his Word to them. They must somehow be caught up in the truth which he addresses to them so that they "correspond" to it, so that it becomes their own word.

But in this picture of a human word which not only says Yes to God's Word, but repeats it back to him, there is an important clue to the meaning of *sacrament*. We can see how this is so, moreover, if we look closely at the traditional definition of *sacrament* which has come down from the Middle Ages—and indeed, as far as its substance goes, from before the Middle Ages. In the English of The Book of Common Prayer, this definition explains that sacrament means the "outward and visible sign of an inward and spiritual grace."

A sacrament, then, is a sign; that is, it is something which means, or points to, something else. It "signifies." In this very general sense, then, a sacrament may be a thing which intimates the presence or nearness of another thing, as heavy clouds betoken rain. It may also be an action or gesture, as dancing can signify joy or a handshake can convey friendship. No matter what specific form it takes, though, *a sacrament is a kind of language.* It is a sign precisely because *it says something.* It expresses and signifies a reality which lies beyond it. To say that a sacrament is a sign, therefore, is the same thing as to say that it is a kind of word.

Furthermore, if we think specifically about the church's sacraments, it is clear enough that they are, in the first instance, words of ours. They are signs which the church enacts in order to say something, to signify something. The church, through its representative minister, pours water over a child's head and accompanies this act by certain words. Or again, the church, through its minister, takes bread and wine and gives thanks over them to God, after which its members consume them. Both of these actions, these sacraments, are signs in and through which the people assembled intend to convey a meaning and to signify something. They are enacted words.

But to whom are these words, these signs, addressed? And what do they signify? These two questions are central and crucial for any understanding of the church's sacraments; and we must therefore be as clear and as careful as we possibly can in trying to answer them.

In the first place, then, to whom are these word-signs addressed? It is not only plausible but correct, from one point of view, to say that they are addressed by the church to itself. Anyone who speaks a word or enacts a sign, of whatever sort, is explaining or clarifying or signifying something for himself; and the same is true of the people of God. By enacting certain ritual signs, the church is reminding itself of what these signs mean. It is saying something to itself.

Furthermore, it is equally plausible and equally correct, from another point of view, to say that these word-signs are addressed to the world in which the people of God live. The sacraments are signs to humanity-at-large of the truth which the church has discovered in Christ.

However plausible and correct these two answers may be, though, they do not get to the heart of the matter. The fact is that, considered as signs or words which the church enacts and speaks, the sacraments are addressed to God. That is why they are regarded, and rightly so, as acts of worship. They shape themselves as acts of obedient thanksgiving, in which people open themselves to God by trustfully acknowledging the love which he has made known in Christ. The first, though not the only, audience of the sacraments is God himself, to whom these signs express faith, gratitude, and commitment.

But this brings us to our second question. What are we saying to God in these word-signs? The answer is plain. We are signifying—speaking—Christ. The act of washing with water means Christ as the one in whom people have forgiveness of sins and fellowship with God. The giving of thanks over bread and wine means Christ as the one whose death and Resurrection inaugurate a new life for humanity—the life of the New Covenant, which was effected through his body broken and his blood poured out. What the sacraments enact—and therefore speak and mean—is the truth which Christ is for his people. They signify the reality of God-with-us in his Word incarnate. By speaking this word to God in thanksgiving, the church worships God. By speaking the very same word, it also reminds itself of the basis of its existence and reminds the world of God's purpose for humanity.

In all of this, however, we are still speaking only of the "outward sign"—the sacrament. What of the "inward and spiritual grace"? Where does that come in? It is often said that what is characteristic of the proper sacraments of the church, as distinct from most other signs, is the fact that they effectively convey what they signify. This means, though, that they are not merely signs. Somehow they not only point, but actually reach, beyond themselves. They touch and involve the reality to which they point. They have, we might say, a spiritual "inside" which is more than just a human act of pointing at something or of trying to indicate something.

But how is this possible? From a purely human point of view, that question is unanswerable. There is nothing we can say which will reveal the mechanics of how a sacrament "works"—how it effectively conveys what it signifies. The reason for this, moreover, is plain; and it is simply this: that a sacrament is not something mechanical.

If a sacrament like Baptism or the Eucharist truly does convey what it signifies, if what it says happens, that is not something which human beings bring about, but rather something which God brings about. The sacrament must be not only what we, the church, say, but also what God says; and God's speaking is not something whose mechanics we can either control or understand. There is another party involved in our action. The sign is the church's attempt to speak Christ, to signify him, by its ritual words and deeds. The "inward and spiritual" reality, though, is Christ himself; and if he identifies himself with our word about him, that is not a matter of mechanics at all, but rather a matter (as the definition says clearly enough) of "grace." It is by God's grace—that is, by his working in the Holy Spirit—that our word to God coincides with God's Word to us, and "sign" is at one with "thing which is signified."

But even though it is impossible to explain this mystery, it is possible to see what the mystery is. What it amounts to is this: that God takes our word to him and lets it be his Word to us, so that in speaking our word, enacting our sign, we receive Christ. The human actions and symbols of the sacrament get caught up in a higher action; and from being our attempt to reach out to God, they become God's way of reaching out to us. God actually involves us with the new life to which our sacrament points.

In the sacraments, therefore, the church enacts not merely its own word, but God's Word. Through actions accompanied by words, it symbolizes the grace and truth which are God's Word incarnate. In this way, it tries to make its word agree with God's—to "get with" the Christ whom the Scriptures proclaim. And the miracle and mystery of the sacrament is that this actually happens. The church's word becomes God's Word, and it is possible to say that in such an action we "dwell in him, and he in us."

So the sacraments too are part of the very constitution of the church. The church cannot be itself apart from the hearing of God's Word through the Scriptures and the proclamation of their message. No more, however, can it be itself apart from the grace by which this Word gets internalized—by which the *ekklesia* is enabled to agree from the inside with Christ who is its life. And that, by God's grace, is what happens in the carrying out of the sacraments.

Baptism

Of the two normative Christian sacraments, the creeds refer explicitly only to one: namely, Baptism, the basic sacrament of membership in Christ.

The reason why this is so, why the creeds mention Baptism alone of the two basic sacraments of the Church is not hard to discover. Nowadays Christians associate the creeds with eucharistic worship or with the prayer and praise of the morning and evening offices. Originally, however, the creeds were employed in the setting of the rites of Baptism. They provided the form of words which converts used to express their acceptance of the Gospel, and thus to signalize their entrance into a new life of open fellowship with God in Christ. The creeds, as a matter of fact, are nothing more or less than verbal actions by which individuals bind themselves to the "grace and truth" of the Word incarnate, and so claim to belong to Christ. They naturally single out Baptism, therefore; for the confession of faith which they embody is a part of the baptismal sign—a part of what happens in the performance of the sacrament itself.

It is only a part, though; for in fact, two things happen in Baptism. On the one hand, the person who is being baptized reaches out in faith to say Yes to God's Word, and the form in which this Yes is said is a creed. On the other hand, the believer's profession of faith is answered and accompanied by an act of washing in water; and as this act is performed, the minister presiding announces that the washing brings this person into a new state of life—a state in which he or she belongs to God, in Christ, through the power of the Holy

Spirit. "I baptize you in the name of the Father, and of the Son, and of the Holy Spirit."

The "sign" in Baptism, therefore, speaks of the creation of a new relationship of which Christ is the basis. Like all relationships, this one has two sides. On the one hand, there is the faith of the persons being baptized, who accept Christ as the truth for themselves and about themselves. On the other hand, there is the action of God, who accepts the believer as his own child in Christ. Baptism, in fact, symbolically enacts an agreement between human faith and God's Word. It is the "sign" of the New Covenant in Christ.

Once this truth is grasped, we can comprehend some of the other ways in which the meaning of Baptism has been expressed. The creeds, for example, following the New Testament, associate Baptism with "forgiveness of sins"; for the New Covenant between God and humanity is based on God's covering of human sin in Christ. To be with God in Christ is to live on the basis of that divine love which has neutralized the power of human sin through the death of Jesus. It is, in a word, to live as one set free by forgiveness.

Baptism is also described as an action which signifies "incorporation" into Christ—what we have called sharing the identity of Christ. To be set free by forgiveness, to live as a "child of God and an inheritor of the Kingdom of Heaven," means to stand with Christ in his relationship to God, and thus to be bound up with him in his life. To be baptized, then, means to accept a name, an identity—that of Christ— and with that name goes a way of life and a calling. The baptized person is a representative in what he or she says and does of the destiny which God wills for all his people, the destiny which Christ embodies, and which we share as we are embodied in him.

Forgiveness of sins and incorporation into Christ, however, are only made possible for people by the action of the Holy Spirit. It is the Spirit who, as we have seen, is God working within people to connect them with Christ and thus to set them in their proper relation with the Father. Baptism, consequently, has always been understood as a sacrament which signifies the gift of the Holy Spirit. There is no being "in

Christ," no sharing his identity and his life, and hence no participation in the forgiveness which that involves, apart from the presence and operation of the Holy Spirit. The action of Baptism, then, speaks of the conferring of the Holy Spirit upon all who are washed in its waters.

These are some of the basic things which the church says—signifies—when it performs the sacrament of Baptism. It says that a particular person is being brought into a new relationship with God, a relationship of faith based upon what God has accomplished in Christ. It says that this relationship is actualized by the power of the Holy Spirit, and that it involves forgiveness of sins, a sharing in the life and identity of Christ, and a vocation to live in accordance with that identity.

This is the church's word; and when we say that this sign, this word of the church, really means what it signifies, we are saying that all of these things truly happen in Baptism—that the church's word, acted out sacramentally, is one with God's Word of salvation in Christ.

The Eucharist

Baptism is the unrepeatable beginning of Christian life. It marks the point at which an individual person's calling and identity in Christ are, so to speak, brought home to that person. From the moment of their Baptism, people stand in a new situation, a new context of relationships. The logic of their personal and common lives has been shown to be that of Christ's life. Like Jesus at his own Baptism, they have been singled out as children of God and recipients of the gift of the Holy Spirit.

A beginning, however, is only a beginning. The foundation, once laid, must be built on. The reality which Baptism signifies and actualizes for people has to be lived out in the changing circumstances of daily existence. In other words, the identity which Baptism assigns must become a principle of constant growth and renewal in people's lives; and this happens through the sacramental action of the Eucharist—

Holy Communion—in which the church enacts and enters into the life of the crucified and risen Christ.

It is no easy matter to describe the significance of the human "sign" which the Eucharist is. One can, to be sure, say quickly enough what the performance of this sign involves: indeed we have already done so. It involves taking bread and wine, giving thanks over them to God for his creation of the world and his redemption of it in Christ, breaking the bread, and distributing the bread and wine to the community. The question is, though: What is this action intended to mean? What word does the church speak to God when it carries out the Eucharist? That question, however, cannot be answered abstractly. The meaning of this sign is not to be discovered from general considerations about its symbolism. What determines its meaning is, in fact, a quite particular set of historical events.

For Jesus himself, just before his execution, performed a sign; and the Eucharist, considered purely as a human action, is a repetition of that sign of his. Its meaning, therefore, is tied up with the meaning of what Jesus did and said on that occasion. One can only understand the Eucharist by understanding what happened at the Last Supper.

What happened, of course, was a solemn, ceremonial meal. It may well have been a Passover meal. Jesus presided over the meal, and his closest disciples were with him. At certain moments in the meal, which had been decreed by long custom, he gave thanks to God over a cup of wine and over bread, each of which he then distributed to his friends. He did not, however, follow custom in his explanation of the meaning of these actions. Instead, he gave a novel interpretation of them. He explained that they had reference to what was about to happen to him—to the fate he was about to meet. Of the bread, as he broke it, he said: "This is my Body for you." Of the cup of wine, he said: "This cup is the New Covenant in my blood."

In other words, Jesus took the ceremonial actions which were customarily performed at such a meal and explained them as signifying his forthcoming death. His body was to be broken, like the bread; and his blood was to be poured out, like the wine. These events, moreover, would have a larger significance. What was about to happen would not be just another unhappy dying. It would be a death through which God would create a New Covenant with his people. It was that sort of death—a death with that intrinsic significance—which the actions of Jesus' meal with his disciples signified.

When, therefore, Jesus said: "Do this for my recalling," people could easily understand what he meant. He was not just saying: "Do this to call me to mind." He was saying: "Do this to enter into the meaning of my life and death." People who take bread and wine, and give thanks over them for the New Covenant which God has made with humanity in Christ, perform an action through which they enter into Jesus' dying and the new life which came through it. In fact, *they are symbolically enacting the creation of the New Covenant.* At the level of their outward actions, to be sure, they are simply repeating the "business" of the Last Supper. At the level of the meaning of these actions, however, they are joining themselves with Jesus in his death and Resurrection.

Let us say, then, that when the church assembles and performs the sign which is a eucharistic celebration, what it means by this action—the word it speaks—is Christ himself, considered as the one who, in his sacrificial dying, is the bearer of a new life of fellowship with God. In doing this, however, the church is not simply pointing to Christ, as if he were someone "over there" to whom it wished to call people's attention. It signifies and speaks Christ by enacting symbolically the meaning of his life, death, and Resurrection. In other words, it speaks Christ in this action by identifying itself with him through the bread and the wine—by doing sacramentally what he did, once and for all, on the Cross.

And because this word which the church speaks, this sign which it acts out, is, at the very same time, God's Word to his people, the sacrament of the Eucharist is not a mere human gesture. It is not just the church's attempt at trying to "get with" its Lord. It is also, and more significantly, the Lord's way of being with his assembled people. The sign carries with it its "inward and spiritual" reality because the truth which it means is God's effective Word. The bread and wine, given to God in thanksgiving, is God's way of speaking Christ to us in the very word which we speak to him. What is signified is conveyed.

That is why Christian tradition has always spoken of the "real presence" of Christ in the sacrament of the Eucharist. That phrase does not mean that the literal, physical "flesh and blood" of the historical Jesus are there to be seen and touched. It means that in taking, blessing, and receiving the eucharistic bread and wine, the church knows and receives Christ as the active principle of its own life; or, in other words, that the reality which the sacrament means is truly and objectively given in it.

And, because this is so, every eucharistic celebration has a sacrificial character. This is true, of course, simply at the human level; for the Eucharist is an act of thanksgiving, and therefore an act of self-giving, to God. It is also true, however, at a much deeper level. In this sacrament, people are joined to Christ. In being joined to Christ, they enter into his life—which was a life of self-offering to God—fulfilled in the triumph of his sacrificial death. And being thus caught up in Christ, they are caught up in his self-giving to God. Their "praise and thanksgiving," human, limited, and inadequate as these are, are seized up in his definitive act of praise and thanksgiving to God. The Eucharist is a sharing in the sacrifice of Christ.

Consequently, and finally, the Eucharist is an action in which the church rehearses and anticipates the fulfilled human life of the Kingdom of God. Receiving Christ and entering into his relationship of self-giving openness to God, the *ekklesia* celebrates the joy of the coming New Age. It looks forward in confidence to the final triumph of that "grace and truth" which Christ himself is.

Conclusion

The church lives by obediently hearing God's scriptural Word proclaimed and by thankfully performing that Word as its own word in the sacraments. Christ preached, and Christ sacramentally received as the principle of its own living and acting: these are the twin pillars upon which the church rests. One implication of this fact we have already stated and explored. The church lives, in every moment, by grace: that is, it derives its life and its identity, not from itself but from God in Christ through the power of the Holy Spirit. Word and Sacrament are institutions through which the church is referred beyond itself to the Christ who calls it into being.

If this is true, though, there is necessarily more to be said. A society which lives not in and of itself but rather in Christ must ask what it means to share the life of Christ. What is the shape of a human existence whose character is defined by the call of God in his incarnate Word? What is the nature of a human existence which—by God's grace in the sacraments—has that incarnate Word as the interior principle of its own growth? What does it mean for people that they are involved, through the Holy Spirit, in what God has done in Christ? These questions point ahead to a new, and final, topic: that of the style of Christian living and hoping.

· 12 ·

Forgiven Sinners

The Holy Spirit, we have said, involves people with the new life which God both makes known and realizes in Christ. This new life is not intended merely for a few people, but for all. It is God's will for humanity as a whole. God intends "to sum up all things in Christ" (Eph. 1:10). The grace of the Holy Spirit's presence, therefore, is not confined to this or that nation or class or group—any more than is the presence of God or of God's Word. In the Spirit, God is at work everywhere—helping people to recognize the truth about themselves and to choose it. Sometimes he works openly, and sometimes he works secretly and anonymously. But he is always at work.

Central to God's purpose, however, is the calling of a people in whose common life the meaning of what God is doing in Christ can be openly and explicitly lived out. This people, the church, is sustained in its life by Word and Sacrament. Hearing God's Word proclaimed, it knows that it has its identity in Christ. Thankfully celebrating the sacraments, it is joined to Christ and so has God's Word as the truth of its own being and acting. The church, in short, is the assembly of people in which God's purpose for humanity has its "public showing."

When all this is said, however, another question still remains. What does it mean for people here and now, in this world and under the conditions of human life as we know it, to have a share in the new life which the Spirit gives us in Christ? What is the shape, the logic, of such Christian and spiritual existence? Saint Paul is the one who says that it is life "in the Spirit" and life "in Christ." But what do those phrases mean?

The creeds have an answer to this question, a terse, easily recited answer. What both say is that people who know God in Christ through the power of the Spirit live a *forgiven life*. They have "forgiveness" or "remission of sins." But these phrases, easy as they may be to recite, are not for that reason easy to understand. *Forgiveness* is a very familiar word, and one which people use all the time. What does it mean, though, when used to describe a whole way of life in relation to God? What is a *forgiven* life like? Those are the questions with which this chapter must be concerned.

What Is Forgiving?

The best way to approach this question is to take a brief look at the meaning of forgiveness itself. When we do that, one thing becomes clear from the very start. What the word *forgiveness* refers to is a special kind of relationship between two people. It does not refer to any sort of "thing," like an idea or a quality or some item of property. It signifies a way in which I can be related to someone else, or in which someone else can be related to me. To forgive (or, for that matter, to be forgiven) means to take a certain stance toward another person.

Another thing which is clear from the very start about forgiveness is the fact that it only makes sense in a special kind of situation. This relationship, as we have called it, can only happen when the two persons whom it affects are angry at each other, afraid of each other, or distrustful of each other. A genuine wrong must have been committed, through some word or action; and as a result, the two parties are alienated, separated, turned away, and isolated from each other. Only when this sort of thing is going on does it truly make sense to talk about forgiveness. Only in a setting of real alienation is forgiveness called for.

That is why some of the ways in which we habitually use the word *forgiveness* are improper and even a bit trivial. Take an example. Suppose that one individual has spoken or acted in a way that might hurt or displease a friend. The friend, however, says: "Oh, that's all right," or "Don't worry; it doesn't make any difference." If the friend is speaking honestly, then this is not a situation in which forgiveness is needed: that is the whole point of his saying, "It doesn't make any difference." Those words are not an act of forgiveness; they are a denial that forgiveness would be appropriate in the circumstances.

Consider another example, of a different sort, of the misuse of the term *forgiveness.* Imagine two long-time friends whose association has been troubled and impaired by the fact that one owes the other one a sum of money, the payment of which is long overdue. Imagine further that at last the debt has been paid in full, and that this action restores the cordiality of the relationship. We might, if we chose, say that the person to whom the debt has been paid "forgave" his or her friend as a result of the payment; it would probably be more correct, however, to say that the payment of the debt in good will created a situation in which forgiveness in the fullest sense was not necessary. The relationship is put right once the debt is discharged; and when a relationship has been put right, forgiveness is not called for.

The truth is, then, that forgiveness is real only where alienation is also real. To forgive is not to say, "It makes no difference"; nor is it to say, "Everything is really all right." To forgive means to reach out to someone who has done wrong and who is therefore, as we say, "in the wrong." Readers of the New Testament often chuckle condescendingly at what is called the "idealism" of Jesus' command to forgive one's enemies. The fact of the matter is, however, that enemies are the only people whom anyone has to forgive. The person who needs my forgiveness is always someone who, in one way or another, has truly hurt or rejected me, and who, to that extent, is my enemy. To forgive, therefore, is never an airy waving of the hand which says, "Think nothing of it." It is a gesture of risk, even of costly love. The person who forgives someone sacrifices his or her right for the sake of someone else, and at the same time shares the burden of fear and guilt and isolation which doing wrong always generates. Forgiveness, then, is an act of grace and of sacrifice. That is why God's forgiveness is effected only through a Cross.

What Is Being Forgiven?

When all of this is said, however, there is still another fact to note. To accept forgiveness—to be forgiven—also involves self-giving and love. This is a hard thing to understand, perhaps; but it is nonetheless true. If I allow myself to be forgiven, that itself is a gesture which involves a kind of giving up, even a kind of death-to-self.

Why is this? Well, why is it that people do not like to need forgiveness or to accept it? The reason seems to be that someone who accepts forgiveness also accepts judgment. In other words, the person who accepts forgiveness from someone admits to being in the wrong; and that is not an easy thing to do. Pride rebels against such an admission. A proper spirit of independence forbids it. Our most likely reaction to any gesture of forgiveness is (as we know from long experience) simply a denial of the necessity for it. This denial may, for public purposes, take the form of an assertion that no wrong has been done and therefore no forgiveness is needed; but at the bottom, what is at work is our fear of being dependent, of being "beholden." What, after all, do I need from you? Why should I accept a gift from you? Why should I admit that I need you to make room for me in the world?

Being forgiven, therefore, is not a merely passive thing. One must accept forgiveness. One must conquer pointless pride and the fear of dependence and the hostility which these engender, in order to say Yes to a gesture of forgiveness. The person who forgives someone sacrifices his or her right for the sake of the other. The person who is forgiven, however, also makes a sacrifice—the sacrifice of the instinct not to need or not to want the other person.

This relationship (let us call it "forgiving-and-being-forgiven"), then, is one in which two agents give themselves to one another through costly actions of love. Graciousness on the one hand calls out trust on the other; and these two gestures, each of which entails self-giving, produce reconciliation and the possibility of a new beginning. All of this occurs, however, not in the absence, but in the presence, of genuine wrong and of the alienation which that wrong produces. Forgiveness, in other words, always goes beyond what is just and due. It is not a matter of justice but an affair of grace.

Forgiveness and Forgiveness in Christ

In the light of this discussion of the meaning of forgiveness, can we go on to say why the creeds single forgiveness out as the characteristic note of Christian existence? Is there something about people's relationship to God in Christ which makes forgiveness a specially useful term to describe it?

Yes, there is. That relationship, as we know, is marred by the profound wrong of human sin. People fearfully and proudly reject God even though he is the source of their being and their identity. In doing so, they put themselves in a wrong relationship not only to God but also to other human beings. It is this sin, as we have already seen, which is definitively revealed and judged in the dying of Jesus. His death shows sin up for what it really is. It shows the human world engaged in the tragic business of killing off its own hope and refusing its own fulfillment. When the world judged and condemned Jesus, it judged and condemned itself.

But the death of Christ means more than just this. It also means "God with us," in spite of and in the very midst of the sin by which we turn our backs on him. In other words, the Cross, as we have said, spells forgiveness. It is an act of divine self-giving in which God affirms the very world which rejects and fears him. For, "while we were yet sinners, Christ died for us" (Rom. 5:8). The dying of Jesus shows humanity alienated from God. Yet, at the same time, it shows God standing with the world which will not have him. The Cross indeed means forgiveness; and so it also means *forgiven-ness*—of the very sin which it reveals and judges.

And that is why forgiveness always appears as the central note of people's relationship to God in Christ. In the first place, being "in Christ" means to know oneself as part of a community of forgiven sinners, one of a people whom God takes on in spite of the wrong which continues to infect their relationship with him. At the same time, therefore, it also means to know God as the one who forgives, whose love is more powerful than either human anxiety or the fearful pride which it engenders. To be a Christian is to know oneself as a forgiven sinner and to know God as forgiving grace.

"Justified by Faith"

Saint Paul describes this situation—the situation of being a forgiven sinner—by saying that in Christ people are "justified" or "made righteous" by an act which is God's and not their own. To understand this language of Paul's, we have to be very sure that we first grasp what he means by the word *righteous*. It is easy enough to say what we mean by it. We mean something like *virtuous* or *sternly and nobly good*. That, however, is not what it means in the language of Saint Paul. For him, *righteous* is a term which is applied to someone whom God has affirmed and set in a right relationship to himself. People are justified when they have a place with God, when he takes them in and so takes them on.

The question is: How does this happen? How are people justified? How do they get "in the right" with God? The popular impression about Christian teaching on this subject (an impression which the church does little to contradict) is that people get taken on by God when, and only when, they have proved to him that they are satisfactorily good, that they have kept his laws and are therefore qualified for his company. In other words, justification is something you have to earn, to deserve, or to merit—like a week's pay.

This notion of the way in which people are justified is, however, precisely the one which Paul is most concerned to repudiate. It is the way which he calls justification "by works of the law" (Rom. 3:28). We might call it self-justification; for that is what it amounts to. People who adopt a strategy of justification "by works" are taking complete charge of their own destiny. They intend to put themselves in a position where God has a kind of moral obligation to acknowledge them as good enough for his company. In other words, they want to be in a position to negotiate from strength when the day of judgment arrives, to stand on their own and claim the justification they have deserved.

The trouble with this strategy is twofold. In the first place, as Paul never tires of reminding people (see Rom. 3:9–18, 23), it is not easy to be good enough to measure up to God. In fact, he doubts whether anyone has ever managed it. The tactic of self-justification invariably fails. There is more to the matter than this, however, as a moment's reflection will reveal. There is a reason why the strategy of self-justification fails. The reason is that self-justification is an attempt to assert human self-sufficiency and independence in relation to God; and as such it is a symptom of the very sin which it professes to be fighting. To be justified "by works" would be to have a basis for one's being apart from—independent of—the goodness and love of God; and this repudiation of dependence on the ultimate "other" is exactly what we mean by sin.

What is the alternative to such a strategy then? From Saint Paul's point of view, the proper answer to this question is simply: no strategy at all, at least, no *human* strategy. People's "all-rightness" with God does not depend on what they do or on what they make of themselves. It depends, in the last resort, on the fact that in Jesus the Christ God takes upon himself the weight of the alienation which is caused by sin; and by giving himself for his people, "justifies the ungodly" (Rom. 4:5). God is not with us or for us because we charm or compel or cajole him to take us on. He is with us and for us because he wants to be, because of his love. It is thus by grace that humanity is forgiven and justified. If there is indeed a strategy being worked out in the relationship between God and his people, the strategy is God's and it is being carried out in Christ.

This explains what Saint Paul means when he says that we are justified "by faith." That assertion is often misun-

derstood, and dangerously misunderstood. The point of it is
not that human faith is the basis of human justification. The
point is that God's love in Christ is the basis of our justification. Faith is simply our way of acknowledging that love and
letting it have its way. To be justified "by faith" means to
have the basis of one's existence and one's hope not in
oneself—and therefore, above all, *not* in the strength or
warmth or depth of one's faith—but in God. Faith, in other
words, is the shape of a human life which has begun to stop
depending on itself and has started to live in the strength of
God's self-communicating love.

Faith itself, then, depends completely on the love, the
grace, which calls it out. Faith is possible for people because,
in the Word and through the Holy Spirit, God communicates
himself as love and thus creates in us an answering trust and
an answering love. That, when you think about it, is the
whole point of the ministry, death, and Resurrection of
Jesus—to make the gracious love of God not just apparent but
also effective in human history. In a derivative way, this is
also the point of the Christian community's proclamation of
the Word and its celebration of the sacraments. The meaning
of these actions is that the grace of God in Christ is effectively
present for people in the world. That grace, the strong love of
God, overcomes the power of sin to keep men and women
separated from God and tied up in themselves. In its
strength, therefore, humanity can live in a new relationship
with God, the relationship in which divine forgiveness
evokes and shapes human faith, and people live as forgiven
sinners; that is to say, as sinners whose future is with God.

Forgiveness and Freedom

That phrase, "sinners with a future," may be a helpful one;
for it calls attention to two matters which are all too often
forgotten and on which we must dwell for a moment here in
order to complete our picture of the meaning of forgiveness.

First of all, the forgiveness of which the New Testament
and the creeds speak is not something purely negative. It is
not merely a getting rid, a putting away, of something. To

live the forgiven life is not simply a matter of being cut loose from wrongs done in the past. On the contrary, the whole point of the forgiven life is that it is one which is now, in this moment, open to the love of God and, therefore, to the future which that love is creating through Christ. Forgiven-ness, in short, is our way of participating *now* in the New Creation.

Furthermore, this participation in the new life in Christ touches human existence in its every dimension. We have a way of limiting the meaning of forgiveness, not only by confining its effects to the past, but also by seeing them solely in relation to the consequences of our conscious moral acts. Forgiveness, we think, releases us from the just and natural results of our misdeeds—period. Actually, though, it does a lot more than that. God's forgiveness reaches deeper than that. It touches not only our deciding, but our wanting; not only our acting, but the springs of our action. It affects all aspects of our life.

Saint Paul knew this very well; and he shows that he does by the way in which he pictures the results or effects of God's forgiveness in people's lives. Christian existence, he insists, is a life *set free,* liberated, by the forgiving grace of God; and he describes this Christian freedom under three heads.

In the first place, God's forgiveness means that people are *liberated from sin and made free for righteousness.* This, and Saint Paul knows it well, is a large claim. Forgiveness, he thinks, does not just free us from the guilt of sin or from the moral indebtedness which our misdeeds have created. It does more than that. It breaks the hold of sin itself. It opens people up to God. It is (as we might say) the beginning and the basis of a reorientation in the shape of human existence. Where sin sets us free *from* God and our neighbor (or at any rate attempts to), God's forgiveness, his justifying grace, sets us free *for* God and our neighbor. And by so much it introduces us to righteousness: that is, to the fulfilled relationship with God which already belongs to Christ and which God's forgiveness establishes as our future.

To understand this line of thought it is necessary to recall that, in the last analysis, sin means closing oneself off from

God, from other people, and indeed from the natural world which God has created. Sin is not just "bad behavior." As a matter of fact, sin can often express itself in what we consider good behavior. It shows itself whenever people's deeds are acts of self-assertion against God or against his creatures; and it is not seldom, as we know well enough, that people use their good behavior as a way of denying or hurting others, or as a way of guaranteeing themselves against vulnerability to God's love. No, sin lies much deeper than behavior, whether good or bad. It is a way of seeing and being related to things which is built, not only into the attitudes of our individual selves but into the structures and values of our common social and political life. It is like a net in which we are tangled, and which seems to draw tighter and tighter the more we struggle against it. The strength of this net, however, comes from ourselves, not from outside us. It stems from our rooted conviction that we can only be ourselves by being independent and self-sufficient, by expelling, ignoring, or dominating others.

God's forgiveness in Christ, then, as it is brought home to people through the Holy Spirit, is indeed an act of liberation from a situation of slavery and imprisonment. The fact that the prison is one which people, individually and collectively, have built for themselves hardly makes any difference. They are still penned up in it. But God's act of justification in Christ, his taking of sinners into his household as sons and daughters, is like the opening of a long-shut gate. It lets people first look, and then venture, though ever so cautiously, into a world where they can begin to share themselves. Because they live in the strength of divine love, and not in the strength of their own power to manage things, they can begin to peer out of their shells—or better, to come out of themselves. And it is this liberation which Saint Paul means when he speaks of freedom from sin.

He does not stop there, however. He insists, in the second place, that God's justification of people in Christ spells *liberation from death and freedom for a new life:* "For the wages of sin is death, but the free gift of God is eternal life in Christ Jesus our Lord" (Rom. 6:23). To us this sounds, at first, thoroughly farfetched. What, we ask, has dying to do with sinning? Surely sin is not the reason why physical organisms are subject to disease and thus to dissolution; and if Saint Paul thinks that it is, he is just wrong.

In fact, though, that is not the way his thinking runs. When he speaks of death, what he has in mind in not just the physical failure of an organism, but the disappearance or destruction of a moral self. When he says, therefore, that death is an appropriate consequence, or even an appropriate punishment, of sin his point is that sin really does involve a kind of death for the sinner. People who, in their search for final self-sufficiency and independence, actually do achieve what they seek, simply lay hold on death. They disconnect themselves from their fellows and from God; and in doing so, they themselves cease to be anything. In losing their world they lose themselves, they die. That is the ultimate "sense" of sin. Sinners cut themselves off from God and so banish themselves from reality. Their physical death then becomes merely the symbol of a more fundamental dying, that dying which consists in being lost to God.

When Paul says, therefore, that forgiveness spells liberation from death, what he means is that the person who is "in Christ" cannot lose or be lost to God. Even the natural event of physical dying, in which Paul sees a symbol and seal of the death which sin brings, cannot be the final word. The forgiven sinner is involved in the life of Christ, the life of the Resurrection. His future, therefore, is not death, but life; not the powerless emptiness of sin, but a vitality rooted in fellowship with God.

Finally, though, and most characteristically, Paul argues that God's forgiveness accepted in faith means *liberation from law and freedom for love*. In a way, of all Paul's statements about the meaning of Christian life, this is the hardest for people to understand. It does not just sound farfetched or obscure or strange; it sounds dangerous. After all, we might ask, do we not need law to guide and to control our behavior? What would happen if people were left free simply to do as they pleased? What would happen if there were no moral rules to keep them in hand?

The very assumptions on which these questions are asked

go a long way toward explaining what Saint Paul has in mind when he talks about freedom from law. Paul thinks that law, a set of rules laid down and imposed to control people's behavior, is the form which God's will takes for people who see God as their enemy. What God wants for people appears to them as "law" precisely when it is not what they want for themselves. To be under law, then, is to be controlled from outside, like an animal which has been penned in or tied down. It is a state which is only possible for one who is alienated from God. *Law* is a word for the way God looks to the sinner. It is what you have to live up to when you would rather not.

The forgiven person, however, knows God not only as law, but as love and grace. That is the whole meaning of God's Word enacted in the ministry, death, and Resurrection of Jesus. To live as a forgiven sinner, therefore, and as one whom God's love has reconciled, is to be in principle free of law. Life is no longer a matter of living up to some standard imposed from outside, a standard which is always secretly violated because it always appears as the contrary of one's own desire. Rather, life is now a matter of finding ways to let the meaning of God's love show in human activity. When people move from being sinners to being forgiven sinners, they stop having to live up to something and begin to live out from something. They possess themselves in God's love and can live freely. They have discovered who they are—children of God called in Christ Jesus—and can set about being themselves. That is what Paul means by freedom from law.

And he means it quite seriously. He is no less aware than anyone else that people who are looking for ways to enact the implications of the love and forgiveness which they have found in Christ can make terrifying mistakes and clumsy errors. He does not think, however, that the remedy for such errors is a return to the system of law; for to live under law is to live not as a forgiven sinner but as an accused sinner. It is to exist as a slave, and so as one who is ultimately without responsibility. What the law demands, however, can only get done when faith responsibly answers love; that is, it can only get done in the freedom which God gives with his forgiveness.

Liberation for Love

And here of course we come to the nub of the matter. Human beings, sinful as they are, can only conceive of freedom in negative terms. For them it always appears simply as freedom *from* something. It always means self-sufficiency and independence. When Saint Paul speaks of freedom in Christ, however, he has something else in mind. Liberation—from sin, from death, and from law—means, for him, to be free in and for God. It is important to remember that the liberation about which he is talking exists for us only in God's grace, in God's self-giving. For just that reason, though, the one form this freedom can never take is that of independence and self-sufficiency. This freedom is, rather, a thankful and spontaneous *giving of oneself* in answer to God's gift of himself in Christ. It is always freedom to love. It is rooted in faith; but faith works, as Paul says, "by love" (Gal. 5:6). And, therefore, "love is the fulfilling of the law," the way in which God's will is truly—because freely—done.

That is why, when Paul finds his converts at Corinth boasting of a "knowledge" and a "freedom" which permit them to take actions that hurt or offend others, he reminds them that love is the form of Christian freedom (1 Cor. 8:1, 13). He himself, he says, is as "free" as anyone (1 Cor. 9:1). This freedom as he sees it, however, is a freedom for service (1 Cor. 9:19). In other words, it is a freedom which is unreal except when it affirms, makes room for, and benefits others. Of all the gifts which the Holy Spirit gives, the highest and best is love, which is: "patient . . . kind . . . not jealous or boastful . . . not arrogant or rude. Love does not insist on its own way; it is not irritable or resentful; it does not rejoice at wrong, but rejoices in the right . . ." (1 Cor. 13:4–6).

What we have to say, then, is that the freedom—from sin, from death, from law—which God confers on people in Christ, takes the form of love; or better, perhaps, that love growing in the soil of faith is the way human beings mirror the divine love which sets us free. In this way, the human being really does "answer to" and "image" God. Love answers love; and the creature participates in the life of the

Creator. In the last resort, then, the forgiven, liberated life becomes the forgiving and liberating life in which the graciousness of God is not only celebrated but mirrored.

Conclusion

The forgiven sinner—set free for righteousness, for life in Christ, and for love—is nevertheless a sinner; and this is a fact which must not be concealed or forgotten. Saint Paul and his converts, and their sisters and brothers in the Christian community down to this day, have always, at least in practice, acknowledged this. They have experienced the righteousness, the new life, and the power of love for which the Holy Spirit sets them free when he brings home to them their identity in Christ. Nevertheless, at the very same time, they see themselves fearfully maintaining the posture of sin, that posture of would-be self-sufficiency and independence which issues in death and knows God only as alien "law." The fact is that Christian existence, the existence of forgiven sinners, is always, at every point, a life in transition. The believer in Christ lives on an edge, in a borderland, where the old is passing over into the new, where death remains real even as the power of life is being asserted. Such an existence is inevitably experimental. It is occupied with the exploring and living out of an identity which we have not fully comprehended or fully accepted. Growing up into Christ is not an easy or an automatic process: and as we know it in this life, it is always incomplete. We share the new life, the new order of things, by being forgiven and so set free to share God's life; but it is as sinners, as people who retreat from God and neighbor, that we need and receive this forgiveness.

By its transitional character, then, and by its incompleteness, the life of the forgiven sinner points beyond itself. It looks for a fulfillment: "for we through the Spirit by faith wait for the hope of righteousness" (Gal. 5:5). That means the life of faith waits for the moment when the new reality of God's Kingdom is present for people in an unqualified and unambiguous way. The final word of faith is: "I look for the resurrection of the dead and the life of the world to come."

· 13 ·

". . . and the Life of the World to Come"

In Christian faith there is a built-in orientation to the future. It has been there from the beginning. Jesus proclaimed that God's Kingdom was at hand and that its powers were at work even in the present. In this way he created expectancy. He pointed people ahead to a future in which the promise of their present, the promise which Jesus himself represented, would be fulfilled. Furthermore, Jesus' disciples understood his Resurrection to be the beginning of that fulfillment. When God raised Jesus from the dead, they insisted, he opened the door leading to that New Age for which the faithful had always hoped. They were certain, therefore, that their own time was the era of the inauguration of God's Rule, of "the world to come"; and that they could, for that reason, look confidently forward to its complete actualization. Saint Paul even describes the gift of the Holy Spirit as a "down payment" or "first installment" which assures that "what is mortal" will be "swallowed up by life" (1 Cor. 5:4–5).

Thus Christian life is governed not only by faith and love, but also by hope: that is, by a confident expectation that God will bring to fulfillment the promise contained in people's present life in Christ. An essential aspect of the relationship with God which the creeds portray is, therefore, this: that when we stand in that relationship, we are stretched out in hope toward "the resurrection of the dead and the life of the world to come."

The full meaning of this Christian hopefulness, however, is not easy to grasp. One might choose to understand it as just an instance or illustration of the fact that all human existence is directed toward the future—as indeed it is. The poet's saying, "Hope springs eternal," does not apply only to Christians. It describes everyone. All of us are compelled to look ahead to the "not yet" and to depend upon it. This is not only because we want the future to provide what the present and past have denied us. It is also because only the future can guarantee our secure possession of what the past and the present have already given us. Until tomorrow, all is uncertain.

The meaning of Christian hope, however, is not exhausted in this commonplace dependence on the future. Far from it. Christian hope is rooted in present reality—in the fact of God's self-giving in Christ and the Holy Spirit. For that reason it goes beyond wishing or wanting. It becomes a kind of expecting. "The life of the world to come" is not a dream or an ideal to be realized. It is a reality which God is even now creating in Christ; and that fact makes Christian hoping distinctive in its quality.

To say this, however, does not make such hope any easier to understand. In the course of the church's history, it has expressed itself in a number of different ways; and some of these seem difficult to justify or to make sense of. Every now and then, for example, a movement appears which announces "the end of the world"; and we ask ourselves whether this indeed is the sole content of Christian hope for the human world. Or again, as many critics of Christianity have pointed out, this hope sometimes takes a form which encourages people to care nothing for the problems of the here and now because they are taught to look for "pie in the sky by and by." But if things of this sort do not represent full or authentic Christian hoping, what does?

So there are many questions to ask about "the life of the world to come." In the first place, we want to know what the content of that hope is. In the second place, we want to know what effect Christian hoping has on the character of Christian life here and now. What does it mean to lead a life formed by this hope in God's "new thing"? These are the questions which this chapter will address.

Heaven and Hell

Before we can set about this task directly, however, there is a preliminary job to be done. There is a popular version of Christian hope which is current among churchgoers and non-churchgoers alike. It is familiar, in one form or another, to almost everyone, and it provides the framework within which most people understand phrases like "the life of the world to come." In fact, however, it distorts the meaning of biblical and creedal teaching about human destiny. By looking critically at this understanding of Christian hope, therefore, we can hope to get some of the issues straight and even begin to see something of the true sense of New Testament language about human destiny.

In fact this popular version of Christian hope does not often use the classical language of Christian teaching. It does not talk much about the life of the world to come or the Kingdom of God or resurrection. Its central symbols are the words *heaven* and *hell,* and the context in which they are used is that of belief in the survival, or "immortality," of the human soul. Heaven is understood to be a place or a state of being in which people are forever happy and blessed—in which things are "right." Men and women go to heaven after their deaths on certain conditions. If they have believed the Gospel and kept God's commandments, they will be sent to this place of happiness when they die. If on the contrary they are disobedient, they run the risk of torment, of punishment in hell, which is also pictured as a present and available "place" or "state."

For centuries this set of ideas and images has been central for people's picture of their ultimate future. It has represented all that they have known or understood of Christian hope. Today, perhaps, the situation is somewhat different.

There are few persons now who thoroughly accept this understanding of their situation. Many have doubts about, say, hell, or about the survival of the soul. Many reject the whole picture outright. Even the latter, however, are convinced that this scheme gives a true account of the Christian hope. Yet it takes only a brief look at the Scriptures, and especially the New Testament, to see that this picture of things distorts the thrust of their witness.

Consider first of all the idea of survival, of what we nowadays call "immortality." The New Testament only infrequently uses the term *immortality*, and its primary affirmation is that immortality, properly speaking, belongs only to God (1 Tim. 6:16, 1:17). When immortality is ascribed to human beings (1 Cor. 15:53, 54), therefore, it appears not as a natural possession, but as a gift from God. Immortality in fact is used to talk, not about survival, but about the quality of life in the New Age. It is a gift of the Holy Spirit in the resurrection, not something that people have in their own right.

Our popular version of Christian hope, therefore, gets the Scriptures' conception of immortality slightly askew. It uses it not to describe the glory of a human life shared with God in the Kingdom, but more or less neutrally, to speak of the automatic persistence of the human self beyond the grave. Yet on the latter subject, the Scriptures are strangely silent. The Old Testament knows nothing of an automatic "life after death"—except, of course, the shadow existence of *Sheol*, which hardly qualifies as life. And if the New Testament speaks of life after death, it is always a matter of a life shared with Jesus—that is, a *new* life conferred by God's gift, and not an automatic possession (Lk. 23:43, 2 Cor. 4:10–11, 5:8). To be immortal is to share through Jesus in the life of the Coming Age.

Then, in the second place, consider the idea of heaven as it is used in this popular version of Christian hope. One of the phrases which the New Testament uses to refer to the future which God has inaugurated in Christ is *Kingdom of Heaven*. Saint Matthew uses it, as we have seen, to mean the same thing as *Kingdom of God* because, for reasons of reverence, he does not wish to refer directly to God. It was easy enough, however, for later readers of his Gospel to think that he was talking, not about the Rule of God, but about "the realm of heaven" or "the celestial realm." This misunderstanding was encouraged by two other factors. One of these was the biblical imagery which portrays "heaven" or "the heavens" as the place from which God and the Messiah and his angels would come to consummate the New Age. Another factor was the belief, encouraged by a long tradition of pagan philosophy and religion, in a separate, heavenly "world" of the gods. The writers of the New Testament, however, did not think of this celestial realm as identical with, or as a substitute for, the Age to Come; and it is this identification which makes, or starts, the trouble, by turning heaven into an alternative or parallel world where things are better than they are in this one.

And finally, what about the picture of hell in this popular version of Christian hope? People often go to the pages of the New Testament to "prove" the reality of hell. What one finds there, though, is not a concept of hell in the modern sense, but a conviction that the coming of God's Rule is a moment of judgment for all the forces that oppose it. When the New Age appears, as indeed it began to appear in the ministry of Jesus, those who reject it shall find the reward which accords with their choice. That is what the New Testament, and the apocalyptic tradition on which it draws at this point, firmly believes. When God acts to put things right, they will be put right; and if that means the rejection of some people because they have finally and irrevocably rejected God, then so it must be.

In primitive Christianity, to be sure, this rejection of the wicked was pictured in several alternative ways. Some held that the wicked would simply be left to death—forgotten because destroyed. Others held that the wicked would be raised from the dead for eternal punishment. Still others, while they agreed that the wicked would be raised from the dead and punished, were sure that this punishment would be therapeutic and educational—that in the end all would be brought into God's Kingdom. No matter which of these views one held, however, hell was not conceived of as a permanent "world" in itself, permanently available for occupancy. It was a product or an aspect of the action in which God did final right—in which he consummated the New Age; and the emphasis was not on punishment, but on God's desire, indeed his solemn purpose, to consummate the good thing which he had done in Christ.

Problems in the Popular Version of Christian Hope

Let us turn, however, from the imagery of this popular version of Christian hope—from the ideas of immortality, heaven, and hell as it conceives them—and look at the meaning of the over-all picture of human destiny which they are used to convey. Here too we see serious distortion of the sense of Christian hoping.

Notice first of all that this popular scheme offers very little hope and breeds very little hopefulness. Jesus came calling for repentance because the Kingdom of God, the promised New Age, was at hand. Thus his message was indeed one of hope. It proclaimed that the promises of God through the prophets were already being fulfilled—that the blind were receiving their sight and the poor hearing good news. What though is the message of our popular version of Christian hope? Heaven is not a good thing coming, least of all a good thing which has appeared in our midst. On the contrary, it is a good thing waiting for us to win it; and the usefulness of achieving it is underscored by the fact that the only alternative is hell. Consequently, it is not very frequently "eager longing" (Rom. 8:19) which inspires people when they think of heaven. It is just as likely to be a sense of having a task to perform in order to avoid torment or in order to prove oneself. And that is not hopefulness.

This, however, is not the only problem with this version of Christian belief in the future. There is also the fact that it concentrates wholly on the fate of the individual. So used are we to thinking in individualistic terms, that we hardly notice the difference between the image of heaven as popularly conceived and that of the Kingdom of God or the World to Come. These, when you stop to consider them, turn out to be images of a *world transformed*. They point to the prospect that the purpose of God's creation shall be realized: that the whole human world, in all its variety, shall enter upon a new age by truly becoming *God's* world. This prospect certainly involves and affects individuals, but it does not come about merely through individual choice or private goodness. Consequently, any version of Christian hope which centers only on the question, *What becomes of me?*, is one which falsifies both the New Testament and the creeds. True Christian hope has social and indeed cosmic dimensions. It answers the question, *What becomes of us?*

Further, as we have seen, this popular version of Christian hope seems to understand heaven as another world alongside this one—a world which is coexistent with ours and parallels it, but nevertheless remains separate from it. That is what appears to be implied by such expressions as "this world" or "the world beyond" or "going to heaven." The idea is, presumably, that under certain circumstances one can leave "here" and go "there." Philosophers have often criticized this picture, arguing that what it adds up to is a devaluation of human life here in this world. Christians are said to teach that it is the heavenly world alone which is ultimately real and worth caring about. They are accused, therefore, of regarding this world as a "vale of tears," in which wrong must simply be endured for the sake of earning heaven.

Such a duality of worlds, however, is no part of what is truly meant by hope in "the life of the world to come." On the contrary, "the world to come" is this world—but transformed, altered, and renewed. To use the language of popular belief, heaven is not "another" world at all. It is our present life re-formed according to God's will. What God is organizing in this world through the ministry, death, and Resurrection of Jesus is its redemption, not its evacuation.

And that, we must finally add, is the whole point of the idea of "the resurrection of the dead," which the creeds mention in close conjunction with "the life of the world to come." The popular version, as we are calling it, of Christian hope has a hard time making sense of this idea of resurrection. Just as, in the particular case of Jesus, we moderns will take resurrection to mean mere resuscitation of a dead organism, so in the face of the idea of the "general resurrection" we tend to conceive it (if we think about it at all) as a matter of an individual's body coming suddenly back to life and getting reattached to its soul, now located in heaven (or perhaps in hell).

This misses the whole point of the New Testament idea of resurrection. Resurrection is the beginning of the New Age. It is the event through which those who have died have the new life in God made real for them. The term *resurrection,* therefore, does not refer to the bringing of corpses back to life—and for two good reasons. In the first place, the life to which those who are awakened from death are raised is a new, transformed life. It is not the old sort of life in the old sort of context. Resurrection does not bring people *back* to anything. It takes them into a new context of living, a world in which all things are summed up in Christ (Eph. 1:10). In the second place, that word *body* in the phrase "resurrection of the body" can be misleading to people who do not talk in the way Saint Paul did. The phrase is his; and since he distinguishes body very carefully from "flesh and blood" (1 Cor. 15:50) which is "perishable," we can be sure that "resurrection of the body" does not mean bringing corpses back to life. Most interpreters think that *body,* when used in this connection, means, for Paul, the individual person as a whole, taken apart from any distinction between flesh and soul. My body is simply myself as I am real for others in my world. To speak of resurrection of the body, therefore, is to speak of the re-bodying of the human person in the context of the new life of Christ.

What we have to say in the end, therefore, is something like this. The world as we now know and experience it is a world in which death comes as the final word spoken to everyone and everything; and death cuts people off in an absolute way. When one speaks of resurrection, however, one is speaking of this same human world so transformed and renewed that the final word is *life in God. Resurrection,* in other words, has two dimensions of meaning which people normally miss. First of all, it stands for something which happens in and for a whole world, a whole context of life, and not just for individuals. Second, it is a symbol which means not so much revival, as it does renewal and transformation. Resurrection is the transfer of our individual and common lives in all their dimensions and relations to a new level of existence "in Christ."

Hope in the God Who Raised Jesus

In the light of this long and critical look at the popular version of Christian hope, it ought to be possible to return to our original question about the content of Christian hope. This question itself, however, has two parts, and they need to be kept distinct from each other for purposes of theological discussion. The content of Christian hope includes both what Christians hope *in* and what they hope *for;* and these are, at least in part, different.

Christian hoping is like Christian believing. That is, it is directed to God. Whatever it is that Christians hope for, the reason why they can hope at all is that they know God has given them a basis for their hope by raising Jesus from the dead and by involving them with his new life. Thus the answer to the question, "In what do Christians hope?" is the simplest answer possible. "They hope in God." Jesus reveals God to be the one who does right and who gives himself in love to be with his people. He also reveals God to be the one who can bring good out of evil and life out of death. And that is why Christians live hopefully—not as naive optimists about human goodness or human intentions, but as people who have learned that God's love has transforming power and that it can be trusted.

And maybe this is the point at which the essential difference between true Christian hoping and that popular version of Christian hope which we have just examined becomes clear. For if it is true that the "getting to heaven" syndrome really does not involve much hopefulness at all, the reason is that it sees God merely as the operator of a cosmic reward-and-punishment system. It has never grasped the fact that God, as seen in the Gospel which Jesus and his apostles preached, is at work in the world to fulfill the purpose of his creation, which means to bring about the good thing which his act of creation has intended from the beginning. That good thing, which we have learned to call "the Kingdom of God" and "the life of the world to come," is not, therefore, just a given and available reality which people have to possess for themselves by playing the game according to the rules. No, it is something which God is up to in Christ—something which he is already bringing about in them, through them, and with them. That is the reason why they can hope; and that is the reason why their hope is centered on God. They do not hope in themselves, or in any objective system of rewards and punishments. They hope in the God who brought the children of Israel out of bondage and who raised Jesus from the dead.

Hope for This World

But if God is the one *in whom* Christians hope, what is it *for which* they hope?

From one point of view, that question is easy enough to answer. People who hope in God take delight in God and trust God. Consequently, what they hope for is simply the fulfillment of his purposes and of their relationship with him. To say the same thing in another way, the object of their hope is the full realization of the life in Christ; for that defines both God's purposes for humanity and humanity's proper relationship to God.

In other words, the content of Christian hope, that to which Christians look forward, is the perfection of something which is already real in Christ and of which they already have a taste through the gift of the Holy Spirit.

It is important, moreover, to say this and to say it emphatically. Often the imagery of Christian hope gives, falsely, the impression that what the church hopes for is something which is absolutely "not of this world," something of which no one has ever heard or dreamt, much less experienced. It is understandable, moreover, how this impression could be given. The rhetoric of Christian hoping is high and enthusiastic, to say the least. It pictures a world of "endless sabbaths" and "golden slippers"—a new Jerusalem come down out of heaven, "its radiance like a most rare jewel, like a jasper, clear as crystal" (Rev. 21:11). Such language is hardly likely to make people think it is referring to hard, salty reality.

On the other hand, this rhetoric must be taken as more than a way of tossing up idle, and ultimately meaningless, images of happiness. In the first place, all of these images grow directly out of the realities of human life as we know it. They point to good things in human life of whose goodness we are intensely aware from time to time. To describe the Kingdom of God as a feast is to remember the joys of a solemnly happy party with good friends. To describe the world to come as a new Jerusalem is to acknowledge the grandeur and splendor of the life of a great city, a city at whose center is the presence of the Holy One. To speak of endless sabbaths and golden slippers is to recall the deep refreshment of contemplative rest, and the sense of fulfillment which sometimes occurs when people "dress up" for a special occasion or event. These images may sound fantastic; but in fact they all grow out of real experience.

But there is more to say than just this. For what these images are trying to describe—and not just the terms in which they describe it—is itself a part of experience and of the real world. To hope for the Kingdom of God is not to hope for a never-never land. It is to hope for the fulfillment of what people have already begun to know and experience in Christ. The imagery of Christian hoping is calculated to suggest not that believers' minds are focused on some dream, but that they hardly know how to express their wonder at the prospect of the full actualization of something which, in its bare beginnings, is already with them. What these images convey, in other words, is the idea of a final enhancement, fulfillment, or realization of a good which has already entered into the present order of things. "World to come" is the name of this world when its affairs are put right and it "graduates," so to speak, to a new form of relationship to God. It is not the name of a substitute world of a quite different sort.

Hope for a World Transformed

Yet clearly enough the life of the world to come is no mere reproduction of the present state of affairs; and this side of the picture must be emphasized as well. It is true that "world to come" refers to the world of God's original creation. At the same time, however, it pictures that world as existing and being experienced on a higher plane. Saint Paul, as we have seen, insists that "flesh and blood cannot inherit the kingdom of God" (1 Cor. 15:50). By the same token he implies that to share in the Resurrection involves making a transition through death from one level of existence to a new one.

> So it is with the resurrection of the dead. What is sown is perishable, what is raised is imperishable. It is sown in dishonor, it is raised in glory. It is sown in weakness, it is raised in power. It is sown a physical body, it is raised a spiritual body (1 Cor. 15:42–44).

In other words, the life of the world to come really does involve a change in the way things are. The change is so profound that it involves a kind of dying and rebirth, whose end product is the same people, making up the same world, but people whose life is led in an entirely different mode, a revised relationship to God. It is as though human existence, like an old melody, were to be transposed into a new key. There is continuity between the two—real continuity; but there is also real discontinuity.

And these two truths must be held in balance in any account of Christian hoping. Throughout the New Testament, and indeed throughout Christian history, there runs a contrast between a tendency to see the New Age as utterly different from the present and a tendency to emphasize its continuity with experience and life here and now. It is the latter tendency, for example, which surfaces when, in the Gospels, emphasis is laid on the bodily, physical reality of the risen Christ and his recognizability. The point of that emphasis is to insist that the Jesus of the New Creation is the same person with whom the disciples walked and talked in Galilee. On the other hand, these same Gospels insist also that the risen Christ is a mysterious and awesome figure, one who very obviously does not belong to the present order of things, but one who comes to it bearing its future. In this way the Gospels call attention to what we have called the discontinuity between old and new, then and now.

This tension, which must be present in any honest account of Christian hoping, is embodied in the important but unfashionable word *supernatural*. That word has, at least recently, been almost universally misused and misunderstood. In popular speech its meaning has been degraded. It is thought to refer to the magical or the "spooky" or the merely miraculous. In academic circles, on the other hand, it is employed as a shorthand way of referring to that "other world," the heavenly parallel of this, which it is believed that Christian faith affirms. Talk of the supernatural, therefore, is naturally condemned either as sheer superstition or as a kind of dualism; that is, a division of reality into inferior and superior worlds.

In fact, however, the term *supernatural* has a perfectly proper meaning. Correctly understood, it means human life as we have it (that is, the "natural") enhanced and taken beyond itself through a perfected relationship with God. And that precisely defines the nature of Christian hope. Such hope does not focus on another world, but on this world. On the other hand, it sees this world surpassing anything that it has ever been before through participation in the life of the risen Christ—life in a "new key." You might say that Christian hoping amounts to a settled confidence that God is completing his work of bringing people to share Jesus' new life, "the life of the world to come," the resurrected life. And that is precisely a *super*natural, but not an *un*natural, goal.

That is why all efforts to picture "what it will be like" must fail. All that human language can do when it tries to grasp "the life of the world to come" is to extrapolate in various ways. It can talk of *final* victory over the things which cut people off from God and their neighbor—i.e., death and sin. It can try to imagine what this might be like by using terms such as "light" and "immortality" and "the vision of God." Nevertheless there are limits to the usefulness of such language. The supernatural can only be pointed to; it cannot be described. What happens when people truly share the life of God in love cannot be said except figuratively; and the most important figure for us is not one of our own images, but the person of Jesus himself. He is the one whose human living and dying, in their moral quality, embody the presence of God for us, and so reach out and touch "the life of the world to come."

Life Shaped by Hope

Even though it is impossible to describe "the life of the world to come" in any save indirect terms, it is by no means impossible to say how hoping in God affects human existence here and now. For hope does make a difference. It is an essential factor in the life of a community of forgiven sinners.

In the first place, hope makes a difference because it rescues people from the abyss of despair and cynicism on the one hand, and from the cloud lands of naive optimism on the other. The Christian believer is not the sort of uncritical idealist who has to hide from the realities of human perversity and meanness behind a mist of illusion. Neither is the believer the sort of person who, when illusion is dispelled, becomes embittered, disappointed, and hopeless. Trusting in God and in the power of God's love, such a person has no need to be deceived about things as they are. It is not necessary to believe that everything is really all right; or, having discovered that it is not, to think the exact contrary—that everything is all wrong. Christians can perceive the imperfection and willful wrongness which infects not just the world but even themselves, and yet know that God works with people and in them and that his grace will ultimately triumph. Christian hope is not optimism; it is trust in God.

There is, however, still another way in which Christian hoping makes a difference for the way people think and live. In a profound and permanent way, it affects the manner in which they understand and face the fact of death—both their own death and that of others.

There is, of course, a terror which is occasioned by dying itself, as distinct from death. In these days, more often than in the past, dying is a protracted process. It involves increasing illness, helplessness, pain, and, above all, a sense of uselessness and isolation. To persons in these circumstances the Gospel offers genuine, though not easy, assurance. It is not the assurance that they will always or necessarily get well or get better. It is, rather, the assurance that their dying is not without meaning. Self-surrender through silent and patient self-giving was the way in which God made himself present for us in Christ. It is also, if Saint Paul is right about the manner in which the new life is born, a way in which people like us can find God. Dying, with all the trouble it inevitably brings upon people's spirits, can in Christ be a pointer to life, the embodiment of hope for new life.

The ultimate terror, however, does not lie in the process of dying. It lies in death itself. For death is rightly and instinctively perceived, not just as the disintegration of an organism, but as the violation of a positive moral good. It is the final cutting off of the self from all that it loves and from all that has given it life. It is true that for many people death is the end of a great deal of pain and trouble. Strangely, though, it is the rare person who sees death, when actually facing it, as relief. Most people fear death, or at least reject it; and the reason for this is not just their fear of ceasing to be. Rather, the reason is that they do not want to be separated either from the other human beings or from the God with whom they have shared themselves and in whom they have discovered themselves. Death is the end of loving and being loved. That is why it means extinction and why it is supremely hated and feared.

Christian faith, however, is based on a story which tells of love's triumph over sin and death—over the two things in this world that have seemed irrevocably to cut people off from the "other." Christian faith affirms, on the basis of Jesus' Resurrection, that death cannot finally "disconnect" the life with which God shares himself in love: that, in fact, death is one step on the way to the fulfillment of life in the New Creation. In this way Christian faith helps people to hope in the midst of death. It enables them to face death with a sense both that it means something positive in human experience, and that it does not bring the world to an end. The world's end, in Christian faith, is not its finish for me in death, but its renewal in the world to come.

Finally, though, hope makes a difference in the way people live and act here and now. Those who, through faith, have caught a glimpse of the love of God as it touches them in Christ, and who therefore hope for the Kingdom of God, become understandably impatient with the present state of human affairs. Hoping, for them, becomes a kind of reaching out for the future God is bringing. It translates itself into efforts to make the world in which we presently live look, if only a little bit, like the New Creation which God is bringing.

There are two very good reasons why hope has this effect. In the first place, hope which focuses on a real prospect of good is bound to make people critical of whatever in their present situation falls short of that for which they hope. Hopeless people are always passive. They do not see how things can be much better than they are; so they cannot be persuaded to stir themselves to try to improve them. Hopeful people, however, are a different breed. They see the present state of affairs in the light of the things for which they hope, and they set about trying to make those good things real even here and now.

In the second place, hope which is genuine fills people with joy, in the same way that the prospect of Christmas fills small children with joy. And in their joy they begin to rehearse the good thing which is coming—to run through it in their minds and to act it out in reality. They begin to behave as though it were already here, out of sheer pleasure.

Christian history is full of such dress rehearsals for the Kingdom of God. In a way, all Christian worship, all enacting of the church's liturgy, is just such an affair, an attempt to actualize in the present moment, through words and music and ritual dance, the beauty and the goodness of the new creation in Christ. In quite another way, but in line with the same logic, such a movement as monasticism attempts to find a social form within which to actualize, and so symbolize for the world, certain dimensions of "the life of the world to come." The same can be said of many other phenomena in the life of the church, from its perpetual singing of hymns to its perpetual fostering of political and social reform in the world. The church is a community which is getting itself and its world ready for the life of the world to come, even while others see, on every hand, only the prospect of death.

Thus, hope throws people into action in the effort to conform the world now to its future in Christ. This indeed is one way of understanding the whole realm of what is studied in Christian ethics as well as in the theological sciences of the interior life. Think, on the one hand, of an individual act of kindness, or of the attempt of a group of people to achieve social justice for others, or of public acts of philanthropy. Then think, on the other hand, of the practice of spirituality—the cultivation of habits of prayer and meditation and interior collectedness before God. Both of these kinds of activity can be seen as expressions of hope—as attempts to actualize in the present, if only in a partial way, the glory of what will be in "the life of the age to come."

Conclusion

It is important not to forget, however, that these forms of Christian action really are expressions of *hope*. The people who engage in them are people who live as forgiven sinners in a world which in fact is not conformed to its supernatural future. Their own hoping, and the action to which it gives rise, may well be touched by the very evil it seeks to overcome. That is why, in the end, the creeds present us with a declaration not of present fulfillment, but precisely of future hope. Even when our attempts to live up to the Kingdom fall short of perfection, even when we know that after all the future which God is bringing cannot be fully experienced here and now, it is still possible to trust God in the power of the Holy Spirit on the basis of his work in Christ, and to say, "We look for the resurrection of the dead and the life of the world to come."

Suggestions
for Further Reading

For persons who wish to read further expositions of the creeds, or brief introductions to Christian doctrine, there are several useful volumes now available. John Burnaby, in *The Belief of Christendom* (available now in the United States from The Seabury Press, 1959) gives a careful exposition of the Nicene Creed. The Apostles' Creed is treated, from differing points of view, by Karl Barth in his *Dogmatics in Outline* (SCM, 1949; Harper Torchbooks); by Joseph Ratzinger in *Introduction to Christianity* (Seabury Press, 1969); and by Wolfhart Pannenberg in *The Apostles' Creed* (Westminster Press, 1972). A thorough introduction to systematic theology can be found in John Macquarrie, *Principles of Christian Theology* (Scribner, 1977). Macquarrie's *The Faith of the People of God* (Scribner, 1973) is more elementary.

Index